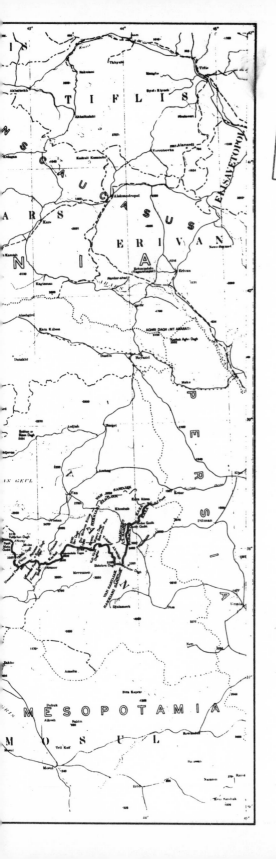

A Mandate for Armenia

A Mandate for Armenia

JAMES B. GIDNEY

The Kent State University Press

For Ruth

Library of Congress Card Catalog Number 67-63733
Copyright © 1967 by The Kent State University Press
All rights reserved
Manufactured in the United States of America
at the Oberlin Printing Company, Oberlin, Ohio
Designed by Merald E. Wrolstad

Contents

If a scepter of diamonds, a glittering crown
Were mine, at thy feet I would lay them both down,
 Queen of queens, Armenia!

If a mantle of purple were given to me,
A mantle for kings, I would wrap it round thee,
 My lady Armenia!

If the fire of my youth and its sinews of steel
Could return, I would offer its raptures and zeal
 All to thee, Armenia!

Had a lifetime of ages been granted to me,
I had given it gladly and freely to thee,
 Oh my life, Armenia!

Were I offered the love of a maid lily fair,
I would choose thee alone for my joy and my care,
 My one love, Armenia!

Were I given a crown of rich pearls I should prize
Far more than their beauty one tear from thy eyes,
 Oh weeping Armenia!

If freedom unbounded were proffered to me,
I would choose still to share thy sublime slavery,
 Oh my mother, Armenia!

Were I offered proud Europe to take or refuse,
Thee alone, with thy griefs on thy head, would I choose,
 My country, Armenia!

Might I choose from the world where my dwelling should be,
I would say, still thy ruins are Eden to me,
 My beloved Armenia!

Were I given a seraph's celestial lyre,
I would sing with my soul to its chords of pure fire,
 Thy sweet name, Armenia!

    Khorene Narbe de Lusignan

Introduction

$\mathcal{I}$N THIS VOLUME I have tried to tell the story of Armenia in the settlement following the First World War with particular reference to the proposal that it be placed under an American mandate. Although parts of the story have been told before, some of them perhaps definitively, it has never been told as a whole. Writers whose focus is on President Wilson or the Paris Peace Conference are chiefly interested in the German, rather than the Turkish, settlement while those who direct their attention to the breakup of the Ottoman Empire deal only peripherally with the American involvement. It could hardly be otherwise, for the subject is one of endless ramifications whose temptations must be resisted if the researcher is not to spend a lifetime tracking them with no ultimate satisfaction to anyone but himself. Even in dealing with a small part of the total I have met such temptations and can only hope I have resisted enough of them to maintain some coherence in my treatment of the Armenian problem.

Although I have occasionally experienced the excitement of what seemed at the time to be a minor discovery, it would be misleading to place much emphasis on that aspect of my work. The problem has been much more one of selection than of discovery. Nonetheless the book could not have been written if I had not had access to a large amount of unpublished material. I acknowledge with gratitude my indebtedness to the Manuscript Division of the Library of Congress, Washington, D.C. which put the Woodrow Wilson Papers at my disposal, the Sterling Memorial Library of Yale University, New Haven, Connecticut which made the papers of Colonel Edward M. House and Undersecretary of State Frank L. Polk available, the National Archives of the United States whose State Department and Peace Conference records proved an indispensable—and inexhaustible—source, the Historical Section of the U. S. Department of State whose files yielded valuable clues, and the University of Michigan Press at Ann Arbor, Michigan for permission to examine the papers of William Yale.

Thanks are due also for the assistance of the staffs of the I. F. Freiberger Library of Western Reserve University in Cleveland, Ohio, the Library of the University of Michigan at Ann Arbor, and the Public Libraries of Cleveland, Ohio and Detroit, Michigan.

It is a pleasure to thank Dean C. H. Cramer of Adelbert College, Western Reserve University for his advice and encouragement. I have profited also from the suggestions of Dean Carl Wittke and Professors Marion C. Siney, Arvel B. Erickson, and Harvey Wish, all of Western Reserve University. Dean Wittke and Professors Siney and Erickson read the manuscript in its original form when it was offered as a doctoral dissertation. Professor Wish presided over the birth of the project when I prepared a paper on the King-Crane Commission for his seminar in twentieth-century American history. The advice and criticism of Professor William Yale of Boston University have been invaluable for the chapter on the King-Crane Commission of which Professor Yale was a member, and there is hardly a chapter that has not benefited from the experience of Professor Harry N. Howard of the School of International Service of The American University in Washington, D.C. Mrs. Nancy G. Giesey cheerfully typed the entire manuscript twice.

Finally, my gratitude to my wife and friends who must feel by now that I have told them more about Armenia than they were ever interested in knowing.

A Word on Terminology and Nomenclature

A special difficulty has been the spelling of numerous words and names which any writer on the Ottoman Empire has to use. The Armenians have an alphabet of their own and the Turks used the Arabic alphabet until the 1930's. Europeans transliterating from these scripts have produced a wide variety of spellings. I have seen at least four ways of writing *Erzerum* and I doubt that it is the worst. Even in the simplest cases French and English transliterations differ. I thought at one time I would get rid of this difficulty, at least for Turkish words, by using only the present official spelling, but I abandoned the idea when it occurred to me that readers with a half-dozen Turkish words might not even recognize those in the new spelling. At about the same time I gave up all effort to be "scholarly" about it and chose in each case the spelling that seemed to have been most commonly offered to English-speaking readers at the time of the events I was describing. This resolution at least had the virtue of bringing my spelling into line with that of some of the sources I quoted.

Needless to say, I cannot guarantee uniformity in my sources. An example which is neither Turkish nor Armenian but mere English is the doublet "mandatory" and "mandatary". In 1919 both forms were used as nouns, "mandatary" being apparently the more common. "Mandatory" has won out since then so I use it exclusively but the reader will frequently run into "mandatary" when I am citing someone else.

Some confusion may be caused by the use of "near east" and "middle east" as synonyms. I regret it, but it can't be avoided. I would much prefer to distinguish, as Arnold J. Toynbee does, between the Christian "near east," i.e., Greece and the Balkans, and the Moslem "middle east," a somewhat elastic term but one which certainly includes Turkey and the Arab countries. No such distinction was observed in 1919. Writers used both terms indiscriminately to designate an area of vague contour at the eastern end of the Mediterranean.

Even today one of the most useful general works on the region, William Yale's *The Near East: A Modern History* deals chiefly with what I would like to call the "middle east." In these pages, therefore, "middle east" and "near east" may be taken to refer generally to the area of the Ottoman Empire. I hope that, however vague these and other geographical terms may be, the context will make their application clear.

Where names have changed I have stuck to the form that was common at the time of which I have been writing, e.g., *Constantinople* rather than *Istanbul*. If *Iraq* and *Mesopotamia* have been used interchangeably, it is because they were equally acceptable in the years following the First World War.

Since the names of Ottoman political subdivisions and their officials are used frequently, the following explanation is offered in the hope of making them clear without excessive resort to footnotes.

The Ottoman Empire was divided into *vilayets*, roughly analagous to American states, which in turn were broken into *sanjaks*. Between the *sanjak* and the village was a further subdivision called a *caza*. The chief official of a *vilayet* was a *vali*. A *mutesarrif* presided over a *sanjak* and a *kaimakam* over a *caza*.

JAMES B. GIDNEY

Kent, Ohio
September 1966

Armenia and the Armenians

$\mathscr{I}$N JANUARY 1919 the victorious Allies of the First World War assembled in Paris for the largest peace conference the world has ever seen. They had come together to settle the affairs of the world as statesmen of the European great powers had settled those of the continent a century earlier at Vienna. The new stage was far larger than the old. This time Japan and the United States sat at the table as great powers. Nations of Africa, Asia, and South America sent delegations. Islands of the Pacific and a Chinese peninsula were among the stakes.

On the other hand the conference was smaller by the absence of Russia, working out its own destiny in civil war, and by that of the losers. No Talleyrand was to be allowed to return a defeated nation to the councils of the victors. In the new democratic age the winners were to decide things for themselves; the inevitable conflicts would have to take place among themselves.

Yet the most striking difference was neither of these. It lay in the role of the smaller nations and the deference paid to the popular will. At Vienna the fate of Europe had been settled by the great powers

and, in the main, for them. The exceptions—for example, the excessive
solicitude for the greatest collaborator of them all, the King of Saxony
—were prompted by dynastic, rather than democratic, considerations.
There was no thought of creating a new age for Europe, even in theory;
the watchwords were order and legitimacy.

The intervening century had seen the growth of two new political
ideals—democracy and nationalism. Today we may wonder if they
are even compatible; the tendency of the nineteenth century was to
make them almost identical. Hence, the new conference, while obliged to deal with the power realities as its predecessor had been,
had to moderate its judgments in appearance and to some extent
even in fact to take account of the "rights" of small nations, to accom-
modate a new concept born of the marriage of democracy and nationalism—the "self-determination of peoples."

The first year of the peace was the high water mark of irreden-
tism. Representatives of the small nations, both those who represented political states and those who did not, received a full hearing.
Some wanted increases in territory to take in more people of their
own "nationality." Some, which had been restricted to a subordinate
status, wanted self-government for the first time. Others wanted a
former state restored.

Among the suppliants who thronged the corridors none represented
a more ancient land nor carried more western sympathies than the
Armenians. While it is probable that many were always sceptical of
their maximum demands, no nation seemed to have a truer grievance
nor a better chance of obtaining some kind of redress, if only because
with the withdrawal of the Russians from the allied coalition no great
power had any serious design on the bulk of Armenia.

The nature of the Armenians' claim and the way in which it slipped
through their fingers form the subject of this study.

✻   ✻   ✻

"Armenia" is the homeland of a Christian people of Indo-European
speech in eastern Asia Minor. Since the fourteenth century the name
has designated no political state, except the short-lived Armenian
Republic of 1918-1920, which comprised a small part of Armenia, and

the present Soviet Republic of Armenia, a still more truncated portion. Moreover, when Armenia was a state, independent or partially
so, its borders were variable—and even within them, the nature of the
country made the exercise of sovereignty minimal in some of its regions. Finally, the last area in which the Armenians prior to 1914
enjoyed, or at least possessed, a political state was not part of ancient
Armenia at all. Consequently, the only useful location of the region
will be historical and topographical rather than political.

Armenia is, with the exception of Cilicia (see below), virtually all
highland—high but fertile valleys, higher, rugged mountains. To the
east and northeast it extends roughly to the present boundaries of
Iran and the Soviet Republics of Georgia and Azerbaijan. To the
south it borders Syria and Iraq. Its northern and western limits are
harder to define. Maps of the Armenian delegation at Paris in 1919
show the Black Sea as the northern extremity, thus taking in the city
and vilayet of Trebizond, but that is a debatable inclusion. The extreme western boundary might be a line drawn from the Black Sea
to the Mediterranean passing somewhat to the west of Sivas and
Adana.

The heartland was the region around Lake Van, the headwaters of
the Tigris and Euphrates, and Ararat, a name used by foreigners to
designate Armenia's highest mountain, but which Armenians use
for the region in which it is located, consisting of a cluster of mountains and a surrounding plain. (Armenians call Mt. Ararat *Massis*.)

Armenian poets have sung the beauty of their country, but its
effect on outsiders has not been so happy. Sir Charles Eliot, an exceptional scholar and linguist who was for some years an official of the
British embassy in Constantinople, knew all parts of Asia Minor from
personal visits. He described northern Armenia in lugubrious terms:

> Northern Armenia is one of the gloomiest and dreariest countries
> in the world. It may have some brief spell of tenderness and
> grace in the spring, which I have never seen, but in the summer
> and winter alike it is hard, repulsive, and terrible. During the
> heat everything is baked to a dry, muddy yellow, from the spiky
> grass on the plains to the scanty brushwood on the mountains,
> which is hardly distinguishable from the rocks. A village is indi-

cated by heaps of grey stones on a mountainside suggesting the remains of a landslip . . .

If Armenia is not a pleasant land in summer, it is still less so in winter. Every country which is periodically overwhelmed with snow must present a terrible monotony of whiteness but in Russia and Siberia mankind have learnt, if not to conquer, at least to cope successfully with the all-pervading phenomenon. They have snow roads and sledges, well-warmed houses, suitable exercise, and food. But in Anatolia man lets himself be helplessly overwhelmed by the annual avalanche. The roads are blocked, life is at a standstill. There are no amusements, no resources, no means of getting about. The earth, the mountains, and the sky are full of snow, and the human race sit huddled together like sheep in a pen trying to keep themselves warm.[1]

Sir Mark Sykes, an English writer and traveler who knew the country well, took a somewhat less unfavorable view, but agreed that Armenia's winters are "more severe than those of Switzerland."[2]

Another characteristic of the mountains is the east-west direction of the ranges, which has made Asia Minor from ancient times a relatively easy country to invade from the east, but difficult from the south. The Armenians, never thoroughly conquered by the Arabs in four centuries, fled from the Seljuk Turks within a few years of the first appearance of those Central Asian migrants.

None of the foregoing description applies to Cilicia, the medieval Armenian kingdom, which owed its existence to the pressure of the Seljuks and the consequent southwestward migration of large numbers of Armenians. Known from ancient times because the *Cilician Gates* were the invasion route to Syria for conquering armies like that of Alexander the Great—perhaps also because Cicero was its governor—Cilicia is the triangle formed by the Mediterranean to the south, the Taurus Mountains to the northwest, and the Amanus range to the east. Its mountains surround a fertile lowland like the seats of

---

[1] Sir Charles Eliot, *Turkey in Europe* (London: Edward Arnold, 1908), 403-404.
[2] Mark Sykes, *The Caliph's Last Heritage* (London: MacMillan and Co., Ltd., 1915), 3.

an amphitheatre. It can be easily identified on any topographical map as the patch of green north of the Gulf of Alexandretta. On the political map of 1919 it meant the vilayet of Adana and the sanjak of Marash, which had once been part of Adana but had been transferred in the 1880's to the neighboring vilayet of Aleppo. The districts of Aintab and Urfa to the east were also sometimes included in references to Cilicia. Unlike other parts of Armenia, Cilicia is a conspicuously rich country. Edouard Brémond, the French administrator in 1919-1920, compared it to Egypt, but "an Egypt with Alps."[3]

By locating the maximum Armenia on the same political map, we will find that it embraces, in addition to Cilicia, seven vilayets of Asiatic Turkey—Van, Bitlis, Diarbekir, Kharput,[4] Sivas, Erzerum, and Trebizond—as well as the Republic of Armenia lying to the northeast along the Araxes River, sometimes called *Transcaucasian* or *Russian Armenia*.[5]

This region is not inhabited solely by Armenians but by a mixture of peoples. If it is not an ethnologist's paradise, like the northern Caucasus, it exhibits a sufficient variety of its own. Three elements

[3] E. Brémond, *La Cilicie en 1919-1920* (Paris: Imprimerie Nationale, 1921), 76.

[4] Ottoman vilayets usually had the same name as their provincial capitals; when they didn't, they were frequently called by those names. Thus, the vilayet of *Mamouret-ul-Aziz* may be called *Kharput* and will be so called throughout this work.

[5] I have called this the "maximum" Armenia because it was the most asked for by the Armenian delegations at the peace conference and the most that was discussed by allied statesmen. It was not the most that could be conceived by the minds of enthusiasts. A map prepared by *The New Armenia*, a periodical published in New York, claimed northwestern Iran down to a line drawn through Lake Urmia and just north of Tabriz. It extended Armenia beyond Sinope on the Black Sea, from where the boundary ran south to the Anti-Taurus, thence turning west to include a coastal strip as far as Antalya. (*The New Armenia*, XIII, no. 5, September-October 1916, inside front cover.) The map was reprinted in *The Literary Digest*, LX (March 29, 1919), 36, and *Asia*, XIX (April, 1919), 421. Such a claim would include in Armenia parts of the vilayets of Kastamuni, Ankara, and Konia whose Turkish character has never, so far as I know, been questioned. If what I have called "maximum" Armenia was somewhat unrealistic, this one was an absurdity.

prior to the First World War made up, as they had for some centuries, the bulk of the population—Armenians, Kurds, and Turks.

It is impossible to say when the Armenians came into the country but we know they were there by the fifth century B.C. The Armenian language has left some traces even from that distant past although it had no alphabet of its own until almost a millennium later.

Armenia rarely enjoyed complete political sovereignty even in its heartland. Exceptional periods of independence were those under King Tigranes, whose misfortune it was to be dragged into war with Rome by his father-in-law, Mithridates of Pontus, and under the Bagratid dynasty in the ninth and tenth centuries. The status of client or feudatory was a more normal one and at many periods Armenia was divided between two powers, e.g., Roman and Parthian, Byzantine and Persian, and, in the nineteenth century, Russian and Turkish.

More important than politics in determining the autonomous character of the nation was its religion. Armenians claim to be the oldest Christian people. Obviously they were not the first Christians, but they were the first to accept the new faith as a nation and to establish a national church. In 301 A.D., before the Emperor Constantine had even granted toleration to the new cult, King Trdat (Tiridates) had embraced it as his own. With the royal example and authority behind him, Saint Gregory the Illuminator set about to teach Christianity to the Armenian people. In honor of its first leader the Armenian Apostolic Church is still sometimes called the "Gregorian Church."

Gregory's work was completed a century later by Mesrop, who devised a thirty-seven-letter alphabet for the Armenian language (it is still in use) and then spent thirty years translating the Scriptures. He paralleled for the Armenian Church the work that St. Jerome did for the Roman Catholic Church—but Jerome had a ready-made alphabet and centuries of literary tradition behind him.

Armenia thus became a Christian nation surrounded by pagans and later by Moslems. Its people have stuck to their faith ever since with a tenacity that has won the respect even of some who are not particularly sympathetic toward them in other ways. Eliot, for example, wrote: "Peculiarly admirable is their fidelity to Christianity, for few races have produced more martyrs in ancient as well as in modern times, or come in contact with more persecutors."[6]

The Armenians were not represented at the Council of Chalcedon in 451 A.D. and never accepted its decision with respect to the two natures of Christ. Their Church has always remained schismatic, adhering to the monophysite belief in a single nature like the Syrian Jacobites and the Copts. It is episcopal in structure with the *catholicos*, who resides at Etchmiadzin, at the summit. It remains the church of the great majority of Armenians; among the minority are Catholics, some of them dating from the period when the Armenian kingdom of Cilicia enjoyed close and cordial relations with the Church of Rome and the crusader states of the Levant; Protestants, the result of missionary work in the nineteenth century;[7] and a few Orthodox.

The difference between the Orthodox and Gregorian forms of Christianity was a constant bone of contention between Byzantium and Armenia. There is some reason to believe the Armenians, like other non-orthodox eastern Christians, preferred the rule of Moslem Arabs to that of Greek Christians, since the Arabs, while by no means ready to grant social equality to the bulk of their Christian subjects, recognized their right to their own religion. The Byzantines were always exerting pressure on other Christians to enter the Orthodox fold. Even when the invasion of the Seljuk Turks menaced the very existence of their empire and when the most elementary common sense would have counseled support of Armenia as a valuable buffer, they were concerned only with exploiting Armenian misfortunes to achieve political and religious control for themselves.

The Armenian state in Cilicia grew out of the migration of Armenians from the highlands in the eleventh century at the time of the Seljuk invasion. It became a kingdom in 1199 and remained one until

---

[6] Eliot, *op. cit.*, 387.

[7] An Armenian writer believes that the Paulician heresy never died out in Armenia, as is usually supposed, and that it provided a fertile soil for Protestantism. Leon Arpee, *The Armenian Awakening* (Chicago: University of Chicago Press, 1909), 66-67.

the deposition of Leon V in 1375. Crowned king in 1374 with both Armenian and Latin rites, Leon held out against the Mamluk rulers of Egypt for less than two years before losing his throne. He was taken as a captive to Cairo, but ransomed a few years later through the intercession of the friar Jehan Dardel. From Cairo Leon went to Paris where he was graciously received by Charles VI. He pleaded eloquently in the Parlement de Paris for peace between France and England and later carried the same message to London where Richard II and his court gave him a warm welcome. For the rest of his life he continued to advocate peace between the two nations; English and French alike applauded, shed a tear or two, and went back to fighting. Leon was convinced that Anglo-French harmony was essential to the existence of an Armenian state. Had he been alive in 1919, he would in all likelihood have thought the same, and with the same effect.

Although after 1375 the Armenians had no vestige of a political state, they continued to reside in Anatolia which became increasingly Turkish throughout the fifteenth century. With the conquest of Constantinople in 1453 the *Osmanli* or *Ottoman* Turks completed the destruction of the Byzantine Empire and erected their own on its ruins. The bulk of the Armenian population thus fell under Turkish rule.

The state the Ottomans created was as unlike the modern western conception of the state as could well be imagined; its structure must be understood if the position of the Armenians is to be made clear.

In the fifteenth century, essential community loyalty in the middle east was not given to the nation or state but to the religious sect. Recognizing this, the Turks, while exercising sovereignty over all parts of their empire, conceded to each religious group within it a large right to manage its own affairs. In theory this grant should have been limited to ecclesiastical matters, but when primary civil loyalty is religious rather than national, ecclesiastical matters are much broader in scope than we think them today. In effect, church officials had complete authority over civil matters in their communities, subject only to appeal to the sultan. The generally unflattering name given to these communities was *rayah* (flock). The religious state within the political state was called a *millet*.[8] In the case of the Armenian community, responsibility rested with the patriarch of Constantinople, rather than with the *catholicos* in far-off Etchmiadzin. Within the church the patriarch was only a bishop, but to the Turks he was the head of the Armenian *millet*.

There were thus in the Turkish empire no minorities at permanent odds with the state or in greater or less degree of assimilation to the majority. To the extent that the system worked efficiently and harmoniously there was no reason for being at odds, while neither the *rayah* nor the Turks had any expectation of assimilation. Westerners who think this an outlandish political institution should remember that the Ottoman state was a theocracy; its law was the *sheriat*, the law of Islam. Unlike some westerners the Turks never believed their religious regulations should be binding on people of other faiths. The *millet* system permitted groups of diverse beliefs to live peacefully on the same land, each one so far as possible following its own religious laws and customs. The chief difference between Moslems and Christians was that the former were subject at all times to be called up for military service, from which the latter were barred. In return for this exemption Christians paid a special tax for protection.

A feature of the system was the power it gave to church officials. It was an extensive power and naturally was sometimes abused, but it was not absolute. On occasion a Christian *millet* was protected from its ecclesiastical authorities by the sultan. When Armenians began turning to Protestantism, for example, officials of the Grego-

---

[8] In the earlier years of the Ottoman Empire the term *rayah* was applied to all the sultan's subjects, but by the nineteenth century it was confined to non-Moslems. Because *millet* is used in modern Turkish in the sense of "nation," it must be made clear that no such sense was ever intended under the Ottoman Empire. The *millet* differed from the "nation" in three ways: 1) it had no jurisdiction in criminal cases; 2) it enjoyed no ultimate sovereignty, which remained in the hands of the sultan; 3) its domain was in no way geographical, except that it was limited in all cases to the Ottoman Empire. On the other hand, if "nation" is understood in its earlier sense, i.e., a group having, or believing itself to have, a common origin, it is not a bad equivalent of *millet*.

rian Church, their wrath unappeased by a mere theological ban, obliged them to leave their families and made it impossible for them to earn a living. They appealed to the Sultan Abdul Mejid who issued a *firman* constituting them a separate community with the same rights as the *millets*.[9]

In the nineteenth century numerous efforts were made to modify the millet system in the direction of the western national state. We will notice a few of them later, but it may be instructive now to observe why they usually didn't work. An example is the law of 1855 admitting Christians to the army. Eliot wrote of it:

> Nothing could be more plausible than this law. It is one of the first conditions for the unity and homogeneity of a State that all classes of the population should have the same right of bearing arms and defending their country. Yet the measure was never executed, simply because all sections of Ottoman subjects objected to it. The Moslems said that their lives would be in danger if the Christians were armed; and the Christians said that they could not fight under the standard of the Prophet or against other Christians.[10]

Living contentedly with a law no one enforces or is expected to enforce is not a peculiarly Ottoman habit, but the reason for non-enforcement in this case is rather characteristically Ottoman. The "unity and homogeneity of the state" were western, not Ottoman ideals. The law was probably forced on the Turks by their European allies in the Crimean War. Having fought to deny to the Russians the status of protectors of the Christians in the empire, they felt they ought to offer some protection themselves, but in the form in which it was offered by the law of 1855, it was just as distasteful to Christians as to Moslems.[11]

---

[9] For the Armenian Protestant Church see Arpee, *op. cit.*, 93-171. An interesting example of protection of Gregorian Armenians against their own clergy will be found in Geoffrey Lewis, *Turkey* (New York: Frederick A. Praeger, 1955), 23-24.

[10] Eliot, *op. cit.*, 293.

[11] Since the Christians were to lose their exemption from military service under

So much has been truly said and written about the miseries of the Armenians that it is necessary to caution against supposing they were always singled out for special hatred by the Turks. On the contrary, credible writers have asserted that before the nineteenth century they were the Turks' favorite minority, enjoying the epithet *millet-i-sadiqa* (the faithful nation) and valued not only for their loyalty but for the services they performed for the Turks.

The reason for such favoritism, if it existed, was less the Armenians' character than their want of outside connections. Greeks and Slavs within the empire felt the pull of Greeks and Slavs without; moreover, their Orthodox faith gave them a relationship to a Russian protector, more or less formalized in the Treaty of Kuchuk Kainarji (1774), that could not fail to arouse resentment among the Turks.

The Armenians, whose church had no institutional ties to any outside of Armenia, and whose people had no self-governing cousins of their own nationality anywhere, gave no similar cause for uneasiness until the Russians crossed the Caucasus early in the nineteenth century and established themselves in Transcaucasia. The Turks then faced one of the most formidable Christian powers across an eastern frontier, a situation made more menacing by the fact that the Turkish side of the frontier held the bulk of the Armenian Christian population. Even if the Russians had been content to advance no further and had shown no interest in intervening between Turks and Armenians, their presence in such a strategic location could hardly have failed to alarm an imperial government increasingly aware of its own weaknesses, nor could it have failed to raise doubts about the loyalty of Armenian subjects.

At no time were the Armenians as monolithic as propaganda, both for and against them, has represented them. They appear rather to have been from ancient times a faction-ridden people. Even the threat of national extinction has never kept them from internal squabbling.

---

this law, it was only fair that they should be freed of the special tax for protection to which they were liable. Consequently, the law abolished the tax. When Christians subsequently failed to enter the army, they were made subject to a new tax, collected in the same way as the old one, but under a new name.

Nor did they all follow the same trade, live in the same kind of community nor enjoy the same prosperity or the same consideration from their neighbors.

In western Anatolia the Armenians were scattered, generally engaged in business and finance, respected and prosperous, though perhaps not loved. In the east they were more numerous; many of them were peasants who lived together in villages. Although there can be no question that they were poor, they were not necessarily poorer than other peoples in the same region. On the contrary, in spite of a unique disability, to be discussed shortly, they seem to have done rather better than other peoples in the east. One thing on which there is virtually universal agreement is that Armenians were more prosperous than Turks.

Their affluence was usually attributed to some kind of personal superiority or to a difference between Christianity and Islam. Sarkis Atamian has ascribed it somewhat more reflectively to the contrasting family life of the two peoples. The Armenians had strong family loyalties and easily identified their welfare with that of their group. "For the Armenian family," he writes, "suppression of individual desires for the common family good was perhaps the dominant value."[12] Their distaste for improvidence and sexual freedom was almost a taboo. Under these circumstances, the Armenian had every reason to work hard and save, since economic self-sufficiency was a family incentive.

The Turk, on the other hand, had no incentive either to get or to keep, since he had nothing that the Christian could identify as family life at all. The men and women lived in separate parts of the house, the *selamlik* and the *haremlik*. They did not mix socially, the women being kept in an unmistakably subordinate position. Promiscuity and the pursuit of pleasure of all kinds were accepted behavior. Atamian quotes the Turkish saying: "*Ishim yok, keifim chok.*" (Work not, play a lot.) These are not ideals that make work a religious duty;

[12] Sarkis Atamian, *The Armenian Community* (New York: Philosophical Library, 1955), 136.

on the contrary, they served to keep Turkish money flowing into Armenian and Greek coffers.[13]

Another possibility is suggested by Arnold J. Toynbee in his theory of "penalizations." He compares the Christians of Turkey with the Jews of eastern Europe and other people denied access to many normal forms of activity, showing that in each case exceptional energy was channeled into the pursuits that were left open. Because they lived on the sufferance of a ruling people they acquired an obsequious manner, a large measure of adaptability, and nimble wits. Under this theory the Armenians were good at business because they had to be.

Toynbee's explanation is impressive because of the abundance of evidence with which he supports it, evidence drawn from all over the world. He shows, for example, that the Moslem minority in Kazan exhibited the same traits that the Turks ascribed to their Christian subjects.[14]

Although there is agreement on the Armenians' prosperity, there is less on their other characteristics. Sir Edwin Pears, who practiced law in Constantinople throughout most of his adult life, thought them a highly artistic people:

> It is rare to visit the house of an Armenian in a fairly prosperous condition where there is not evidence of artistic and musical taste: pictures or a piano, or other musical instruments.[15]

The artistic achievements of Armenians in diaspora would seem to confirm this view, yet Eliot, who also had substantial experience in Asia Minor, disagreed with it. He found them "wanting . . . in artistic sense."[16] He also believed they had no capacity for governing themselves,[17] although the Turks used many of them in government.

---

[13] *Ibid.*, 136-137.

[14] Arnold J. Toynbee, *A Study of History*, 12 vols. (London: Oxford University Press, 1955), II, 208-259.

[15] Sir Edwin Pears, *Forty Years in Constantinople* (New York: D. Appleton and Co., 1916), 151.

[16] Eliot, *op. cit.*, 391.

[17] *Ibid.*, 383.

Some foreign observers treated them as paragons—"the Europeans of Asia"—while others frankly disliked them or regarded them with a kind of scorn apparently learned from upper-class Turks. Sir Mark Sykes had some good words for the rural Armenians, but portrayed the town-dwellers of Van, Bitlis, and Erzerum as hateful in the extreme, devoid of even physical resemblance to their country cousins.[18] The archeologist D. G. Hogarth, a more objective writer than Sykes, noted their "passion for plotting" and "fanatical intolerance."[19] General James G. Harbord, who led the American Military Mission to Armenia in 1919 reported that even the missionaries who risked their lives for their Armenian charges liked the Turks better. The general did not cite his authority for the statement, but by a curious coincidence Gregory Mason, correspondent for *The Outlook*, who was in Turkey at the same time as Harbord and might have talked to him, said much the same thing and illustrated it with some curious examples.[20]

Undoubtedly, the Armenians were people of all sorts like the rest of us, lacking none of the qualities of humanity, good and bad, and with a normal range of individual variations, but with characteristics, some admirable, some less so, peculiar to their circumstances. Banal as this conclusion may appear, the "character" of the Armenians must be discussed for the reactions they aroused in foreigners, to be considered further in Chapter III, constitute one of the elements in their fate. It is as sad as it is odd that outsiders were rarely able to like both Turks and Armenians.

Allusion has been made to a special disability suffered by Armenians in the east. Much of the territory here called *Armenia* may also be called *Kurdistan*. The presence of large numbers of Kurds in eastern Turkey was an affliction to the Armenians. Linguistically Iranian, in religion Moslem, but of a very lax sort, these rude tribesmen behaved in a way that may be typical of mountain people generally.

[18] Sykes, *op. cit.*, 414-418.
[19] David G. Hogarth, *A Wandering Scholar in the Levant* (London: John Murray, 1896), 147.
[20] *The Outlook*, CXXIII (October 29, 1919), 86.

Fierce, wild, ruthless, with little respect for law or property, they spent much of the time not devoted to harassing the sedentary Armenians in endless blood feuds among themselves. At the same time they were warm-hearted and hospitable, with a code of behavior no less real and binding because it is unfamiliar to people who live under more settled conditions.

The antagonism between the Kurds and the Armenians, and the suffering of the latter at the hands of the former, were such a permanent feature of life in eastern Anatolia in the years before the First World War that there is a tendency to believe it was always so. It appears, however, that in earlier times there was a sort of rough but workable feudal arrangement between them. The fierce, hard-fighting Kurds took a part of the peaceable Armenians' crop in exchange for protection. A tribe of Kurds would go to war with another which it had found molesting "its Armenians."[21]

This symbiosis worked well enough while Ottoman power was weak in Armenia, for the Kurds provided a protection the government was unable to give, while the Armenians were able to turn over a portion of their crops to the Kurds and still retain enough for themselves. The increase in Turkish authority in the nineteenth century destroyed the relationship. A chief feature of the Ottoman power, indeed the only one that must have been visible to many Ottoman subjects, was the power to tax. The Armenians could not survive if they had to make payments both to their Kurdish overlords and the Ottoman tax-gatherer. If they chose to stick with the Kurds, they were harassed by the Turks; if they paid taxes to the legal government and complained to the authorities about the exactions of the Kurds, they were subject to savage reprisals against which, being unarmed, they had no defense.

Such a state of affairs was bad enough when it represented merely a lag in adjustment to circumstances. Transformed into a weapon in a campaign of repression, it became utterly intolerable. After the

[21] For a good description of this relationship and the stages of its breakdown see S. Zarzecki, "La Question Kurdo-Arménienne" in *Revue de Paris*, April 15, 1914, 884-888.

Treaty of Berlin in 1878, the Sultan Abdul Hamid was determined to suppress the Armenians for good and all. In pursuit of this objective he created a new paramilitary organization in the east, patterned on that of the Cossacks and called, to leave no doubt of its origin, the *Hamidieh*. It was made up of Kurds who were given a virtually free hand against the Armenians. Foreign observers said the corps was useless for genuine military purposes, but it terrorized the Armenians with impunity.

If we can imagine public authorities calling on mountain moonshiners to keep order in the fastnesses of Appalachia, we may form some appreciation of the imbecility of this manoeuvre. It increased the hatred many of the Sultan's subjects felt for him—and not all of them Armenian subjects—and it provided additional justification for intervention by foreign powers in favor of Ottoman Christians.

Armenia also counted among its inhabitants a number of Turks, both in cities and in villages. The city-dwellers differed from their Armenian neighbors in that they shunned commerce. As professional work was scarce and their narrow education would in any case not have fitted them to do it, they had a choice between becoming a part of the bureaucracy and doing very little or staying out of the bureaucracy and doing nothing.

The rural Turk was a different sort altogether. He was a hard-working peasant like the rural Armenian; according to some who knew the old regime well, the Turkish peasant was the chief victim of imperial oppression. He was liable to military service as the Christian was not. He had no ecclesiastical authority to fight his battles and no foreign powers to defend him.[22] When we speak of France or Great Britain

---

22 This point of view is expressed with moderation by Sir Harry Luke, *The Old Turkey and the New*, revised edition (London: Geoffrey Bles, 1956), 201-202. Sir Harry concedes that by 1913 the Armenians were being treated worse than the Turks, but the latter aroused his sympathy, particularly when they had to leave their crops unharvested to fight in a war, while their Christian neighbors prepared to pile up profits that reduced their military exemption tax to insignificance. Eliot thought the Turks got the worst of it even in the capital: "The Christians in Constantinople have relatively little to complain of in the way of permanent oppression, because some Power or other is always ready to air their

defending Turkey, we mean protecting the Turkish government and ruling class, not their victims, many of whom were Turks.

It would be hard to prove that these Turks entertained feelings of unquenchable hostility toward the Armenians. In a land in which religion was the individual's chief loyalty, there must always have been some gulf between them. There may also have been mutual disdain for their contrasting ways of life, the Turk despising the Armenian's endless fuss over business and profits, the Armenian equally despising the Turk's idleness. The latter difference would not be operative in the case of tillers of the soil, who had to work hard, whether Turk or Armenian, but religious loyalties would probably have influenced them to some extent.

The nature of the disabilities suffered by Christians is described with a wealth of detail in reports submitted in 1867 by all the British consular officials in the Turkish Empire.[23] There is a wide agreement that they were subject to social and legal discrimination ranging from the relatively mild in towns where there were European residents to very severe in the interior where foreigners were rare. The worst aspect of the prejudice was the refusal to accept the testimony of Christians in court, but this was to some extent mitigated by judges who found ingenious ways to reconcile law with justice and on occasion by the greater wealth of the Christians which made it possible to employ Moslem witnesses.

Some of the consuls exonerated the central government, accepting as sincere its efforts at reform which broke down on the backwardness, incompetence, and corruption of local officials. The Christians themselves were assigned a share of blame, one consul testifying that at Kars they were so fanatical as to render the application of the provisions of the *Hatt-i-Humayun*[24] quite impractical, another charging

grievances. But there is no one to protect the Turks, and prevent their own government from pressing upon them." Eliot, *op. cit.*, 140.

[23] Great Britain, House of Commons, *Reports Received from Her Majesty's Ambassador and Consuls relating to the Condition of Christians in Turkey.* 1867 (Sessional Papers 3854 and 3944).

[24] The imperial rescript of 1856 which guaranteed equality and civil rights to non-Moslems.

that assaults on Armenian Protestants were instigated by leaders of the Armenian communities.

The discrimination described in these reports and elsewhere, however deplorable, is not hatred. The consuls maintain there was little violence against the Christians. There are many accounts of personal friendship between the two peoples in various sources as well as in stories any visitor to the east is certain to hear. Even where friendship was absent, the two peoples accepted coexistence as natural. The American missionary Grace Knapp gave this account of an exchange of messages between the Armenians besieged in Van in 1915 and their Turkish assailants:

> They sent a manifesto to the Turks to the effect that their quarrel was with one man and not with their Turkish neighbors. Valis might come and go, but the two races must continue to live together, and they hoped that after Djevdet went there might be peaceful and friendly relations between them. The Turks answered in the same spirit, saying that they were forced to fight. Indeed, a protest against the war was signed by many prominent Turks, but Djevdet would pay no attention to it.[25]

Many Turks' resentment at the power of the Kurds must have exceeded any distaste they felt for the Armenians. Sykes related an incident he witnessed when, traveling through eastern Turkey, he saw the Turkish captain of his escort beat a Kurd with his whip. The victim, a thief who preyed on Armenians, was a member of the *Hamidieh*; he had fired on Sykes' party thinking they were defenseless villagers. The Turk conceded that if the Kurd had merely robbed a Turk he would have been powerless to intervene, but by firing on the escort of a foreign consul, he had lost his immunity. The delight of the captain in beating up the Kurd was obviously shared by his English companion.

After the beating, the Turk tied the man's wrists to a saddle and led him to the nearest police post two hours away. There the Kurd freely

---

[25] Viscount Bryce, *The Treatment of Armenians in the Ottoman Empire 1915-1916.* Documents presented to Viscount Grey of Fallodon, Secretary of State for Foreign Affairs, with a preface by Viscount Bryce. Blue Book Miscellaneous No. 31 (1916) (London: Sir Joseph Causton and Sons Limited), 35.

admitted he had been engaged in robbing the Armenian villagers and would not have fired if he had known the Turkish force was still in the neighborhood. Riding away, the Turk informed Sykes that the thief would be free in an hour, as they never did anything to the Kurds—but expressed satisfaction that the presence of the Englishman had given him a chance to break his whip on "one of the favorites."[26]

In the same year, however, the Armenian Catholic bishop at Mush told Sykes the Armenians suffered little from the Kurds or the Turkish soldiers, but a great deal from the police. The vali, he said, was a good man but so surrounded by spies and incompetents that he could do nothing.[27] What Ottoman subjects said to foreigners should be accepted with reserve, but Sykes was a Catholic and the bishop might well have talked to him with more frankness than to someone of another faith.

The same journey produced another and more striking revelation of the attitude of the Turkish regulars toward the *Hamidieh*. At a village south of Van, Sykes found the soldiers on excellent terms with the Armenian revolutionaries to whom on occasion they furnished food and from whom they borrowed money. This state of affairs came about because of the resentment of the Turkish soldiery toward the *Hamidieh* whom they knew to be openly disloyal but could not punish. Secret orders obliged the courts-martial, the only courts that had jurisdiction over the *Hamidieh*, to let offenders go with little or no punishment. This made the army the butt of jeers from the civil service; military resentment was increased by the fact that the civil service received their salaries regularly and in full, while the army did not. Sykes noted that the revolutionaries "were not slow to appreciate the possibilities of these circumstances."[28]

British consuls on the scene confirm the role of the Kurds in persecuting the Armenians while emphasizing the complicity of Turkish of-

[26] Sykes, *op. cit.*, 421-422.

[27] *Ibid.*, 409. See Eliot, *op. cit.*, 138-139 for a description of the role of spies in the imperial government.

[28] Sykes, *op. cit.*, 420-421.

ficialdom. Consul Clifford Lloyd wrote from Erzerum on January 31, 1890:

> If the Turkish government locally can be induced to insist on
> the maintenance of order among the Kurdish population, from
> whose acts of violence the Armenians hitherto have suffered
> much and often, the chief cause of the unhappy condition of
> many of the Christians in Armenia will have been removed.[29]

Vice-Consul C. M. Hallward reported from Diarbekir on October 26, 1896:

> Everything depends on the attitude of the Government. The
> Kurds have, generally speaking, no importance as an element
> of disorder unless they act with the connivance of the authori-
> ties.[30]

As for the quality of the officials charged with such a heavy responsibility, Hallward summed it up effectively:

> In this province, besides the vali, whom I have had frequent
> occasion to criticize unfavorably, there are two Mutesarrifs, the
> one very corrupt and the other very incompetent, and eleven
> Kaimakams, of whom perhaps two or three would pass muster
> as relatively good officials, and most of whom exercize less
> practical authority in their districts than the Kurdish Beys
> and Aghas.[31]

Hogarth blamed Turks, Kurds, and Armenians alike for the disorders—for sloppiness, lawlessness, and fractiousness respectively—but stressed the evil effect of foreign meddling:

> If the Kurdish question could be settled by a vigorous Marshal,
> and the Porte secured against the irresponsible European sup-

---

[29] House of Commons, *Correspondence Respecting the Conditions of the Populations in Asiatic Turkey and the Proceedings in the Case of Moussa Bey. 1890-
1891* (C-6214) (London: Printed for Her Majesty's Government by Harrison
and Sons), 13.

[30] House of Commons, *Further Correspondence respecting the Asiatic Provinces
of Turkey and Events in Constantinople. 1897* (C-8395), 38.

[31] *Ibid.*, 39.

port of sedition, I believe that the Armenians would not have much more to complain of.[32]

Kurds and Turks were both minorities but in Armenia every people, including the Armenians, was a minority. According to the Armenian patriarchate's population figures for 1912, Kurds constituted sixteen per cent of the population of the six Armenian vilayets,[33] Turks twenty-five per cent, and Armenians thirty-nine per cent. These statistics do not cover all of the territory of the six vilayets, some districts in which the Armenians were very few having been omitted. If Sivas and Erzerum had been left out entirely, Kurds and Armenians would have shown substantially higher percentages, Turks lower. In those two vilayets Turks were more numerous than any other ethnic group, although not a majority. In only one vilayet, Van, did any element have an absolute majority. The Armenians had it there but with less than fifty-three per cent.[34]

In addition to Turks, Kurds, and Armenians, there was a host of other peoples, divided for purposes of enumeration into "other Christians, other Moslems, and other religions." The Christians, about seven per cent of the total, were significant only in Diarbekir where the "Assyrians," descendants of the Nestorian Christians, together with some smaller sects, brought them up to twenty per cent. The Moslems, including Persians, Circassians, and Lazes, were only three per cent but

---

[32] Hogarth, op. cit., 149.

[33] Sivas, Erzerum, Van, Bitlis, Diarbekir, Kharput. These were the six in which the Sultan had been obliged to promise reforms to the European powers after the massacres of 1894-1895.

[34] This figure contrasts glaringly with that in the French Yellow Book on Armenian Affairs which puts the Armenians as low as seventeen per cent in Van. France, Ministère des Affaires Etrangères, Documents Diplomatiques: Affaires Arméniennes. Projets de réforme dans l'Empire Ottoman. 1893-1897, no. 6 (Paris: Imprimerie Nationale, 1897), 7. Such a discrepancy tempts the observer to dismiss all population estimates for eastern Turkey as mere fancy—or mere fakery. There is, however, no necessary conflict between them, since the French figure includes the entire vilayet while that of the patriarchate, as explained above, excludes areas not considered Armenian. The differences in calculation produced a wider divergence in Van than almost anywhere else, since the Lake Van region was the most densely Armenian in Turkey, while the large Hakkiari district between Lake Van and Mesopotamia was heavily Kurdish.

might have been considerably higher if the Kizilbashis, whose faith is a variation of Shi'a Islam, had been included. Instead, they are lumped with such "other religions" as the Yezidis, bringing that category to ten per cent of the total.

The following table shows the figures for the six vilayets as a whole, but excluding those areas the patriarchate did not consider Armenian. It will be noted that the Armenians were more numerous than any other group, but at the same time less than two-fifths of the population. Christians of all types were less than half. Among the three chief elements, the Armenians, although outnumbering either Turks or Kurds, were slightly outnumbered by the two in combination.

POPULATION OF THE SIX VILAYETS IN 1912[35]

Group	Population	Per cent of Total
Turks	666,000	25
Kurds	424,000	16
Other Moslems	88,000	3
Armenians	1,018,000	39
Other Christians	165,000	7
Other Religions	254,000	10
TOTAL	2,615,000	100

[35] Marcel Léart, *La Question arménienne à la lumière des documents* (Paris: Challamel, 1913), 60-61. (I have simplified the table by rounding out the percentages.) Léart, a careful writer even though undisguisedly a partisan of the Armenians, accepts these figures as being as accurate as can be expected in the circumstances. It should be borne in mind that no census in pre-1914 Turkey had the accuracy demanded in western countries, that the six vilayets had more than their share of wild country, and that many of the Kurds were semi-nomadic, migrating south to Syria or Iraq in the winter.

Figures presented to the Paris Peace Conference by the Armenian delegation show 1,403,000 Armenians in Turkish Armenia out of a total of 4,470,000 in the world. The discrepancy between this figure and Léart's is partly accounted for by the delegation's inclusion of all the territory of the six vilayets as well as Cilicia and Trebizond. The same tabulation shows Armenians in other parts of the world as follows: Caucasian Armenia 1,296,000; other parts of Transcaucasia 508,000; Asiatic Turkey 440,000; Persia 140,000; elsewhere 683,000.

An obvious objection to these statistics as a measure of the density of Armenian population is that they do not include Russian Armenia where the Armenian percentage was higher than in most parts of Turkish Armenia. On the other hand they also do not include Cilicia and Trebizond; in Trebizond at least it was lower.

Another and more justified objection is that the Armenian population in 1912 had been diminished by the massacres of 1895-1896 and in all likelihood by emigration from the six vilayets which was prompted by fear of a recurrence of the massacres and which would not otherwise have taken place. If this is left out of account, the figures might be taken to mean that the more Armenians they killed, the better the claim of the Turks to govern Armenia. They are not included here, however, with any thought of supporting or refuting the Armenian claim to independence, for that claim rested not on a numerical majority, but on the sufferings of the Armenians and the apparent futility of trying to end them under Turkish rule.

The figures show, however, that an Armenian state could not be established by plebiscite as an expression of the "self-determination of peoples" in the rather mechanical way in which that concept seems to have been understood, since they had not had a majority in the area claimed even before their ranks were thinned by the massacres and deportations of 1915-1916. They also show that if an Armenian state were formed in virtually any part of what was called Armenia, it would face a serious minority problem of its own. Not an insoluble problem certainly; it is possible that the Kurds would have ceased being a troublesome element on a large scale as soon as they found themselves under a government that could and would control them (as now seems to be the case under the Turkish Republic). Nonetheless, in asking for an independent state, the Armenians were, however unwillingly, asking to govern others as well as themselves, and as the size of their claim increased, the others grew more and themselves, relatively fewer.

"Elsewhere" is large because it includes Constantinople. *La Question arménienne* (a pamphlet presented by the Armenian National Delegation), *annexe 4* in Papers of Edward M. House, hereafter referred to as House Papers, dr. 30, f. 21.

2

Reforms and Persecutions

*I*T MAY BE ADMITTED that the position of the Armenians and other subject nationalities was not at any time ideal, but it visibly worsened as the empire began to imitate the liberal institutions of the west. No purpose would be served by entering into the argument for and against westernization, whether it offered the Ottoman state its only chance to stay alive and competitive in the contemporary world or whether it was a snare to be avoided at all costs because it destroyed the very basis of that state.[1] It is hard to see how Turkey could have avoided it. Successive defeats at the hands of Russia, the growing awareness of her own most alert minds that the nation could not compete with Europe, the pressure of foreign powers upon her, the relinquishment of a portion of her sovereignty, vague though the terms of surrender may have been, in the Treaty of Kuchuk Kainarji, all con-

[1] The argument that westernization was inevitably fatal to the empire has been put with vigor and force (and, I think, exaggeration) by Elie Kedouri, *England and the Middle East. The Destruction of the Ottoman Empire 1914-1921* (London: Bowes and Bowes, 1956). The opposite viewpoint is such a commonplace that no citation is necessary.

tributed to a westernizing movement that, once begun by Selim III
and successfully forwarded by Mahmud II, could hardly have been
indefinitely resisted even under those of their successors who detested
it.

Effective reform began in 1826 when Mahmud II succeeded in
breaking the power of the janissaries who had grown into a kind of
Praetorian Guard, commanding the government at least as much as
they served it. Mahmud's rule was marked by administrative reforms,
by opening the country to European influences, and by consolidating
power over the empire at Constantinople.

Abdul Mejid, who succeeded his father in 1839, inaugurated his
reign by an act of toleration, the *Hatt-i-Sharif of Gulhane* (Illustrious
Rescript of the Rose Garden). Tax-farming was abolished, a Council
of State was created along with a Penal Code, naturally based on European models, and a state bank; most important, the new sultan proclaimed the absolute equality before the law of all of his subjects. Not
all Christian subjects rejoiced at equality, however, if the abolition of
tax-farming went with it. The Christian *sarrafs* (magnates or financiers) objected strenuously to the inroads such a reform might make
on their profits. Two years later the whole project was tacitly abandoned.

It came to life again after the Crimean War with the issuance of a
new rescript, the *Hatt-i-Humayun* (Imperial Rescript).[2] In addition
to administrative, financial, ecclesiastical, and judicial reforms, it abolished tax-farming all over again, and this time bribery with it, and
once again announced toleration and equality for all religions. Unfortunately, one of the ecclesiastical reforms provided fixed stipends for
the clergy in place of whatever they could squeeze out of their flocks,
an innovation that was particularly objectionable to the Greek church.
It is said that when the Archbishop of Izmit saw the rescript replaced
in its silken envelope after its official promulgation, he exclaimed,

---

[2] *Hatt-i-Sharif* and *Hatt-i-Humayun* are essentially synonymous terms since they
were used for the same purpose. Each designated an executive order of the Sultan. However, western writers have generally applied the first to the order of
1839 and the second to that of 1856.

"Pray God it may stay there!" "No supernatural intervention was necessary to produce that result," is the comment of Sir Charles Eliot, who noted that the powers recognized "the high value" of the rescript in the Treaty of Paris, "but no one else paid any attention to most of its provisions."[3]

One effect it did have. The government, having noticed a growing antagonism between lay and clerical elements in the *millets*, took advantage of it to reorganize them in such a way as to strengthen the laity. Among the Armenians (as among the Greek Orthodox and the Jews) the rescript paved the way for a "constitution."[4] Whether it led to a more democratic community life or to domination by the bourgeoisie of Constantinople is a matter of interpretation. Sarkis Atamian holds the latter view; Leon Arpee saw the constitution as the beginning of democracy not only for the Armenians but for all of Turkey.[5] The governing General Assembly was heavily weighted in favor of Constantinople, which had one hundred members, against the rest of Asia Minor which had only forty, but this may not have had the importance Atamian ascribes to it. He may be oversimplifying in dividing the Armenian *millet* into liberal, patriotic peasants in the east and reactionary, collaborationist bourgeois in the capital.[6]

With the coming to power of Abdul Aziz in 1861, the curve of reform began to turn downward. Lacking his brother's amiable disposition, and less European in outlook—Abdul Mejid was the first sultan to read French newspapers—he leaned toward absolutism. Nonetheless, some of the chief reformers were still alive and the western pow-

---

[3] Eliot, *op. cit.*, 293.

[4] For a discussion of the reorganization of the non-Moslem *millets* cf. Roderic H. Davison, *Reform in the Ottoman Empire 1856-1876* (Princeton: Princeton University Press, 1963), Chapter IV.

[5] Atamian, *op. cit.*, 33-41; Arpee, *op. cit.*, 185-194.

[6] James Bryce believed the constitution and the representative council had been beneficial to the Armenians because they had assisted in the spread of education among them and taught them "to apply for the common good such funds as they can save from the rapacity of their enemies." James Bryce, *Transcaucasia and Ararat*, 4th ed. (New York and London: The Macmillan Company, 1896), 430.

ers still pressing for reform. Hence, the fifteen year reign of Abdul Aziz appears in retrospect as a continuation of the reforming era, the more so by comparison with the dark pall of despotism that fell upon the empire with the advent of his successor.

Abdul Hamid, who came to the throne in 1876, did more than anyone else to create the character of the "terrible Turk," until recently so familiar to Americans. He was narrow, fanatical, ruthless to the point of savagery. Some say he was also crafty and resourceful. Certainly he ruled for over thirty years, yet so many of his policies led to exactly the kind of internal revolt and foreign interference that brought about his undoing that we must question whether his abilities represented more than mediocrity joined to luck, the latter in the form of a division of Europe into two hostile camps which could not act together in the east.

When Abdul Hamid entered on his long rule, Turkey was involved in trouble over its European provinces which led to war with Serbia and Montenegro. At the same time a rising in Bulgaria was ferociously repressed. Feeling in the west ran high—Gladstone's "bag and baggage" pamphlet dates from this period—while Russian opinion clamored for war in defense of the southern Slavs. In 1877 the war began; in 1878, in spite of a determined Turkish defense, it ended in an overwhelming Russian victory.

The terms of peace, imposed in the Treaty of San Stefano, were severe. They stripped the empire of much of its authority and a substantial piece of its territory in the Balkans. Their harshness brought the other European powers into the game.

To understand the attitude of those powers, we must bear in mind that Turkey's might and influence had been waning for several centuries. Thrust back from the gates of Vienna in 1683, the Turks had had to withdraw from Hungary, which they had never really conquered but for which they had contended for a century and a half. They never again penetrated so far into Europe. In the early nineteenth century the Russians brought Transcaucasia under their rule. In 1830, Greece was finally lost. Following the Crimean War, Article 9 of the Treaty of Paris marked the beginning of regular western intervention in Ottoman affairs. Europe was nibbling at Turkish territories in Africa. Egypt had been only nominally Turkish since Napoleon's invasion three-quarters of a century before. Indeed, the Egyptians had outstripped the Turks in power. Only the intervention of Russia in 1833 and Great Britain in 1840 had kept the vassal from taking over the empire. In 1860, war between Maronites and Druses had brought the west, led by France, into action to create a semi-autonomous sanjak in Lebanon under the protection of Europe.

While these losses were being digested, the Russians had been trying to give life to the vague concessions in the Treaty of Kuchuk Kainarji by assuming an active role as protector of Orthodox Christians within the empire. The attempt had been foiled in the 1850's when French and British troops had gone to the Crimea to defend the Turks. The massacres in Bulgaria gave the Russians another chance which they meant to exploit. However, the strategic importance of the Ottoman Empire was such that none of the great powers could allow it to fall under the sole domination of any other. In trying to clip the Turks' wings too closely, the Russians got their own clipped.

The great powers assembled at Berlin in June 1878 to write a new treaty, one in which the Russian gains were much reduced. Serbia, Montenegro, and Rumania were recognized as independent states but the Russian plan to create a greater Bulgarian vassal state through the annexation of Macedonia was shelved. Bulgaria north of the Balkan range became an autonomous principality, to the south it became an "autonomous Ottoman province" to be called "East Rumelia," while Macedonia remained Turkish.

These rectifications may have been necessary to keep the Russians from dominating the Straits and hence the entire eastern Mediterranean. It is harder to see the point of western abandonment of Armenia which the Russians were offering to protect. Article 16 of the Treaty of San Stefano provided that the Russians were to maintain troops in occupied areas until satisfied the Turks had made adequate reforms in the "provinces inhabited by the Armenians."[7] Under Article 61 of the Treaty of Berlin, which replaced it, the Russians had to

[7] *British and Foreign State Papers, 1877-1878* (London: William Ridgway, 1885), 739-740.

Ott. falling apart cuz of internl's + Arm. land in hot area + "protected" by Russ.... makes them suspect of anti T.

REFORMS AND PERSECUTIONS   29

withdraw and the Turks merely "engaged" to make the reforms.[8] This arrangement would have been of dubious value at any time; with Abdul Hamid at the head of the Turkish government, it was a cynical farce. Most cynical of all was the secret Anglo-Turkish Convention of June 4, 1878,[9] under which Great Britain was to occupy the island of Cyprus if the Berlin negotiations allowed Russia to retain the districts of Batum, Kars, and Ardahan, a point the British and Russians had already settled.[10]

European intervention on behalf of Turkey had its effect on the Armenians. Angered by Armenian partiality for the Russians—or what they took to be such—the Turks had destroyed many villages and massacred thousands of Armenians, particularly at Bayazid and on the plains of Alashkerd. Destroying Armenian villages in reprisal for Russian attacks had begun with the Crimean War; the reprisals of 1877-1878 were more severe than the earlier ones. Armenian desire for autonomy was inflamed. Representatives made the long journey to Berlin to ask for it under the protection of the great powers. They came home feeling that a reasonable presentation of their case had done no good at all. If Armenia wanted justice, she would have to fight for it. Revolutionary societies began to appear among the Armenians.

The first of these was organized in 1880 at Erzerum. Called *Defenders of the Fatherland*, it lasted only two years before many of its members were brought to trial. Others followed—the *Armenakan* at Van, which was concerned only with resisting the Turks, the *Hunchaks*, who represented the penetration of Marxism into both Turkish and Russian Armenia, and most important, the *Dashnaktzoutyoun*[11] (Armenian Revolutionary Federation) which was organized in 1890 with the intention of unifying the revolutionary movement.

Rev. grps

---

[8] *Ibid.*, 766.

[9] *Ibid.*, 748.

[10] For a somewhat more favorable view of this transaction see Dwight E. Lee, *Great Britain and the Cyprus Convention Policy of 1878* (Cambridge: Harvard University Press, 1934), Chapters II and III.

[11] The possible spellings of this name are almost equal to the number of letters in it. I have adopted the one used by Atamian, *op. cit.*

The *Dashnaktzoutyoun*, identified by Russian Communists as "Mensheviks," were essentially nationalistic. It is true they supported the peasants rather than the bourgeoisie, but their objection to the latter (unlike that of the *Hunchaks*, who were Marxists) had nothing to do with class struggle. To them the bourgeoisie were not patriotic Armenians but collaborationists who would make any deal with the Turks to maintain their own position.

It is natural that the *Dashnaks* should be controversial, since they were at all times the leaders in the attempt to satisfy Armenian demands for autonomy and later for nationhood. Except for a brief period at the beginning of the rule of the Young Turks, their methods were revolutionary. Other Armenians who opposed revolutionary action found a political voice in the *Ramgavar* party, always the enemy of the *Dashnaktzoutyoun*.

Abdul Hamid was also affected by the Treaty of Berlin. Relieved no doubt to be saved from Russian domination, he was humiliated and apprehensive at the same time to owe his safety to Europeans. Nor did he relish paying for it by western-style reforms. He wanted to free his empire of outside interference and win back those portions of it which had been lost. In pursuit of these ends he fought relentlessly against reformers within the empire, and against the Christian minorities he never trusted.

Ironically, the very westernization of the country facilitated the achievement of his aims. Reform had been effected by his predecessors over the last half-century by centering power in the capital. Europeans seem to have believed that the sultan had always been absolute. Perhaps he was in the time of Suleiman the Magnificent, but the same centuries that saw the power of the European monarchs increase witnessed the limitation of that of the sultan by an intricate system of checks and balances, none the less effective for being completely unplanned. While Europe's feudal lords were losing their function, Turkey's *ayans* and *derebeys* were exercising very nearly sovereign rule in Rumelia and Anatolia. The religious leaders represented a quasi-independent authority under the *sheikh-ul-islam* and the *ulema*. Even the janissaries were a check on the sultan's power.

By 1878 the janissaries were gone, the feudal lords reduced to rela-

tive impotence, and the religious leaders much weakened. Thanks to
the growth of liberalism, Abdul Hamid could do what he liked—and
what he liked was not liberal.

The effect of Russian power in Transcaucasia on relations between
Turks and Armenians has already been suggested. The work of the
missionaries, particularly the American Protestants, may also have
contributed to the Armenian tragedy. These teachers unselfishly aided
the Armenians to a better life, but their effect may have been to make
the Armenians think of themselves as a special people with a special
relation to the growing power across the Atlantic. Similarly, the Turks,
already harassed by all the might of Europe, could not have been expected to react well to an American disposition to regard the Armenians as their wards. The complete uselessness to the Armenians of
both European and American friendships must have ultimately surprised the Turks as much as anyone else.

Finally, there was the Treaty of Berlin. Nothing better calculated to
create antagonism between Turks and Armenians could be imagined.
It is intriguing to speculate what might have been the effect of a plain
declaration by the European powers one way or the other. They
might, for example, have reaffirmed the complete sovereignty of the
sultan over his domains and expressed confidence that he would treat
all his subjects with fairness. Or they might have provided for a European armed force to assure fairness to Christian subjects when necessary. They did neither. They obliged the Turks to abrogate their sovereignty to the extent of promising fair treatment to the Christians, but
with no specification as to enforcement. The effect was to render the
Armenians aggressive without giving them real security and the Turks
jittery and hence disposed to violence without putting them under
any real control.

Sykes describes the result of this vague "protection":

> How massacres could well have been avoided is hard to imag-
> ine. The Armenians insisted on threatening revolution; openly
> boasted that the Powers would help them. . . . On the other hand,
> their enemies the Turks and Kurds, the bravest and boldest

of men, were so ignorant that they believed the Armenians would be assisted by the Christian powers.[12]

Sykes had, it is true, some feeling against the Armenians[13] and a weakness for rhetorical exaggeration. It is well, therefore, to read him skeptically. However, other witnesses agree with him about the evil effect of making both Armenians and their Moslem oppressors believe the Christian powers would intervene without any stipulation at all as to the circumstances under which such intervention would take place or the form it would assume.

Boasting that a powerful outsider is going to help, however unfortunate the result, is a forgivable, because human, type of behavior. It would be less forgivable to provoke atrocities against one's own people in the hope of bringing in outside help. This the Armenians, particularly the *Dashnaks*, have been charged with doing. To what extent the charge is justified is hard to know; the seizure of the Ottoman Bank has been cited as evidence of such an intention, but that episode followed the massacres of 1894-1895. The men involved were crazed by hatred of the Turks.[14] That the *Dashnaks* consciously pursued a policy of provoking reprisals is at least doubtful.[15]

[12] Mark Sykes, *Dar-ul-Islam* (London: Bickers and Son, 1904), 117.

[13] See Chapter III.

[14] House of Commons, *Correspondence respecting the Disturbances at Constantinople in August 1896* (C-8303), 16-18.

[15] Although William L. Langer accepts the charge against the *Dashnaks*, his own evidence in the case of the bank seizure supports a quite different conclusion. "They had chosen the bank for attack because it contained people of so many nationalities that the representatives of the powers would have to act to save their nationals." If this is true, the powers were being manoeuvred into intervening, not to avenge dead Armenians but to preserve the lives of their own citizens. William L. Langer, *The Diplomacy of Imperialism* (New York: Alfred A. Knopf, 1951), 323.

The author has, however, been advised not to assume that Armenians could not have intentionally provoked massacres. A reliable friend who grew up in Ireland and who took part in meetings of nationalists in the northern counties who wanted union with Eire, recalls that a policy designed to provoke terrorism on the part of the government and, in response to it, intervention by the United States, was quite seriously proposed and debated. It should be understood, therefore, that there is no intention here to maintain that such a policy was impossi-

The decades following the treaty saw the continued decline of Ottoman power, with trouble in Crete and the Balkans, and growing persecution of the Armenians. The role of the *Hamidieh* has already been described. Armenians were also persistently hectored by the Turkish authorities. They were thrown in jail on absurdly trivial charges and kept there for months without trial. In a list of prisoners and the offenses with which they were charged, forwarded by British ambassador Sir William White to Lord Salisbury on April 27, 1891, is the name of Muhuan Aliksan,

> ... an Armenian Catholic [who] was imprisoned about the beginning of December. The only charge against him is that, while coming from Kars [to Erzerum], he wrote down the names of the villages at which he stopped.[16]

This is the most harebrained item on the list but it reflects no more injustice than most of the others.

The massacres of 1895-1896 overshadowed anything that had gone before. They began at Sassun, a wild mountainous area in the vilayet of Bitlis to the west of Lake Van. The Armenians who lived there were a rough mountain folk, indistinguishable, it is said, from the Kurds.

The massacres were set off by the pillaging of the Armenians by Kurds. Fighting ensued and several were killed on each side. The Turkish authorities sent troops, ostensibly to protect the Armenians, but as soon as the latter had laid down their arms, they were massacred.[17]

From Sassun violence spread to surrounding areas and thence throughout Asia Minor. The number killed has been estimated from 50,000 to 350,000. In the face of such discrepancies in contemporary

ble; it is merely suggested that caution be exercised in evaluating inconclusive accusations, particularly when they come from unsympathetic sources.

[16] House of Commons, *Further Correspondence Respecting the Condition of the Populations in Asiatic Turkey, 1892* (C-6632), 41.

[17] This is the account of Vice-Consul Hallward, House of Commons, *Correspondence Relating to the Asiatic Provinces of Turkey, 1895* (C-7894), 13-16. Other versions differ but agree in essentials, i.e., that the trouble started with the Kurds but the massacres were the work of the Turks.

accounts it would be foolish to try to assess the casualties today. There is no doubt, however, that an appalling and widespread slaughter took place. It is not easy to say why it should have been so much worse than previous outbreaks of the same kind. It is possible that the Armenians were readier to resist outrages than they had been in the past. In view of the wildness of the country and its people and of the differences between Christian and Moslem attitudes toward women, we can hardly doubt that there had always been outrages, but before 1878 they had been chiefly individual acts of violence. By 1894 Armenians had had opportunities for better education, knew more about life in the west, and were not willing any longer to take whatever fate sent them. It may also be that the example of the *Dashnaks* made organized resistance more practicable and effective. Envy of the Armenians' cultural and financial superiority may have been a factor in Turkish behavior; fear was probably more important, for, incomprehensible though it was to Europeans at the time, the Turks had become afraid of their Armenian minority. Above all, the belief of the Sultan, sedulously nourished by a net of private informers, that the Armenians were disloyal and a menace to the empire was creating an atmosphere in which atrocities were inevitable.

In August 1896 a group of Armenian revolutionaries seized the Ottoman Bank in Constantinople and remained inside it for some hours, terrorizing the employees and impervious to appeals from outside. They finally agreed to evacuate the building as a result of negotiations with M. Maximoff, the first dragoman of the Russian embassy who, according to the report of the British ambassador, handled the affair with great skill. They were taken aboard a yacht belonging to the British director of the bank where they were questioned.[18] They exhibited a fanatical hatred of the Turks; nonetheless, the statements they made to the embassies of the European powers were sensible enough. They complained that it was impossible to get justice from the Turks and that the Europeans had let them down. They asked for autonomy for Armenia within the empire.

These statements were made in three letters from the revolution-

18 House of Commons (C-8303), 11-13.

aries, the first two directed to all the embassies, the last only to the French *chargé d'affaires*. The first was signed by "the Armenian people," the other two by the *Dashnaktzoutyoun*. The first accused the government of violating the Armenian constitution and putting a puppet patriarch at the head of Armenian affairs.

The other notes charged the Europeans with indifference to their plight and proclaimed that they were therefore taking action themselves. "The time for diplomatic manoeuvre has passed," they declared. "The blood of 100,000 martyrs gives us the right to liberty. Despite all the insinuations of our enemies, we have only asked and will only ask what is absolutely necessary."[19] Liberty did not mean complete independence; "what is absolutely necessary" meant a foreign high commission for Armenia to be chosen by the six powers,[20] such commission to appoint valis, mutesarrifs, and kaimakams with the consent of the sultan.[21]

The government had had wind of an attentat of some kind several days before the seizure took place, but instead of moving to stop it, had used it as a pretext for stirring up the Moslems of the capital. When the hour struck, mobs appeared armed and ready to hunt down any Armenians they could find. Many were killed. The British *chargé d'affaires* asked for sailors and marines from British warships to protect the embassy, consulate, and post office. When this information was conveyed to the grand vizier, the violence came to a sudden halt.[22]

Some Turcophiles have argued, and have cited the seizure of the Ottoman Bank in support of their view, that Armenian revolutionary activity produced a violent reaction in the once easygoing Turks and that Armenian nationalism was the cause of Turkish persecution. Although the point may be somewhat academic today, it is worth noting that it didn't appeal at the time to some very well-informed Europeans. In 1894, Ambassador Paul Cambon maintained in a report to

19 *Ibid.*, 14.
20 Russia, Germany, Austria, France, Great Britain and Italy.
21 House of Commons (C-8303), 14.
22 *Ibid.*, 19.

Casimir-Périer, the French premier and foreign minister, that Armenian nationalism did not exist in 1878, "or, if it existed, it did so only in the minds of a few educated men, who had taken refuge in Europe." It had been created later by massacres, by tax-gouging, by the pillage and persecution of the *Hamadieh*, and by the determination of the Ottoman government that it shouldn't exist. "The Armenians were told for so long they were plotting that they finally plotted," Cambon wrote; "they were told for so long Armenia didn't exist that they finally believed in its existence. . . ."[23] A similar view was expressed by the German missionary Johannes Lepsius who probably knew the Armenians as well as any outsider.[24]

In these circumstances it was natural to think, as some did, that the "solution" to the Armenians' difficulties was to place all of Armenia under the protection of the Russians. Unfortunately, from the Armenian point of view, the Russians had always been repressive, although in a different way than the Turks, and were becoming more so. Armenians living on the Russian side of the border probably enjoyed more security of life and property than the Turks gave anyone, but their national identity was constantly menaced by a determination to assimilate them which would have been quite foreign to Turkish policy. The Russians wanted them to speak Russian, attend Russian schools, and accept the Orthodox faith—in short, to become Russians. Therefore, when the tsar ordered Armenian schools and churches closed in 1903, his *ukaz* represented merely a harsher application of an established policy.

This time he met organized opposition. The *Dashnakzoutyoun* replied with a proclamation calling for armed resistance and a boycott of all government offices. It declared itself in effect the government of Armenia.

The response of the Russian minister Golitsin was to provoke the Tatars against the Armenians. A government renowned for its pogroms against the Jews hoped to serve the Armenians in the same way

[23] Ministères des Affaires Etrangères, *op. cit.*, 11-12.
[24] Johannes Lepsius, *Armenia and Europe, An Indictment*, Eng. trans. (London: Hodder and Stoughton, 1897), 19, 70-71.

through the agency of a culturally backward people. The Armenians fought back hard; their own apologists do not deny there were excesses on both sides, but the Armenians were the injured party. Russian agents engaged in stirring up the Tatars met death by assassination. Golitsin himself was attacked but recovered. By the end of 1905 the tsar had dismissed Golitsin and rescinded the edict of 1903. The Armenian community in Transcaucasia was saved from extinction. Small wonder the *Dashnaks* were the recognized leaders of that community until it was crushed by the Bolsheviks in 1921. Even today they are banned by the constitution of the Armenian Socialist Soviet Republic, the only political party that is proscribed by name in any Soviet constitution.

The triumph in Russia was quickly followed by what appeared to be a greater one in Turkey. Abdul Hamid had never been able to kill the reform movement; he had, in a sense, driven it underground. As his despotism increased both the desire and the need for change, he blocked the normal avenues to it. Earlier reformers had won places in the government; their successors could only overthrow the government. In 1908 they did.

The group that came to power is known variously as the Committee of Union and Progress (*Ittihad ve Terakki*) or C. U. P., the "Young Turks," or occasionally the *Ittihadists*.[25] At its core the movement was similar to those of liberal nationalism in Europe in the nineteenth century, although it found its model less in any of them than in Freemasonry. Its aim was to create a modern, constitutional Ottoman nation without distinction of creed or origin. As such it was naturally hailed by those who had been subjected to a subordinate status. So many accounts of the *coup d'état* of July 1908 record that Turks and Armenians embraced in the streets the reader begins to think it no mere turn of phrase but an actual phenomenon.

Like many movements which seek to overthrow a tyranny, however, Union and Progress had attracted diverse elements. Some devout

---

[25] *Ittihad ve Terakki* is the name favored by Turks. "Young Turks" was used in Europe in imitation of similar movements there. It appeared first in France in the form of *la Jeune Turquie*.

Moslems had joined because they felt Abdul Hamid had weakened and discredited Islam. While they wanted a more humane government and one that would command more respect abroad, they had no sympathy with the secularism of the Young Turk leaders. There was also a cleavage between the Ottomanists and the Turkish Nationalists. The former wanted a constitutional regime in which all citizens, regardless of origin or religion, would be equal. The latter had embraced the romantic concept of the nation that had been such a prominent feature of European thought a generation earlier. To them a nation must be homogeneous; the Turkish nation must be Turkish. Other nationalities could be tolerated but could not expect equality with the Turks. The effect of Ziya Gokalp, the theorist of pan-Turanianism, was beneficent or maleficent, according to one's point of view, but it was deep and widespread.

The proclamation of equal rights for all (one of the first acts of the new government was to restore the Constitution wrested from Abdul Hamid in 1876 and suspended by him two years later) did not appease the nationalisms already in full flower in the Balkans. Serbia, Greece, and Bulgaria had won independence, but instead of hailing a new era of better relations with a liberal Turkey, they were bent on "liberating" populations of their own languages in Thrace and Macedonia. There was, therefore, instead of a new dawn, merely a new period of warfare, first between the Balkan states and Turkey, then among the Balkans themselves. This naturally cooled off the ardor of the reformers, at least so far as brotherhood with Christians was concerned.

The actions of the Christian powers did not make things any better. Austria annexed the provinces of Bosnia and Herzegovina in violation of the Treaty of Berlin, Italy took Libya, and Russia, moving with great difficulty toward constitutional government for itself, never slackened in its zeal for pressing it on Turkey.

The decline of the C.U.P. from its high ideals made itself felt almost immediately and as usual the chief victims were the Armenians. In April 1909, when conservatives were attempting a *coup d'état* against the new government, massacres of Armenians took place at Adana. Some blamed the government, others the rebels who were seeking to restore the authority of the sultan. The *Dashnaktzoutyoun* did its best to regard the occurrences as merely local outbreaks and to continue to cooperate with the Young Turks, but it is doubtful that many shared its hopefulness.[26] The new government must have seemed just like the old except that, with the growing rapprochement with Germany, it became more efficient in its ruthlessness.

So precipitous was the descent that it has been customary to treat the Young Turks as fraudulent liberals and to regard them as a further example of the terrible—and incorrigible—Turk. Those who knew them do not seem to share this view. One of Turkey's severest critics, Andrei Nicholaievich Mandelstam, first dragoman of the Russian embassy, was convinced by frequent and friendly contact with the leaders of the movement that they had sincerely embraced the ideal of an Ottoman state in which all citizens would be equal. They failed to understand, however, that none of the non-Turkish peoples of the empire would consent to lose its identity in a "colorless Ottomanism." In recognizing the rights of man the Young Turks had left out an important one, the right to the free development of each "nationality."[27] The minorities saw the realization of their dreams in a decentralized state which the Young Turks could only regard as fatal to their revolution. "As a result relations between Turks and non-Turks inevitably took on a character of mistrust and hostility."[28]

Mandelstam probably came as close as any observer to diagnosing what went wrong with the Union and Progress movement. An empire in which many peoples lived side by side, each observing its own faith, maintaining its own institutions, and loyal to its own "nation," is not necessarily inconsistent with "modernism" and "progress," so long as these are defined to mean technological improvement, universal edu-

---

[26] So far as I can find out, it is still impossible to say who was behind the massacres. In a sense the *Dashnaks* were right in calling them "local" since they did not spread beyond Cilicia and northern Syria, but within their area they were widespread and intensive. See Avedis K. Sanjian, *The Armenian Communities in Syria under Ottoman Dominion* (Cambridge: Harvard University Press, 1965), 279-282.

[27] André N. Mandelstam, *Le Sort de l'Empire Ottoman* (Lausanne and Paris: Payot et cie., 1917), préface, vi.

[28] *Ibid.*, 21.

cation, constitutional restrictions on executive power, a representative legislature, equal manhood and womanhood suffrage, and even the separation of church and state. If, however, "modernism" and "progress" meant nineteenth century nationalism, no ingenious adjustment and no amount of good will could reconcile them with a state like the Ottoman Empire. It was nationalism which first undermined the loyalty of the empire's Christian subjects and ultimately corrupted the Turks themselves. A Christian people could exist and thrive within the empire as a *millet*, but not as a *patrie* or *Vaterland*. All the Christians were going to learn this bitter lesson. The Armenians, as the most vulnerable, would pay the highest price for the instruction.

With this essential contradiction eating away at the heart of the Ottoman state, its ultimate doom was clear. But it had been clear for a long time. Turkey was always falling apart and always confounding those who predicted an early death. It might have continued to do so for an indefinite period. The Young Turks brought it to the ground when they cast their lot with Germany in 1914.

3

Armenia and the Allies

W HEN AN ACQUAINTANCE of the author learned the subject of this work she remarked that she had heard a good deal about
the Armenians when she was a child. Whenever she failed to eat
everything that was put before her, her mother improved the occasion by referring to the Armenians. "The Armenians would be glad to
have that," or "You should be ashamed to leave that when the Armenians are starving."

This seems to accord with other people's memories. Even today one
hears: "All I know about the Armenians is that they were starving."

These and similar comments tell their own story. There once existed
in the United States a widespread sympathy for the Armenians. Nourished by missionary effort, it was kept alive not only by the churches
but by newspapers and magazines, and during the First World War
by official as well as unofficial pleas for charitable relief of Armenian
sufferers from Turkish persecution.

Sympathy was not matched by understanding. There must be mil-
lions of Americans living today who learned in childhood that the
Turks worshipped a false god named "Allah" and that they thought

the way to serve him was to kill anyone who didn't believe in him. The Armenians therefore, because of their steadfast adherence to Christianity, had been murdered.

Since children in the early 1920's were taught this religious version of the persecutions in Sunday schools and Bible classes, the story of the good Samaritan might have usefully illustrated the state of affairs in Armenia. We were not told, however, that in 1920, while Armenia lay dying, a procession of priests and Levites made up of the United States and its former allies walked down the other side of the road. Least of all were we told that the ambiguous Samaritan who nursed the dying organism back to life (after, of course, doing its share to bring the victim to the brink of the grave) was Bolshevist Russia. Most of our elders must have known no better than the young. If they had, we would occasionally have heard fragments of another interpretation. Americans were, in short, fully aware of the hideous treatment of the Armenians by the Turks, but almost universally wrong about the reasons for it and totally unconscious of the part our own and other "Christian" nations had played in it.

Sympathy for the Armenians was no more universal than revulsion against the Turks. This point must be insisted upon because at least a generation of Americans which sees Turkey only as an ally against communism may find it hard to realize that the Turk was once the object of a special odium.

For thirty years and more prior to the outbreak of the war American magazines had opened their columns to Armenian writers and to friends of Armenia. Their pages were full of tales of Armenian suffering and Turkish brutality. One may look hard but in vain for an article or editorial comment defending or even mildly sympathizing with the Turkish position, although it was sometimes conceded that the individual Turk was not a bad fellow, merely quiescent under a hopelessly savage and corrupt government. The evidence of magazines is reinforced by that of newspapers and church activities.

The national concern rose and fell to some extent with circumstances but it never disappeared. However superficial some of its aspects, it had nothing of the quality of fad that disfigures so many movements in America. If it was ready to manifest itself at any and all times, it was so because it lay close to the country's heart. Thus, all sorts of stimuli caused it to find expression. During the clamor for war with Great Britain over the Venezuelan boundary in 1895, a convention of Baptist ministers resolved that if we were to go to war it should be rather to save Armenia from Turkish persecution.[1] When Thomas Emmet Moore, a southern Ohio newspaperman, accepted a challenge to write a novel, he chose as his subject—along with the iniquity of Russian nihilism—the persecutions of the Armenians. *My Lord Farquhar*,[2] appropriately subtitled *A Romance*, adds nothing to American literature, to our understanding of the Ottoman Empire, nor to Moore's reputation as a humorist in the Mark Twain manner, but it clearly got something off its creator's very American chest.

Joined with the deep sympathy for the Armenians to be found in these manifestations is usually an equally deep antipathy for the Turks, and somewhat less frequently a sharp criticism of the European powers for their failure to protect the Armenians. The criticism was sound enough as far as it went, for the powers, having compelled the Russians to withdraw protection from the Armenians in exchange for a simple Turkish pledge to safeguard their rights, had surely some obligation to see the pledge carried out. Americans, on the other hand, might have been more sensitive to the incongruity—to call it nothing worse—of demanding the adoption of policies and the pursuit of objectives in other parts of the world while stoutly insisting that we had nothing at all to do with them. One publication that perceived the incongruity was *The Nation*; when several resolutions dealing with the fate of Armenia were before Congress in 1896, the editors tartly observed that there was no use at all in agitating the issue unless we were ready to abandon jingoism and the Monroe Doctrine and cooperate with the detested British.[3] The writer of a highly emotional article in *The Outlook* in 1904 appeared ready to face that sacrifice and

[1] Thomas A. Bailey, *A Diplomatic History of the American People*, 6th edition (New York: Appleton-Century-Crofts, Inc., 1958), 444.

[2] Thomas Emmet Moore, *My Lord Farquhar, A Romance* (New York: The Abbey Press, 1902).

[3] *The Nation*, LXII (January 30, 1896), 93-94.

even to go to war if necessary but his was a rare point of view. Just as rare was his belief that Secretary of State Hay was in favor of some such démarche.[4] A common feature of virtually all this agitation was the assumption that the Armenians were being persecuted for their religion.

Thus the massacres and deportations of 1915 intensified feelings already common to the American people. If there is anything new in their expression it is to be found in the increased demand for a political solution of the problem which would separate the Armenians forever from Turkish rule. The following comments from *The Independent* of October 18, 1915 may be taken as typical of the attitudes and even to some extent of the style and tone of American magazines of the period, whatever their political viewpoint:

> Intellectually and physically they [the Armenians] are vastly superior to the Turks. In education, enterprise, industry and love of home they surpass all the other races [of the Ottoman Empire]. Among all the peoples of Turkey they have been quickest to catch the spirit of modern education and twentieth century progress. . . . This ancient and proud-spirited race, conscious of its own innate superiority, ambitious to educate its children, Christian in its religion, and eager for progress, cherished the hope of an independent Armenia reestablished upon the ruins of its ancient kingdom.[5]
>
> But the doom of Turkey must be near at hand. The world has endured the intolerable Turk to the end.[6]

By this time, too, a champion had arisen in Congress in the person of Edward C. Little of Kansas, a former consul-general in Egypt, who defended the Armenians as ably as any clergyman or magazine writer and, thanks to the less rigid editorial standards of the *Congressional Record*, at greater length.[7] So great indeed was America's special so-

---

[4] *The Outlook*, LXXVIII (October 8, 1904), 372.

[5] *The Independent*, LXXIV, 96.

[6] *Ibid.*, 83.

[7] See, e.g., his speech in United States *Congressional Record* (hereafter cited as *CR*), 65th Cong., 2nd Sess., Appendix, 175-182.

licitude for the Armenians that when President Wilson proclaimed October 21 and 22, 1916 as Syrian and Armenian Relief Days, the Syrians appear almost as an afterthought.[8]

Although intense sympathy also existed for the Armenians in some other western countries, it was by means so nearly unanimous as in the United States. That there was a substantial pro-Turkish sentiment among Frenchmen, particularly in the army, is well attested. Michel Paillarès, who edited a French-language newspaper, *Le Bosphore*, in Constantinople in 1919, was constantly indignant about its manifestations among French occupation troops. In a way that seems peculiarly French he attributed it to literary conditioning and singled out for special reprobation Pierre Loti and Claude Farrère.[9]

It is hard to image anyone's political opinions or ethnic preferences influenced by the lost loves and vanished yesterdays of the elegiac Loti, but Farrère's work was of a quite different type. In many respects the very opposite of Loti, whose autumnally beautiful prose clothed little in the way of character and nothing that could be identified as plot, the younger writer told a melodramatic story in a racy, colloquial manner. Loti's style moves us to sadness but of an indeterminate kind since his characters are too unreal for any emotion to fix upon them as its object. Farrère's people may be just as phantasmal but the charm and excitement of the story produce a measure of involvement on the part of the reader. The Turkish officer in *L'Homme qui assassina* could have aroused admiration and pro-Turkish sentiment in many a western bosom. (Actually he was not a Turk but a Circassian—as was Loti's Aziyadeh—but the French public was not likely to notice that.)

Contrasting as they were in their works, the two men exhibited some striking similarities. Each was a naval officer, each an "old-fashioned" type who was somewhat out of place in his own time, and each

[8] The correspondence leading to the proclamation as well as the document itself in Woodrow Wilson Papers, File VI, b. 498, f. 2554.

[9] Michel Paillarès, *Le Kémalisme devant les alliés* (Paris and Constantinople: Editions du Bosphore, 1922). There is no purpose to be served by trying to cite pages for this view; the author fulminates against Loti and Farrère throughout the book.

had a particular love for Turkey and Japan. Each was a *turcomane* to Paillarès (equivalent not to "Turkoman" but to "Turkomaniac"). Farrère, equalling Loti in his admiration of the Turks, went well beyond him in his dislike of oriental Christians. He was chiefly offended by their commercial preeminence. He went so far as to put into the mouth of an Armenian character the statement that the Turks massacred Armenians from time to time out of an instinct for self-preservation. "We are too modern and they not enough."[10]

Turks, in his view, are quite unsuited to the contemporary world. They are simple, decent, honest people who never beat a woman, a child, or an animal, but they live by farming and small urban occupations. Vultures in the form of Greeks and Armenians long since descended on them and profited by their lack of guile. These Christians, however, had more greed than imagination. They cleaned up on small operations but lacked the nerve for the big deal. Europeans, suffering no such disability, moved in with the result that the Turks owned virtually nothing. Between the Debt and the Bank they were hamstrung. They were good soldiers, but what good is an army against a joint-stock company?[11]

Against the *turcomanes* there was a strong body of pro-Armenian opinion in France, well represented by the *Association Franco-Arménienne*, a group of intellectuals and parliamentarians. When Turkey entered the war against the Allies, the Association asked the French government to recognize Armenia as a belligerent.[12] Also active was the *Comité de l'Asie Française* which published the well-edited *Bulletin de l'Asie Française*. The Comité was responsible for assembling the Armenian National Conference in Paris in November 1913. In the struggle for Frenchmen's minds, the defenders of Armenia were neither outnumbered nor outclassed.

---

[10] Claude Farrère, *L'Homme qui assassina* (Paris: Flammarion, 1922), 176.

[11] *Ibid.*, 40-46.

[12] Boghos Nubar Pasha, president of the Armenian National Delegation, to Stephen Pichon, French Foreign Minister, October 29, 1918. National Archives of the United States, R. G. 256, Files of the Paris Peace Conference (hereafter cited as NA, Peace Conference), 867B.00/302.

It is hard to believe in any case that even in France political attitudes toward a foreign nation would be determined to a significant extent by imaginative literature. It is likely that strategic and financial considerations bore a greater responsibility for such pro-Turkish feeling as existed than the works of Loti and Farrère, who may be regarded less as creators of the military bias than as exceptionally articulate examples of it. At the same time they were undoubtedly representative of a belief that might be called the "eastern myth." Since the myth had a greater hold on British than French imaginations and continued to some extent to exert it in 1919,[13] we may better understand it by considering the views of British admirers of the Turks.

Like French *turcomanie*, pro-Turkish sentiment in Great Britain is associated with the military and some literary people, but it also had a strong hold on Britons resident in the Ottoman Empire and on the Conservative Party at home. Sir Edwin Pears gives an example of the kind of unreasoning sentiment that prevailed in Constantinople when he arrived there in the 1870's:

> The late Mr. George Crawshay of Newcastle-on-Tyne was a great
> philo-Turk. He belonged to a little company of men . . . [who]
> could not or would not recognize anything wrong about the
> Turk. He was the one gentleman left in Europe.

Moved by this conviction, Crawshay was so determined that his company should install buoys in Constantinople harbor that he put in a bid which just covered his cost. To his chagrin the contract was awarded to a "Belgian or German firm" which bid £ 150 more per buoy—and their buoys turned out to be no good. Crawshay, the story concludes, ". . . fell back upon the usual excuse of the philo-Turks of the day, that the matter had probably been arranged by some Christian employees of the Porte."

Pears conceded that this might well be true, but added that where

---

[13] In a memorandum on "The Disposition of Armenia," Samuel Edelman, for many years an American consular official and interpreter in the Ottoman Empire, wrote that England was the worst offender in "sentimental twaddle" about the Turk as "the gentleman of the East," "the cleanest fighter of the war," etc. *Ibid.*, 869.00/2.

the volume of graft was so enormous and its practice so constant, it was not credible that Turks were not involved in it at all. In any case, since the power to govern the empire resided in the Turks alone, they could hardly be absolved from all responsibility for its persistent misuse. But the ubiquitous philo-Turk blamed everything on the Christian minorities. "The truth is that at that time the whole British community, so far as I could learn, was philo-Turk."[14]

The most eloquent purveyor of the eastern myth in Great Britain and naturally therefore the most articulate philo-Turk in the kingdom was Sir Mark Sykes. The difference between pro-Turkish feeling in Great Britain and that in France may be gauged by that between two nostalgic novelists on the one hand and a member of Parliament and negotiator of the Sykes-Picot Agreement for the liquidation of the Turkish Empire on the other.

Among intellectual Turcophiles Sykes was unusual in two ways. He had a genuine skill as a writer which, joined to a good deal of industry, produced a surprising number of readable books in his short life. (He was just forty when he died.) They contain some dubious judgments, including some that derive from strong prejudice, as well as sound ones, but their primary attraction lies in their vivid pictures of the Ottoman lands. His way of expressing his opinions was equally vivid and is frequently unforgettable even when the opinions are best forgotten. He was, moreover, an apparently sincere Roman Catholic who admired Moslems and disliked Christians as he traveled toward the east.

In other respects Sykes was typical enough. His repeated jibes at non-Turkish Ottoman subjects are less distasteful if we bear in mind that they, particularly the Armenians, that "abominable race" without any good qualities,[15] were to some extent straw men to be knocked down in the service of his myth. He was persuaded that the east enshrined a uniquely happy way of life which was being assaulted by Europeans and undermined by its Christian minorities. Where liberals in the west condemned the Young Turks for being the same old thing, Sykes damned them as a new and most pernicious thing, de-

[14] Pears, *op. cit.*, 6-8.
[15] Mark Sykes, *Through Five Turkish Provinces*, 80, cited by Kedouri, *op. cit.*, 69.

stroying the very foundations of the old ways in the interests of a shabby cosmopolitanism.

Eastern life had consolations of a type forgotten by the west in its race for prosperity and material comforts. In Turkey there were no "poor," since one had only to ask to receive aid.[16] Contrast this with the west:

> We stayed a day in Tiflis and saw poor people for the first time since we left Europe. . . . Tiflis has some fine modern buildings; Tiflis has a picture gallery; Tiflis has a museum; and Tiflis has slums, wretchedness, and want in its back streets. Tiflis is, in fact, a European town; the East has been rolled back for a time, and the happy, swashbuckling, open-handed people who fought and loved and lived their lives, are now ground into the mill of progress; and we must take off our hats and salute that subaltern of Cossacks who is riding down the street at the head of a squadron to save a tramcar from the hands of the strikers.[17]

To Sykes, as to other Englishmen with less than his literary powers, the worst thing in the Ottoman empire was the Levantine or, as Sykes derisively called him, the "Gosmobaleet." A "Levantine" was originally a European who lived in the empire, but the word had gradually come to denote the volatile, adaptable, commercial character of the eastern Mediterranean ports, usually a native Christian. He had a smattering of European languages which he was determined to display, and he had no "roots" of his own. Naturally, such a creature was inferior to the dignified, generous Turk, known to English admirers as the "genuine" or "true" Turk. The orientalist Edward G. Browne expresses this feeling in his preface to Sykes' *Dar-ul-Islam*:

> I speak, of course, of the genuine Turk—not of the hybrid

---

[16] As an infallible sign of the degeneracy initiated by the Young Turks, Sykes points to one of their first enactments, a poor law (*The Caliph's Last Heritage*, 512). It should not be supposed, however, that his objection was the one we are accustomed to hearing from the advocates of a strict laissez-faire, that moral fiber will be undermined if people are given something they haven't earned. It was merely that help was customarily given by private individuals, and to look to government for it betokened a decline in the warmth of personal relationships.

[17] Sykes, *Dar-ul-Islam*, 242-243.

Levantine, who is too often taken by the casual and superficial observer as a national type and still less of that fearful product of misapplied European or American zeal, so faithfully portrayed by the author of this book under the name of "Gosmobaleet." The intrinsic value of "western civilization" in the ordinary newspaper sense is doubtful enough . . . ; but as a "fancy dress," badly fitted on unwilling or unsuitable recipients, it moves to tears rather than laughter.[18]

It will be noted that this predilection for a "pure" national type with its accompanying detestation of the cosmopolitan is in itself an unnatural imposition of nineteenth century European ideals on the Ottoman Empire to which they were supremely unsuited. The empire was always multinational; the man who identified it only with the pure Turk was bending it to a foreign pattern, therefore himself a Levantine or Gosmobaleet.

When this is recognized, there can be no doubt that Sykes and his fellows had something on their side. The westernization of Turkey, like that of other states, was a painful business with the most superficial aspects of western culture grasped first. No one saw the absurdities of the process more clearly or described them more vividly than Sykes. In a small place named Tavshanli he had come across a library of fine old volumes which the elders of the village read and discussed assiduously. Sykes found their dignity and devotion to learning infinitely touching and noble. When he left them he traveled over a new road.

From Tavshanli to Kutahia in an araba along a preposterous road—preposterous, because 1) it had cost £ 15,000; 2) its proper maintenance would cost more than the district could afford; 3) the first section was in ruins before its last was finished; 4) the best part of the district through which it ran was dry, level, and hard, and required no road; 5) the one rough portion of hill country was left untouched. Here was the new learning. Surely it is better to sit in a library and learn about great kings and travelers, of mighty Empires and their rise and fall,

[18] *Ibid.*, x-xi.

to wear a turban and look wise and clever, than to get a degree
in a continental school of engineering, and on the score of
progress but really in a fit of childish vanity, perform such an
act of colossal folly as this.[19]

The prosperous trading center where the peoples of the empire
lived side by side he ticked off summarily:

Mersina is a wretched hole, Greek in its squalor, Armenian in
its ugliness, Turkish in its ruinousness, Arab in its noisiness.
It is a town of some trade, however; and unlike happy, healthy
Ermenek, people make a little money here and lose their appe-
tites and complexion in the getting of it.[20]

A Gosmobaleet may be of any nationality, but to Sykes he was more
likely to be Armenian than anything else. He characterizes the type
scathingly:

[I] had not proceeded any distance before an oily voice at my
elbow cried: "Hallow! good after-nun, mai deah old fellow,
do yew spik English, from ware are you came?" . . . This incident
served to remind me that I was in Armenian lands.[21]

The Armenians of the eastern towns were sketched in several dev-
astating pages of which only a fragment may be quoted here. Com-
menting on their generally hostile and suspicious attitude, Sykes said:

It is very difficult to account for this ill-bred behavior and tone,
and I myself can only attribute it to the fact that the keynote
of the town Armenian's character is a profound distrust of his
own co-religionists and neighbors. Whether this fear arises from
long and sad experience, or from a perverted business instinct,
it is hard to tell; but to say that it is not without cause may
sound a harsh, but perhaps not unjust judgment.[22]

Without blaming the Armenians entirely for the unrest in Turkey,
Sykes suggested that a substantial measure of the fault was theirs:

[19] Sykes, *The Caliph's Last Heritage*, 518-519.
[20] *Ibid.*, 546.
[21] Sykes, *Dar-ul-Islam*, 66-67.
[22] Sykes, *The Caliph's Last Heritage*, 415.

If the object of the English philanthropists and the roving
brigands (who are the active agents of revolution) is to subject the bulk of the Eastern provinces to the tender mercies of
an Armenian oligarchy, then I cannot entirely condemn the
fanatical outbreaks of the Moslems or the repressive measures
of the Turkish government.[23]

The involvement of Mark Sykes as negotiator of the Franco-British
agreement for the partition of the empire of his beloved Turks was
ironical enough; the ultimate irony was the appearance of a pamphlet
from his pen as an item in the case for an independent Armenia.[24]
Perhaps he concluded that a people of such monochromatic hideous-
ness had indeed an unmistakable "national" character and were therefore not Levantines or Gosmobaleets at all.

At his worst Sykes never went so far as to pretend that Armenians
were murdered because they wanted to be. That remained for Colonel
T. E. Lawrence ("Lawrence of Arabia") who told a member of the
American Commission to negotiate peace:

Armenians have a passion for martyrdom, which they find they
can best satisfy by quarrelling with their neighbors. No one
at the present moment particularly wants to massacre them,
but they can be relied on to provoke trouble for themselves in the
near future.[25]

The authenticity of this might be doubted, particularly since the
member of the peace commission who heard it is not named, but a
letter written a decade later to Professor William Yale makes it plausi-
ble enough. Lawrence recalls that at the time of the Arab occupation
of Damascus he had been shocked by the callousness and indifference

23 *Ibid.*, 417-418.

24 *The Future of the Near East* (London: Pelican Press, 1918). This is the best
statement I have seen of the case for liberating the non-Turkish peoples of the
Ottoman Empire from Turkish rule and allowing them to develop under the
protection and guidance of mandatory powers. It is curious only in that it represents such a complete reversal of all of Sykes' earlier stands on the question.

25 "Memorandum of Conversation with Colonel Lawrence by member of American Peace Commission," November 3, 1919 in Papers of Frank L. Polk, hereafter cited as Polk Papers, dr. 78, f. 68.

of the doctors in the military hospital. He had been relieved to learn that they were not Turks, as he had supposed, but merely Armenians.[26]

Obviously there was another point of view in Great Britain and just as obviously it held the center of the stage during the war. While the Conservative Party had traditionally favored the Turks, not all of its followers did so.[27] The Liberals, representing what was undoubtedly a majority of English opinion during the war years, had always been more sympathetic to the Turks' Christian minorities. Sykes' reference to "English philanthropists" points to the existence of a body of Armenian sympathizers both large enough and influential enough to affect policy. Viscount Bryce, the well-known author of *The American Commonwealth* and other works, was one of their champions. The Friends of Armenia, a voluntary society, played a prominent role as did the Lord Mayor's Fund for the Relief of Armenian Refugees.

British periodical references to the problem are comparable to those in the United States both in their frequency and in the prevalence of the hortatory over the analytical in their content. They are similar in their disposition to emphasize religious aspects of the persecutions at the expense of other factors. They differ, however, in that a few journals assumed a position much more favorable to the Turks. As might be expected, these were Conservative publications, notably *Blackwood's Edinburgh Magazine*[28] and *The Saturday Review*. The latter

[26] The letter is dated October 22, 1929 and is among Professor Yale's papers at the University of Michigan Library. Much of it is included in David Garnett, ed., *The Letters of T. E. Lawrence* (New York: Doubleday, Doran, and Co., Inc., 1939), 670, but the thirty-seven lines describing the hospital incident are omitted.

[27] The staunchly conservative *Quarterly Review*, for example, was pro-Armenian and deplored foolish Turcophilia. See "Turkey and Armenia," CXCV (April, 1902), 590-616.

[28] For an interesting and rather unusual analysis of the problem see the article by Walter B. Harris of October, 1895, CLVIII, 483-492. Harris believed that the Turkish policy after 1878 was based on the conviction that the Armenians were subversive to the state, joined to the fear that any attempt to deal with them too harshly would provoke foreign interference. The Sultan therefore decided on a policy of petty persecution which should avoid the violence that would

particularly took the straight Turcophile line, maintaining that atrocities were of local significance only, that they were exaggerated to serve the purposes of Russian imperialism, that the Armenians were largely responsible for their own misfortunes, that misguided "philanthropic" support was to be deplored, and that Turkey, as a nation friendly to Great Britain, should be free of outside interference.[29]

It would be well not to exaggerate the effect of this kind of sentiment, whether pro-Turk or pro-Armenian, on the determination of public policy, or at the very least we must not overlook the importance of other factors, such as the military and financial. Although a pro-Turkish outlook appears to have been much more entrenched in high places in Great Britain than in France, in the postwar showdown Britain supported the Greeks while France backed the Turks. The fact that France had larger investments in Turkey than Britain may be more significant than any "climate of opinion" among the well read and the gently nurtured. Skepticism is enforced when we read the eloquent appeals for the Armenians made by Dr. Lepsius and other German clergymen whose nation not only did nothing to save them but actually collaborated with the Turks in their suppression.[30] At the same time, emotions, even biases, do count for something in policy-making and emotions about the Turkish Empire were a factor is the support of the Armenians during the war; contrary emotions could become a factor in the peace settlement, particularly if endless delays in making the treaties permitted the Turks to regain their former strength.

Pro-Turkish sentiment among the Allies was dealt a blow by the

bring on intervention by the powers while at the same time annoying the Armenians enough to induce them to solve the problem by emigration. This policy turned to indiscriminate violence because the government was unable to control its chosen instruments of persecution, the Kurds.

[29] See, e.g., *The Saturday Review of Politics, Science, Literature and Art*, LXVIII (Aug. 31, 1889), 230-231.

[30] The extent of their collaboration is controversial, but the fact of it is not. Lepsius, given access to the Foreign Office archives, printed the relevant materials in *Deutschland und Armenien. Sammlung Diplomatischer Aktenstücke* (Potsdam: Der Tempelverlag, 1919).

entrance of the Turks into the war on the side of the Germans and probably a much more severe blow by the persecutions which began in 1915 and exceeded in scope and fanatical intensity anything that had preceded them. Again reliable figures are hard to find but there can be no doubt that the bulk of the Armenian people were murdered or expelled from Turkey. Many of those expelled or deported died in circumstances more appalling than those who were killed on the spot. They were obliged to leave their homes, taking virtually none of their belongings, forced to make long marches under Turkish guard, fed inadequately if at all, and left to die when weakness overcame them. German missionaries in Aleppo wrote in protest to the Foreign Office in Berlin:

> Out of the 2,000 to 3,000 peasant women from the Armenian
> Plateau brought here in good health, only forty or fifty skeletons
> are left. The prettier ones are victims of their gaolers' lust;
> the plain ones succumb to blows, hunger and thirst (they lie
> by the water's edge, but are not allowed to quench their
> thirst). The Europeans are forbidden to distribute bread to the
> starving. Every day more than a hundred corpses are carried
> out of Aleppo.
> All this happens under the eyes of the high Turkish officials.[31]

This is a part of one of the 149 eye-witness accounts of Turkish massacres of the Armenians in the British government's Blue Book of 1916. They are 149 tales of savagery and horror with only an occasional partial deliverance for the Armenians, such as that which took place following the determined resistance of a handful of villagers on the slopes and summit of Musa Dagh, made familiar two decades later by Franz Werfel's novel, *The Forty Days of Musa Dagh*. (Werfel shortened the actual ordeal by thirteen days.) Their authenticity can hardly be in doubt. As Viscount Bryce pointed out in his preface, there is remarkable concurrence among survivors who could not have communicated with each other after leaving Turkey. Furthermore, their charges are echoed in numerous other sources.[32]

[31] Bryce, Blue Book, xxxiii.
[32] Too numerous for a detailed listing; see, for example, Lepsius, *Deutschland und*

There was in any case no disposition on the part of the Young Turk leaders to disclaim responsibility. Henry Morgenthau, the American ambassador in Constantinople, was told by two of the ruling Young Turk triumvirate, Minister of War Enver and Minister of the Interior Talaat, that the massacres were no mere outbreak of popular emotion but were ordered by the government with the deliberate purpose of "ending the Armenian problem" by getting rid of the Armenians.

> [Talaat] told me that the Union and Progress Committee had carefully considered the matter in all its details and that the policy which was being pursued was that which they had officially adopted. He said that I must not get the idea that the deportations had been decided upon hastily; in reality, they were the result of prolonged and careful deliberation.[33]

As Morgenthau made many attempts to move Talaat and other Turkish officials to abandon their Armenian policy, he had ample opportunity to become acquainted with their attitude.

> [Talaat] was very willing to grant any request I made in behalf of the Americans or even of the French and English, but I could obtain no general concessions for the Armenians. He seemed to me always to have the deepest personal feeling in this matter, and his antagonism to the Armenians seemed to increase as their sufferings increased. One day, discussing a particular Armenian, I told Talaat that he was mistaken in regarding this man as an enemy of the Turks; that in reality he was their friend.
> "No Armenian," replied Talaat, "can be our friend after what we have done to them."[34]

Enver was a much subtler man and harder to pin down. In Morgenthau's account he was extremely ingenious in confusing cause and

Armenien; Edmund Candler, "The Armenian Tragedy," in Current History. A Monthly Magazine of the New York Times, August 1917, 332-334; Woodrow Wilson Papers, File VI, b. 498, f. 2554.

[33] Henry Morgenthau, Ambassador Morgenthau's Story (Garden City, N.Y.: Doubleday, Page & Co., 1918), 333.

[34] Ibid., 339.

effect—for example, he represented the Armenian resistance to persecutions which had already begun at Van as the reason why the persecutions took place—[35]but he made the same admission as Talaat
under surprising provocation. The ambassador had thought to pave
the way to a change of policy by suggesting that the deportations had
actually been the work of subordinates who had gone farther than
the government intended:

> "You are greatly mistaken," he [Enver] said. "We have this
> country absolutely under our control. I have no desire to shift
> the blame on to our underlings and I am willing to accept the
> responsibility myself for everything that has taken place.
> The Cabinet itself has ordered the deportations. I am convinced
> that we are completely justified in doing this owing to the
> hostile attitude of the Armenians toward the Ottoman Govern-
> ment, but we are the real rulers of Turkey and no underling
> would dare proceed in a matter of this kind without our orders."[36]

If Enver was the more complicated of the two, Talaat was the more
forthright. As Morgenthau represents Enver, he spun out his arguments at length and with ingenuity. Talaat boiled them down to three
reasons for the Armenian policy.

> In the first place, they have enriched themselves at the expense
> of the Turks. In the second place, they are determined to
> domineer over us and to establish a separate state. In the third
> place, they have openly encouraged our enemies. They have
> assisted the Russians in the Caucasus and our failure there is
> largely explained by their actions.[37]

There seems no reason at all to doubt Talaat's sincerity in this;
indeed, there was an element of truth in some of what he said.[38] Even

---

[35] *Ibid.*, 344. See Bryce, Blue Book, 31, for the refutation of this claim.

[36] Morgenthau, *op. cit.*, 351-352.

[37] *Ibid.*, 337.

[38] The Armenians' aid to Russia is presented eloquently as the reason for the deportations in a remarkable nineteen-page memorandum headed "Les Turcs et
la Question d'Arménie," submitted in behalf of Rechid Safvet Bey, a Turkish
diplomat in Switzerland, by Professor George D. Herron and forwarded to the

if it had all been true, it would not have justified the action the Turks took, but it is interesting that this most implacable of the Armenians' enemies never thought of making their religion a reason for suppressing them—at a time when virtually everybody in the United States believed it was the only reason.

Talaat was right that many Armenians wanted a state of their own. It is idle to argue whether this desire for independence was the cause or the result of the bad treatment they received from the Turks. It seems likely that it was originally a result, but that once the Turks had become alarmed by it, it was both cause and result, each Turkish or Kurdish brutality intensifying the desire for independence and each intensification of the desire leading to more savage repression. It is clear that by the time the First World War broke out, there was widespread feeling for Armenian independence, that the war served to focus it by giving it a chance for success, and that the overwhelming majority of the Armenians in Turkey favored the victory of the Entente, however they may have differed on the degree to which the Armenians should actively involve themselves in the struggle. Many of them gave effect to their preference by fighting for the Allies. While most of those who served in the Russian army in the Caucasus were Russian subjects, many had become so only recently, having left Turkey to live in the Russian Armenian provinces because of the sufferings and indignities to which they had been subject under the Turks. Those who fought in the French Foreign Legion on the western front or with the *Troupes Françaises du Levant* were Turkish subjects, giving the most concrete manifestation of their desire to be something else.

It is hard to know exactly what promises the French made to

American Mission to Negotiate Peace on December 18, 1918 by the American Minister in Berne. Safvet severely condemned the way in which the deportations had been carried out but defended them as necessary in the light of widespread Armenian treason. Although this point is surely controversial, it is hard to argue with his contention that the trouble between Turks and Armenians began in the eighteenth century with Russian interference and specifically with the Treaty of Kuchuk Kainarji (1774) in which the Russians inaugurated the policy of exploiting the Ottoman Christians to make trouble for their government. NA, Peace Conference, 867.00/38.

them,[39] but the Armenians had every reason to expect the Allies to reward their fidelity and their contribution to victory. The seizure of power by the Bolsheviks in 1917 put the Armenians in a most difficult position in the Caucasus. The Russian armies were withdrawn, leaving them to face the Turks alone. Nor was that the worst of it. The Treaty of Brest-Litovsk in the spring of 1918 restored to Turkey the districts of Kars and Ardahan, the only direct Russian gain from the war of 1877 that the Treaty of Berlin had allowed them to keep. In 1917 the three Caucasian states attempted to unite into a single Republic of the Caucasus, an attempt which persisted for a year. In 1918 each of the three had to find its way alone. The Georgians did it by allowing the Germans to occupy their country, the Azerbaijanis by drawing closer to the Turks, while the Armenians alone stayed firmly on the side of the Entente.

On May 28, 1918 Caucasian Armenia declared itself an independent republic, severing all ties with Russia. The *Dashnaks* organized the government and filled most of the important posts. They were able to hold out until the Armistice of Mudros on October 31, 1918 removed the Turkish menace for a time and that of November 11 ended the threat of the Germans. They were thus able to come to the peace conference as a state seeking recognition. They also asked to join the eastern vilayets of Turkey to their own territory to form an enlarged Armenia,[40] a demand in which they were seconded by the much more conservative leadership of Turkish Armenia.

[39] Nubar Pasha, president of the Armenian National Delegation, wrote to Baron Sonnino, Italian Foreign Minister, on November 12, 1918: "C'est à la demande même du Gouvernement Français, en 1916, que la Délégation Nationale s'est engagée à fournir des volontaires arméniens au corps expéditionnaire français en Turquie d'Asie." NA, Peace Conference 867B.00/302.

[40] For events in the three Transcaucasian states during this period see Firuz Kazemzadeh, *The Struggle for Transcaucasia 1917-1921* (New York: Philosophical Library, 1951). While Kazemzadeh's interpretations may have been influenced by writers with a strong anti-*Dashnak* bias, he has provided a clear narrative of the turbid currents of the time in all three Caucasian states and has thrown much light on them by his command of Russian sources.

4

Toward an American Policy

*I*F AMERICAN SENTIMENT was strongly in favor of the Armenians, American policy was another story. There was, in fact, no policy toward the Ottoman Empire before the First World War. The establishment of American colleges in the empire during the 1860's interested some Americans; the persecutions of a later date interested more, but these events did not lead to any national action. President Cleveland declined even to protest to the Turkish government during the massacres of 1894-1895, although asked to do so by both houses of Congress.[1] To most Americans the middle east meant the "Holy Land." President Garfield appointed the erratic General Lew Wallace as Minister to the Sublime Porte because he had been impressed with the general's popular novel *Ben-Hur: A Tale of the Christ.*[2]

Since no disaster or even serious inconvenience resulted from the absence of policy, presumably none was needed. However, when we

[1] *CR*, 53rd Cong., 3rd Sess., XXVII, 214-215.
[2] Irving McKee, *"Ben-Hur" Wallace* (Berkeley and Los Angeles: University of California Press, 1947), 189-191.

60

went to war against Germany and Austria-Hungary, our relation to the rest of the world changed drastically. President Wilson's determination that we should play a role in the peace settlement obliged us to acquire information about a number of parts of the world we had previously gotten along without. Turkey's empire, as the richest prize to fall to the victors, was one of these.

In September 1917, at the request of the President, a group of scholars began compiling information on all areas whose destiny might be decided by the peace conference.

General administrative responsibility for the enterprise, which came to be known as "the Inquiry,"[3] fell to Colonel Edward M. House, the ubiquitous Texan who had played so prominent a part in Wilson's nomination in 1912 and had become the president's right hand man. The actual direction House entrusted to his brother-in-law, Dr. S. E. Mezes of the College of the City of New York.

In a memorandum of December 22, 1917, in which the nature and scope of the Inquiry were defined, disposal of the remains of the Turkish Empire received what appears to be its first official American mention:

> It is necessary to free the subject races of the Turkish Empire from oppression and misrule. This implies at the very least autonomy for Armenia and the protection of Palestine, Syria, Mesopotamia and Arabia by the civilized nations. . . . Turkey proper must be justly treated and freed from economic and political bondage.[4]

That it would be difficult to give effect to this recommendation was candidly acknowledged. The experts, well aware of the pitfalls that awaited such an undertaking, produced papers for the guidance of the peace conference that were both solid and extensive. The American delegation was exceptionally well served with background infor-

---

[3] For an amusing account of the origin of the name see James T. Shotwell, *Autobiography* (Indianapolis: Bobbs-Merrill Co., 1961), 79.

[4] U.S. Department of State, *Papers relating to the Foreign Relations of the United States: Paris Peace Conference 1919*, 13 vols. (Washington: Government Printing Office), hereafter cited as *PPC*, I, 52.

mation. It was weakened, however, by paying far too little attention to the secret treaties by which France, Great Britain, Russia and Italy had divided the Ottoman Empire among themselves.

On March 18, 1915 Great Britain and France, renouncing the efforts of more than a century to keep the Russians from controlling Constantinople and the Straits (i.e., the Bosphorus, the Sea of Marmora, and the Dardanelles), conceded it in the "Constantinople Agreement." Russia was to annex Constantinople and the adjacent portions of eastern Thrace as well as an area in Asiatic Turkey from the Bosphorus to the Sakkaria River. In return the Russians agreed to safeguard British and French rights in Constantinople and to join in a later agreement recognizing the claims of both of their allies in Asiatic Turkey.

The Treaty of London, signed on April 26, 1915, which brought the Italians into the war on the side of the Allies, conceded that Italy was interested in a partition of Turkey and "ought to obtain a just share of the Mediterranean region adjacent to the province of Adalia [Turkish Antalya]. . . ."[5] In the event that Turkey should not be partitioned the interests of Italy were to be taken into account in the distribution of spheres of influence.

The division between France and Great Britain, anticipated in the Constantinople pact, was effected in the Sykes-Picot Agreement of May 16, 1916. Negotiated by Sir Mark Sykes and Georges Picot and ratified by the Russians, it gave Russia the vilayets of Trebizond, Erzerum, Van, and Bitlis as well as some additional territories to the south inhabited chiefly by Kurds. France was to have Syria, Cilicia, and a substantial territory to the north as far as Kharput and Sivas and as far as Diarbekir in the east. Thus in effect Turkish Armenia was partitioned between France and Russia. Great Britain was to have Mesopotamia, while the future of Palestine was reserved with a promise that it would be separated from Turkey. The "red" and "blue" Arab zones assigned as French and British spheres of influ-

---

[5] H. W. V. Temperley, ed., A History of the Peace Conference of Paris, 6 vols (Published under the auspices of the Institute of International Affairs. London: Henry Froude and Hodder and Stoughton, 1920), VI, 19.

ence are not discussed here, as they had no bearing on the fate of Armenia except indirectly as part of the Franco-British conflict that weakened the Allied position after the war.

When the provisions of the Sykes-Picot Agreement began to get around, the Italians felt, naturally enough, that the division of the spoils was an unequal one. Moreover, they had designs on the vilayet of Adana which the agreement reserved for France. In early 1917 the war was going badly for the Allies; the continued cooperation of Italy was a necessity. Hence new conversations began at St. Jean de Maurienne in April, 1917. Their upshot was the enlargement of Italy's share to comprise not only Adalia but virtually the entire southwest quarter of Asia Minor, including Smyrna, Turkey's most important seaport. In addition, a valuable area to the north of Smyrna was set aside as an Italian sphere of influence. The Italians agreed to leave Adana to the French.[6]

These treaties would appear to have been of sufficient importance to attract the attention of the State Department. Indeed, they had settled the question of the Ottoman Empire so thoroughly that there would hardly need be any peace conference at all so far as that part of the world was concerned—and other equally secret treaties had disposed of other issues. In the circumstances the determination of the American government to ignore all the many evidences of their existence is only comprehensible if we dismiss the idea that it was the result of mere indifference or carelessness. It was a matter of policy. Our government did not want to know about the treaties officially because, had we known, we would have been obliged to take a stand for or against them. Once we were formally notified, silence would have been a form of acquiescence whereas it committed us to nothing in the absence of official information. For President Wilson to favor the treaties was unthinkable, while opposing them would have created difficulties with our allies while the war was still in progress. By not knowing about them we avoided conflict when unity

[6] For a description of the secret treaties together with a map showing the partition of Turkey and the text of important clauses, see *Ibid*. VI, 1-22.

was essential but retained the right to oppose them at the peace conference.[7]

The principles by which the United States expected to judge the terms of peace were embodied in the President's address to Congress on January 8, 1918. What we asked, he said, was

> ... nothing peculiar to ourselves. It is that the world be made fit
> and safe to live in; and particularly that it be made safe for
> every peace-loving nation which, like our own, wishes to live
> its own life, determine its own institutions, be assured of justice
> and fair dealing by the other peoples of the world as against
> force and selfish aggression. ... The program of the world's peace,
> therefore, is our program; and that program, the only possible
> program, as we see it, is this: ... .[8]

There followed the objectives which came to be known as the Four-teen Points. They embodied in some detail the President's views not only for a just peace but of the principles on which the coexistence of nations was to be based in the future. They included such general principles as the famous "open covenants openly arrived at," freedom of the seas, and removal of economic barriers; they also included specific provisions for Russia, Belgium, France, Italy, Austria-Hungary, Rumania, Servia, Montenegro, Poland, and the Ottoman Empire. The fourteenth point called for the creation of the "general association of nations" which came into being two years later as the League of Nations.

Of chief interest in connection with the Ottoman Empire were Points Five and Twelve:

V.   A free, open-minded, and absolutely impartial adjustment of

---

[7] For a brief but definitive discussion of the American policy toward the secret treaties see Laurence Evans, *United States Policy and the Partition of Turkey 1914-1924* (Baltimore: The Johns Hopkins University Press, 1965), 51-58. Evans establishes incontrovertibly that the American government knew of the treaties and argues persuasively for the interpretation of American motive which I have adopted.

[8] Ray Stannard Baker and William E. Dodd (eds.), *Public Papers of Woodrow Wilson*, 6 vols. (New York: Harper and Brothers, 1927), V, 158-159.

all colonial claims, based upon a strict observance of the principle that in determining all such questions of sovereignty the interests of the populations concerned must have equal weight with the equitable claims of the government whose title is to be determined.

XII.   The Turkish portions of the present Ottoman Empire should be assured a secure sovereignty, but the other nationalities which are now under Turkish rule should be assured an undoubted security of life and an absolutely unmolested opportunity of autonomous development, and the Dardanelles should be permanently opened as a free passage to the ships and commerce of all nations under international guarantees.[9]

These positions were reinforced in a number of subsequent public statements of the President, notably in his Fourth of July address at Mt. Vernon, in which he called for:

The settlement of every question, whether of territory, of sovereignty, of economic arrangement, or of political relationship upon the basis of the free acceptance of that settlement by the people immediately concerned, and not upon the basis of material interest or advantage of any other nation or people which may desire a different settlement for the sake of its own exterior influence or mastery.[10]

Three days before the President's address to the joint session of Congress, Lloyd George had anticipated it in a speech to representatives of the British trade unions. Although freedom of the seas was conspicuously absent, the British program, as the Prime Minister outlined it, was very much like the American. In a passage frequently quoted later, the speech assured the Turks that they were not to lose those parts of the empire chiefly inhabited by Turks, at the same

---

[9] *Ibid.*, V. 159-160. Point Five may not appear applicable to the Ottoman Empire since the non-Turkish portions of the empire were not, strictly speaking, colonies. However, in seeking to divide the empire under the provisions of the secret treaties, the Allies made it applicable.

[10] *Ibid.*, V, 233.

time putting them on notice that they could no longer expect to rule over non-Turkish subjects.[11]

A more general acceptance of the Fourteen Points came with the Allied note of November 5, 1918:

> Subject to the qualifications which follow they declare their willingness to make peace with the Government of Germany on the terms of peace laid down in the President's address to Congress of January 8, 1918, and the principles of settlement enunciated in his subsequent addresses.[12]

Although the note did not apply directly to Turkey, the joint declaration of the French and British governments on November 9 specifically held out hope for self-government to Ottoman peoples:

> The aims which France and Great Britain have in view in prosecuting in the east the war let loose by German ambition is the complete and final liberation of the peoples so long oppressed by the Turks and the establishment of national governments and administrations deriving their authority from the initiative and free choice of the native populations.[13]

A somewhat different note was struck on the French side when Foreign Minister Pichon asserted the determination of France to maintain its rights in Turkey. Speaking in the Chamber of Deputies on December 29, 1918, Pichon referred to the "incontestable rights" of France in Syria, Lebanon, Cilicia, and Palestine. These rights, he said, were based not only on historical titles but on international agreements in which they had been recognized by Great Britain. France expected them to be honored. Aristide Briand, who had been premier at the time of the Sykes-Picot Agreement, asked by Marcel Cachin if this was his interpretation of the matter, answered in the affirmative, adding that there could not be two interpretations.

---

[11] *The Times* (London), January 7, 1918, 8.

[12] U.S. State Department, *Papers Relating to the Foreign Relations of the United States, 1918: Supplement One* (Washington: Government Printing Office, 1933), I, 468-469.

[13] *PPC*, V, 3.

In the same speech Pichon referred to France's continuing interest in "unhappy Armenia" which she might at any time be called upon to "protect against a recurrence of the worst calamities".[14]

The Armenians, who did not want a French mandate, were disturbed by Pichon's statement. Miran Sevasly, then heading the Armenian National Union of America, warned the State Department that Armenians throughout the United States were "seriously apprehensive of the tenor" of the speech.[15]

Their reaction had been anticipated in a memorandum of the Department of Liaison and Diplomatic Intelligence of the American Commission to Negotiate Peace (i.e., the Inquiry) on December 26, 1918, three days before Pichon spoke. Recalling the division of Armenia between France and Russia provided in the Sykes-Picot Agreement, the memorandum pointed out that the French still wanted their share and were trying to get the Armenians to request a French mandate. The Armenians, however, were afraid of the French. They trusted Clemenceau but not the Foreign Office and feared their interests would be subordinated to those of Syria.[16]

Clemenceau, known as the "Tiger of France," was to preside over the peace conference and to head the French delegation. Although almost eighty, he was by no means a weary old man. He had more than a decade of activity ahead of him. A tiger is not the same as an ogre; Americans, particularly those who have confused President Wilson with Parsifal, have not been kind to the old gentleman. His preoccupation was primarily with the safety and integrity of France. He was also determined that Germany should pay for the impoverishment of France. Could any French statesman have asked less? (The elections of January 1920 demonstrated that, in the view of the electorate, he should have asked and got more). Could he have received satisfaction on those points, there is no reason to think he would have

---

[14] France, *Assemblée Nationale, Chambre des Députés. Débats.* December 29, 1918, 3716 (in *Journal Officiel*).

[15] NA, Peace Conference 867B.00/24.

[16] *Ibid.*, 867B.00/17. The memorandum is signed by the initials A.H.L., presumably Albert H. Lybyer.

been illiberal on others. For more narrowly commercial and colonial interests he had less sympathy than the ministry which succeeded his.

When justice has been rendered to the Tiger, it remains true that he was an irascible old man. Amusing though he is in retrospect, he must in person have greatly added to the exasperations of the conference. Yet even at the time there were those who relished some aspects of his behavior. Of the many anecdotes that cry for inclusion, one must suffice:

> [A. J. Balfour] told me that after Saturday's official opening of the Conference he walked down the stairs with Clemenceau. A.J.B. wore a top hat: Clemenceau wore a bowler. A.J.B. apologized for his top hat: "I was told," he said, "that it was obligatory to wear one." "So," Clemenceau answered, "was I."[17]

At the Premier's right hand, although not occupying a prominent place in his esteem, was the foreign minister, Stephen Pichon. Harold Nicolson, one of the British experts, remembered his "fumbling" and "owl-like obstinacy."[18]

The British delegation was headed by the able but mercurial Prime Minister, David Lloyd George. If Pichon was an owl, the Welshman was a swallow, darting constantly in unanticipated directions.

He was seconded by the Foreign Secretary, Arthur James Balfour, a former prime minister himself (1902-1905). Balfour was a man of broad culture—he had written a book on Handel—and of broad sympathies, so far as that was possible for one who set such store by gentlemanly detachment. His colleague, Lord Hardinge, noted "that he cannot help taking the opposite point of view to people who seem excited."[19] Lord Curzon, who succeeded Balfour as Foreign Secretary in October 1919 and played a chief role in the settlement with Turkey, was on the sidelines at the outset, having been left in London to run the Foreign Office in Balfour's absence.

---

[17] Harold Nicolson, *Peacemaking 1919* (Boston and New York: Houghton Mifflin Co., 1933), 245.

[18] *Ibid.*, 120.

[19] *Ibid.*, 340.

Vittorio Orlando, the Italian prime minister, a kindly and generous man, was a victim of public opinion at home. The Italian people, thoroughly sold on the doctrine of *sacro egoismo*, were rabidly bent on cashing in on Allied promises. They wanted nothing in the way of a new world order. They wanted their delegation to get everything it could for Italy.[20]

The foreign minister, Sidney Sonnino, was better equipped to do the job than Orlando. A ruthless, aggressive man, something of an old-fashioned imperialist, he was out to pick up territory. The east coast of the Adriatic was the most coveted region for Italians, but southern and western Anatolia offered greater advantages. Their climate and products were similar to those of Italy and they were, by European standards, underpopulated. Sonnino understood that Adalia and its adjacent provinces would add to Italy's wealth while offering an outlet for its population and that they would establish Italy as a serious intercontinental power. Since they had been promised to Italy at St. Jean de Maurienne, it is not surprising that he was determined to get them.

The British, French, and Italian delegations were those with which President Wilson and his associates had chiefly to deal in disposing of the Ottoman Empire. The outstanding personality in that operation did not, however, represent a great power. The meteoric rise of Eleutherios Venizelos, a native of Crete, to the prime ministership of Greece and his success in bringing the country into the war over the opposition of the king, powerful politicians, and many of the people are of the stuff of which legends are made. Such success was owing in large measure to an extraordinary charm and persuasiveness felt by all who knew him, even by those who opposed him. In the memorable words of his antagonist, Francesco Nitti, who succeeded Orlando as premier of Italy in June 1919: "In asking he had always the air of offering, and, obtaining, he appeared to be conceding something."[21]

---

[20] Naturally, this generalization does not apply to such Italians as Count Carlo Sforza or the historian Guglielmo Ferrero, but they did not play prominent roles in making the peace and in the temper of the time they could not have done so.

[21] Francesco S. Nitti, *Peaceless Europe*, Eng. trans. (London: Cassell and Company, Ltd., 1922), 169.

That he overreached himself in his claims for Greece and in so doing brought much misery on Greeks and non-Greeks alike may now be conceded, but those who have read accounts by participants in the events of the time and sensed the hold he had on his contemporaries may well wonder if he was not among the rare great ones of the earth.

At the head of the American delegation President Wilson placed himself. The other commissioners were Colonel House, Secretary of State Robert Lansing, General Tasker H. Bliss, and the veteran diplomat Henry White. It was a weaker delegation than Wilson should have permitted himself in view of the magnitude of the task he had cut out for them. All were men of ability and distinction. Yet all suffered two disabilities for which they were not to blame. None of them was a prominent Republican—only White was a Republican at all—and none was a member of the United States Senate. Wilson must have been advised more than once to use his commission appointments to conciliate the Republicans and the Senate and to involve them in making the document the Senate would be asked to ratify.[22] For reasons of his own he refused to do so.

The greatest weakness, however, was Wilson's personal participation. Of the President's ability, character and devotion to duty there can be no question, but he lacked experience in negotiation as well as background in the issues under discussion. Had he remained in Washington, decisions could have been referred to him which could have been made after due reflection. In the hurly-burly of Paris his ideals were at the mercy of haste and ignorance. (The haste was in the emotions of the participants, not in the progress of the conference, which moved with glacial deliberation.)

To make matters worse, his contact with three of his fellow-commissioners was minimal.[23] In the early days of the conference he was saved by constant consultation with Colonel House, but follow-

[22] See, e.g., the memorandum by Attorney-General Gregory in Charles Seymour, ed., *The Intimate Papers of Colonel House,* 4 vols. (Boston and New York: Houghton Mifflin Co., 1928), IV, 222-225.
[23] Alexander L. George and Juliette L. George, *Woodrow Wilson and Colonel*

ing his return from the United States in March he apparently lost confidence in his old friend and even this resource was used sparingly. One of the most grotesque examples of the resulting lack of coordination was the simultaneous preparation of two American commissions to visit the middle east.[24] The President not only waved aside the expedition his fellow-commissioners had been preparing for some time and which was almost ready to leave, but he did not even inform them he had done so. Indeed, he hardly seemed aware of its existence.

If the American performance at Paris was less effective than it should have been, the fault assuredly did not lie with the experts of the Inquiry who had been transformed into the Intelligence Section. Harold Nicolson's testimony is unequivocal:

> I have never had to work with a body of men more intelligent, more scholarly, more broad-minded or more accurately informed than were the American delegation to the Peace Conference. . . . Had the Treaty of Peace been drafted solely by the American experts it would have been one of the wisest as well as the most scientific documents ever drafted.[25]

This is satisfying and probably true, but the American delegation suffered a disability shared only by their Greek colleagues. They did not represent their people. Venizelos met his handicaps by trying too hard to satisfy his people; Wilson may have done less damage by pretending the people agreed with him. During the preceding autumn the President had appealed for the election of a Democratic Congress to help him finish the task he had undertaken. The voters replied with a Republican Congress. His defeat put Wilson in a strange position with Lloyd George and Clemenceau, each of whom had received a strong vote of confidence. In the circumstances they may be forgiven

---

House. A Personality Study (New York: John Day Co., 1956), 215-217. The authors, who have examined the relevant material, substantiate the charge that the President neglected Lansing, Bliss, and White almost entirely and that all three were badly frustrated by his treatment.

[24] See Chapter VII.

[25] Nicolson, *op. cit.*, 28.

for wondering if Woodrow Wilson really represented the united resolve of the American people, let alone the aspirations of mankind.

Evidence was not lacking that the American mood had changed, that if the country hadn't repudiated Wilson it was ready to do so. It retained enough of his idealism to be on the alert for shoddy practice on the part of our allies, but there was no call for sacrifice by the United States. "The ghastly suspicion," Nicolson wrote, "that the American people would not honor the signature of their own delegates . . . became the ghost at all our feasts."[26] The only American unaffected by this ambiguous state of affairs, said Nicolson, was Wilson himself.[27]

The point need not be overstated. There is no conclusive reason to believe the game was lost before the conference opened. There was still much support in many countries for the President and his program. Some Britons were beginning to see that a vengeful peace would not be good policy even from the somewhat earthbound point of view of British manufacturers. In the United States some Republicans as well as Democrats still favored the League of Nations. The rights of weaker nations had not lost their appeal to Americans (the fuss they made over the Japanese occupation of China's Shantung Peninsula is eloquent testimony to that) and no one who has looked at the files on Armenia in the National Archives, even if he has got no further than the index, can doubt the continued sympathy for that tragic people.

There were, in short, positive as well as negative factors at work. It is a bold observer who thinks he can say with certainty what would have happened if something had been done differently. Perhaps, however, it is possible to say that the American people have always had a low frustration tolerance, at least in international affairs, and that the way to keep their support for noble purposes was to accomplish them quickly. If the conference was allowed to drag on too long, American interest would wane and the chance for American leadership to effect its objectives would wane with it. This would be unfor-

26 *Ibid.*, 108.
27 *Ibid.*, 58.

tunate for America and more than unfortunate for some other nations. For the Armenians, crushed between two stronger neighbors, decimated, with nothing to trade, dependent totally upon western support and good will, it could be simply fatal.

Yet the conference had to drag on. Even if it had been much better planned and managed than it was, solutions to some of its problems could not have come quickly. The American delegation was not responsible for the grim predicament that resulted, but, because of the situation at home, it must have suffered more from it than any of the others.

5

The Peace Conference

*F*ROM THE MOMENT war was declared, there was not a
British statesmen of any party who did not have it in mind
that if we succeeded in defeating this inhuman Empire, one essential condition of the peace we should impose was the
redemption of the Armenian valleys forever from the bloody
misrule with which they had been stained by the infamies of the
Turk.[1]

Thus Lloyd George. So far as we can know, he was telling the truth.
While actual pledges to the Armenians are hard to find, the expressions of universal sympathy for them are impressive.

The Armenians had taken such expressions seriously. They felt that
their contribution to the Allied cause had been a very substantial one
for a small nation. On October 29, 1918 Boghos Nubar Pasha, president of the Armenian National Delegation (i.e., the delegation of
Turkish Armenia) wrote to Pichon to claim the status of belligerent.

---

[1] David Lloyd George, *The Truth about the Peace Treaties*, 2 vols. (London:
Victor Gollancz, Ltd., 1938), II, 1260.

Between six hundred and eight hundred volunteers, he pointed out, had served on the western front with the French Foreign Legion. Only forty of them were still alive, some in hospitals. Three Armenian battalions of the *Légion d'Orient* had been cited by the French commander for zeal and endurance. Their loyalty to the Entente had never been denied. General Allenby, in command of the Allied forces in the middle east, had also praised them in a telegram to the Armenian National Delegation. Finally, 150,000 Armenians had fought in the Russian army and had held the front in the Caucasus after the Russians had dropped out of the war.[2]

It is easy to conclude, in the light of later happenings, that the Armenians had been duped again into expecting help from the west, that they had been used to promote western purposes only to be heartlessly cast aside when the purposes had been accomplished. Yet they had better reason than some other small peoples to count on western support. There can be no doubt that the sentiments of the Allies were real, however little thought may have been devoted to the means of giving effect to them. Not only was there, particularly in Great Britain, a feeling of guilt about the Armenians—for had they not been cast back into the fiery furnace at Berlin by the western powers, led by Britain, after the Russians had pulled them out at San Stefano?—but there was an equally strong feeling against Turkey. The British considered the Turks guilty of ingratitude. They had turned away from British protection which had saved them so often, had rejected an offer of continued protection in exchange for neutrality, and had joined Britain's enemies. The Turkish side of the case was not a wholly despicable one. It was simply that British protection had meant protection against Russia; when Britain and Russia became allies, they had to look elsewhere. We are not here concerned, however, with the merit

---

[2] NA, Peace Conference 867B.00/302. A French priest, Antoine Poidebard, studied the record of the Armenian army in the Caucasus after the Russian withdrawal and concluded emphatically that the Armenians deserved the title of *puissance alliée* later accorded them—far too much later—by the Treaty of Sèvres. Antoine Poidebard, "Rôle Militaire des Arméniens sur le front du Caucase après la défection de l'armeé russe" in *Revue des Etudes Arméniennes*, I fascicule 2 (1920), 143-161.

of Turkish action but with the way in which the British looked at it. They looked at it unfavorably. Even the pro-Turkish sentiments of the Conservative Party appear to have vanished, or at least gone underground, during the war.

Furthermore, Armenia had little to tempt the ravening imperialist. A small country, the "poor house of Europe", as Food Administrator Herbert Hoover called it,[3] its occupation was not vital to any of the great powers. As an independent nation, on the other hand, it could help to cut the Turks off from the Turkic-speaking peoples of Transcaucasia and central Asia, thus becoming a stumbling block to either pan-Turanian or pan-Islamic ambitions, both of which were taken more seriously than they are now. Armenia as a colonial dependency offered nothing to the west; Armenia as an independent state offered advantages which, although small, were real; Armenia as a part of Turkey meant the same wretched situation all over again. When the most solemn expressions of sympathy are thus joined to the most positive interests, who can refuse to take them seriously? Who can be blamed for overlooking some interests on the other side, such as French investments in Turkey?

If there was anything lacking to complete the conviction, it was supplied by the American entrance into the war. Not only had the Armenians been a favorite of missionary-minded Protestant America, not only was President Wilson known to have deep sympathies for them, but with the American accession to the Allied cause, justice to smaller nations became something like a war aim. It would be a mistake to suppose the Fourteen Points and the doctrine of "self-determination" were mere verbiage, which meant little or nothing to plain people. There is much evidence that all sorts of people, in the middle east as elsewhere, were aware of them and expected them to be put into effect.

With the armistice signed at Mudros on October 31, 1918, the war with Turkey was brought to a successful end. The Turks were shattered and in a mood to accept almost any peace the victors cared to dictate. The Armenians of Turkey therefore declared their independ-

3 *PPC*, XI, 261.

ence and notified the powers of their action on November 30, 1918.

There was, then, every reason to suppose that when the delegates gathered at Paris, the independence of Armenia would at last be recognized. It would be, in all likelihood, a qualified independence, for a new factor had come into the picture. By the end of the war the mandate system, urged by President Wilson and General Smuts, had become increasingly accepted by Allied statesmen as applicable to nations which were not ready for complete self-government. Such nations were to be placed under the guidance of more advanced communities whose function it would be to prepare the mandated nations to govern themselves. Mandates were to be assigned and supervised by the League of Nations.

Armenia stood to gain as much as any by mandated status. It had lost a large proportion of its population through massacre, with much of the rest scattered through various eastern lands. Few of the survivors retained even personal property, to say nothing of liquid capital. Their countryside was devastated, their agriculture ruined, and their villages destroyed. They were surrounded by more powerful neighbors, at least one of which might be expected to be hostile. Armenia would need guidance and protection far more than most of the new states.

The logical power to assume the mandate would have been Russia, since it had had an Armenian province within its own borders, a common frontier with Turkish Armenia, and a half-century's experience as the protector of Armenians against the Turks. However, the defeat of the Russian armies, the Bolshevik revolution, and the Treaty of Brest-Litovsk had taken Russia out of the ranks of the Allies. In publishing the secret treaties the Bolsheviks had disclaimed any intention of accepting the territory accruing to Russia as a result of them; northeastern Turkey, the most likely area for an Armenian state, was included in the renunciation. Furthermore, in 1919 the Russians were still engaged in a civil war; the government, even had it been minded to assume responsibility for Armenia, would actually have been cut off from its ward by the troops of General Denikin.

Great Britain, France, and Italy were little disposed to fill the role themselves. They all had responsibilities elsewhere. The United

States, on the other hand, was interested in Armenia, had conducted extensive missionary enterprises there, and had been generous with money for charitable purposes. Lloyd George wrote that:

> French, British and Italians alike were driven to the conclusion that America alone was capable of discharging adequately the responsibilities of a mandatory. When the delegates of the great Powers assembled at the Conference examined the difficulties, it became clear that America was the only mandatory who would have been acceptable to all alike.[4]

David Hunter Miller, Legal Advisor to the American Delegation, was the guest of Lord Robert Cecil[5] at a dinner party of eight on January 11, 1919, on the eve of the conference. He found ". . . a unanimous opinion among the British present that the United States should take Constantinople, and agreement, although reluctant on the part of Colonel Lawrence, that it would take Armenia."[6]

The experts of the Intelligence Section of the American Commission also favored awarding the mandate to the United States. On January 21, 1919, they submitted their recommendations to the commissioners. Admitting that the creation of an Armenian state was difficult because

> . . . except for a small area north of Lake Van and in Kars and Erivan, the Armenians are everywhere in a minority . . . not more than thirty or thirty-five per cent of the population,

the experts held that the population criterion should not apply because of the hardships the Armenians had suffered and the reduction of their numbers through massacres. There was need for a mandate because of "the inexperience and defects of the population, its mixed character, and its weakness."[7]

---

[4] Lloyd George, op. cit., II, 1260.

[5] Conservative member of the House of Commons from 1906 to 1923, and one of Great Britain's strongest advocates of the League of Nations.

[6] David Hunter Miller, My Diary at the Peace Conference, with Documents, 21 vols. Special edition limited to 40 sets (New York: Appeal Publishing Co., 1924), I, 74.

[7] "Outline of Tentative Report and Recommendations by the Intelligence Sec-

Because of the American tradition of non-involvement in the affairs of the old world, resistance to anything so unprecedented as a mandate was to be anticipated at home. However, the concern of Americans for Armenia might be able to override it. In January seventy-five Congregational ministers telegraphed Wilson:

> Justice to Armenia is demanded alike by the fundamental principles which inspired the Allied Democracies in the world war and by specific pledges made by the Entente to the Armenians.[8]

These clerics may not have spoken for "the Christian people of America," as they claimed, but they certainly spoke for many of them. On February 2 the New York Federation of Churches cabled, urging the President to "champion the right of Armenia to a free national existence within her historic boundaries," and asking that "either Great Britain or America extend to Armenia such aid as she may need during this formative period."[9]

That President Wilson had the same feelings is shown in his reply to a message from James W. Gerard, the former ambassador to Germany who had become chairman of the American Committee for the Independence of Armenia:

> Your cable . . . has struck a responsive chord in my heart and I beg that you will assure the Committees that I shall be as watchful as possible to do my utmost on Armenia's behalf.[10]

Encouragement came from a variety of sources. Viscount Bryce, speaking in London at a Lincoln's Birthday luncheon of the English-speaking Union and the Atlantic Union, called on the United States to guide Armenia to statehood. Recalling the many benefits that America had conferred on the east, he maintained that "America is specially fitted for the job because she stands apart from the jealousies of the European powers and none could suspect her of seeking dominion

---

tion, in Accordance with Instructions for the President and the Plenipotentiaries", 1041-1043. *NA*, Peace Conference, 185.112/1.

[8] Woodrow Wilson Papers, File VIII-A, b. 14, f. January 24.

[9] *New York Times*, February 3, 1919, 14.

[10] Woodrow Wilson Papers, File VIII-A, b. 20, f. February 14.

for herself.[11] The British Armenian Committee, meeting at the House of Commons on February 28, urged the United States to accept the mandate.[12]

At the same time the American Committee for Relief in the Near East was sponsoring a series of showings of its "official photo-drama," *Ravished Armenia*. Following a special preview at New York's Hotel Commodore attended by "leaders of society," the film was exhibited ten times to the public.[13]

The agreement of the Allies was manifested by the heads of the five principal delegations (United States, France, Italy, Great Britain, and Japan) during a "conversation" in Pichon's office at the Quai d'Orsay on January 30, at which they accepted the "Draft Resolution on Mandatories," affirming that Armenia, Syria, Mesopotamia, Palestine, and Arabia must be severed from the Turkish Empire, that they should be governed by more developed nations under mandates assigned by the League of Nations, and that the "wishes of these communities must be a principal consideration in the selection of the mandatory power."[14]

The suggestion that the United States should participate in the administration of mandates was acknowledged by President Wilson with the warning: "The people of America would be most disinclined to do so."[15] Although no precise location for a mandate was mentioned during the conversation, Lloyd George placed it in Armenia at a later meeting on the same day.[16]

Wilson, who recrossed the Atlantic in the middle of February, delivered an off-the-record address to the Democratic National Committee on February 28. Asked whether the United States would ac-

---

[11] *New York Times*, February 13, 1919, 15.

[12] *Ibid.*, March 1, 1919, 4.

[13] *Ibid.*, February 15, 1919, 4.

[14] *PPC*, III, 795-796. According to a letter from David Hunter Miller to Colonel House (Miller, *op. cit.*, IV, 205), the resolution was prepared by Lord Robert Cecil.

[15] *PPC*, III, 788.

[16] *Ibid.*, III, 807.

cept a mandate for Armenia, he replied that the Allies had proposed it. He had told them he was ". . . perfectly willing to go home and stump the country and see if they will do it, but I could not truthfully say offhand that they would, because I did not know."[17]

In the speech he had delivered upon landing in Boston four days earlier, the President had asked: "Have you thought of the sufferings of Armenia? You poured out your money to help succor the Armenians after they suffered. Now set up your strength so that they will never suffer again."[18]

The Armenian National Delegation, representing the Armenians of Turkey, came to the conference with an armory of printed material, whose chief item was a document entitled *La Question arménienne*. It recited the story of Armenian sufferings and participation in the war, concluding with the claims the delegation intended to put before the conference. These were presented under five heads and in more detail than in the personal appearances of Armenian leaders before the Supreme Council.

The conference was swamped by a flood of documents of all kinds; it is impossible to estimate how many of the delegates, or even the experts, read any one of them. Any who took the trouble to read the Armenian case found the following demands:

1) Recognition of an independent Armenian state formed by a union of the seven vilayets (the six plus Trebizond), Cilicia, and the Armenian Republic of the Caucasus, its precise boundaries to be settled by a commission of the great powers;

2) The state thus created to be guaranteed by the powers and the League of Nations in which it claimed membership;

3) A mandate not to exceed twenty years' duration, with the Armenian National Conference, which had been sitting in Paris since before the war, to be consulted on the choice of a mandatory;

---

[17] Papers of Charles L. Swem (President Wilson's personal stenographer), cited by Herbert Hoover, *The Ordeal of Woodrow Wilson* (New York: McGraw-Hill Book Co., 1958), 225.

[18] *Public Papers of Woodrow Wilson*, V, 439.

4) An indemnity for massacres, spoliations, and devastation
to be fixed by the peace conference and paid by Turkey, in
return for which Armenia would assume a share of the Ottoman
debt;

5)   The mandatory to be responsible for the following:
   a) expulsion of all Turkish and Tatar authorities,
   b) disarmament of the population,
   c) expulsion and punishment of those guilty of massacre, violence and pillage or profiting therefrom,
   d) expulsion of disruptive elements and nomad tribes which
   could not be brought under the control of the government,
   e) repatriation of the *muhajjirs*, i.e., Moslem colonists settled
   during the Hamidean and Young Turk periods,
   f) restoration of Christian women forcibly placed in harems,
   with the Turks paying damages in such cases, as well as
   indemnities for the destruction of schools, churches, and
   monasteries.

It was further demanded that Armenian religious authorities should
be allowed to dispose of any Armenian community property remaining in Turkey after the boundaries had been fixed, with the proceeds
of such sales going to their congregations.

Any person of Armenian origin in any other country was to be
given five years in which to choose the new nationality for himself
and his minor children. The document concluded by rejecting all
Syrian and French claims to Cilicia.[19]

The Armenians presented their case to the Supreme Council during
Wilson's absence in America. On February 28 Avetis Aharonian, President of the Republic of Armenia, spoke for his small state. Boghos
Nubar Pasha, son of the former prime minister of Egypt, represented
the Armenians of Turkey. Aharonian, a poet and novelist, was the head
of the more or less democratically elected *Dashnak* government; Nubar headed a delegation of *Ramgavars* chosen by the patriarch in 1912.

Aharonian told the Council there were two million Armenians in

[19] House Papers, dr. 30, f. 21.

Russia's former Transcaucasian provinces, about one-fifth of them in such large cities as Batum, Tiflis, and Baku (none of these is located in Armenia), the remainder, more than one and one-half million, settled compactly around Erivan, Kars, Chucha, and Alexandropol. One hundred eighty thousand of them had fought in the armies of the tsar and had continued to fight under the Kerensky government. When the Bolsheviks signed the Treaty of Brest-Litovsk, they not only removed the Russian armies from the Caucasian front but ceded to Turkey the entire western half of Russian Armenia, including Kars, the natural gateway for Turkish invasion. Completely abandoned to their traditional tormentors, the Armenians had organized their own army, choosing to regard Russia henceforth as a foreign nation.

In setting forth the claim of Armenia to independence, Aharonian referred to the promises of the Allies and the performance of the Armenians: "We were told that the declarations made in the British House of Commons and the French Chamber of Deputies were of such nature as to satisfy our claims."[20]

The Turkish Armenians, he asserted, had been offered autonomy by the Porte if they would join Turkey against Russia. This they had refused to do and had stood by the Entente.

When the Georgians had submitted to German occupation, the Republic of Armenia had broken away from Transcaucasia and declared its independence. The people of the Republic wanted union with their fellow-Armenians in Turkey. They already had 400,000 to 500,000 of them as refugees; some had fought against the Turks. Annexation by the Republic would provide the only possible security for the Armenians of Turkey's devastated and depopulated eastern vilayets.[21]

[20] PPC, IV, 149. An examination of the debates in the House of Commons reveals many expressions of sympathy for the Armenians and indignation against the Turks, but nothing that could be construed as a pledge. The same statement cannot be made with assurance about the Chamber of Deputies since its debates are not indexed by subject like those of the House of Commons, but it is probable that French legislators, like their British counterparts, left such things to executive action. That pledges were made by the British and French governments seems probable in view of the frequent references to them, none of which was apparently ever denied.

[21] Ibid., IV, 147-151.

Nubar, who followed Aharonian, reiterated that the Armenians had been offered autonomy if they would side with Turkey and had refused, preferring to throw in their lot with the Allies. In addition to their heroic stand in the Caucasus, they had, in accordance with their agreement of 1916 with the French, provided 5,000 troops for the French Army in Palestine. A corps of volunteers had fought in Europe with the French Foreign Legion.

Their devotion to the Entente, Nubar maintained, was one of the reasons for the massacres and deportations. They had therefore been belligerents; the "tribute of life paid by Armenia is heavier than that of any other belligerent nation."

The Armenian state, Nubar continued, should include Cilicia (with the sanjak of Marash) and the six vilayets of Erzerum, Bitlis, Van, Diarbekir, Kharput, and Sivas with a portion of Trebizond giv-ing access to the Black Sea—and of course the territory of the Armenian Republic with which the Armenians of Turkey wished to be united in a single nation. (Nubar did not claim the city of Tre-bizond, which he acknowledged to be Greek, but merely enough of the vilayet of the same name to provide access to the sea.) To the objection that these vilayets contained many areas which were not Armenian before the war, Nubar replied that the Armenians were not necessarily claiming all of the territory within the prewar boundaries of the vilayets. These, he asserted, had been gerry-mandered by the Turks to make the Armenians appear an inconse-quential minority. He was willing to have areas with a predomi-nantly Turkish or Kurdish population detached from the Armenian state by a mixed commission. He categorically rejected any Syrian demand for Cilicia, where the Arabic-speaking population was in-significant.

In answer to doubts whether an Armenian state could survive, Nu-bar pointed to the impressive prewar figures on the predominance of Armenians in both foreign and domestic commerce.

The demands of the National Delegation were summed up in three points: 1) liberation from Turkish rule; 2) joint protection by the powers from outside interference; 3) guidance for a time by one of the powers in the form of a mandate.[22]

The National Delegation and that of the Republic were brought together on February 24 to form an "All-Armenia Delegation" (*Délégation de l'Arménie Intégrale*), with Nubar as its president.[23] While it is not to be expected that a popular party like the *Dashnaktzoutyoun* would always see eye to eye with a group backed chiefly by the clergy and the bourgeoisie,[24] the Armenians stuck together during the critical spring months of 1919. There is nothing at all to support the charge that their own factionalism cost them their independence.

President Aharonian was serving the interests of both groups when he addressed a letter to Clemenceau on March 7 requesting that the Armenian Republic be recognized and that the conference authorize refugees from Turkish Armenia to return home under protection. The Republic had 30,000 troops available for this purpose, he said, adding that it was important to act immediately because crops would have to be planted within a month.[25]

The Americans, or at least their most active delegate, appear to have been at this time disposed to support the maximum Armenian demands. On the very day of Aharonian's letter, Colonel House recorded in his diary:

> We [House, Clemenceau, and Lloyd George] discussed
> whether Armenia should remain whole or whether France should
> take Cilicia, for which Clemenceau contended. George [*sic*] was
> disposed to fight this contention, but I quieted him and told
> him aside that I understood the question thoroughly and had

[22] *Ibid.*, IV, 151-157.

[23] Nubar explained this in a letter to William M. Buckler of the American delegation dated August 18, 1919. NA, Peace Conference 867B.00/236.

[24] Noradunghian, president of the Armenian National Conference in Paris, admitted to Leon Dominian of the American Intelligence Section that the delegates from Turkish Armenia were property-owners while those from the Republic were revolutionaries. Dominian's memorandum, *Ibid.*, 867B.00/81.

[25] House Papers, dr. 30, f. 26.

no notion of allowing Armenia to be broken up in this way
without a fight.[26]

It may be doubted that the colonel knew the situation as thoroughly
as he thought—although the fact that France had a claim to Cilicia
under a treaty signed by Lloyd George's government may have been
as much a matter of indifference to him as it obviously was to Lloyd
George—but he was getting an education on it.

On March 12 Nubar charged that the Armenians were being massacred in Cilicia. He demanded that the Turks be disarmed and their
authorities expelled from Cilicia to be replaced by a police force of
Armenians and occupying Allies.[27]

Throughout the ensuing month House was to be the target of numerous appeals, among them those of the American Committee for
the Independence of Armenia. House wired Gerard on March 17:
"Armenian cause being well taken care of at Peace Conference.
Everything possible is being done for the future of Armenia."[28]

A cable from Gerard among House's papers, undated but subsequent to House's, mentioned that the Armenians were uneasy as their
case was about to go before the conference. (This is unfortunately
no clue to the date, for virtually anything could be said to be about to
go before this badly organized conference at any time.) They had
asked him to come to Paris to help them, but he had replied with
House's assurance that they were being well cared for.[29]

Fears for the fate of Armenia continued to be expressed throughout the spring[30] and with them a growing uneasiness about the
determination of the great powers to stand behind their pledges. Re-

---

[26] Diary of Edward M. House, XV, 84 (entry of March 7, 1919).

[27] House Papers, dr. 30, f. 26. Nubar's note is in French but across the top of
Colonel House's copy an unknown hand has written in English: "The poor
devils are being massacred again."

[28] *Ibid.*, dr. 8, f. 34.

[29] *Ibid.*

[30] See, for example, the summary of a report received by the Presbyterian Board
of Foreign Missions from President G. H. T. Main of Grinnell College in *The
Literary Digest*, LXI (May 17, 1919), 32-33.

ports of Turkish brutality were heard at Paris. Since the Allies were not in control of the Turkish interior, such reports could well be true. It is natural that they should cause alarm. Why, therefore, was the conference so remiss in dealing with the situation?

In the first place, there was substantial difference of opinion as to how seriously warnings about the plight of the Armenians should be taken. Lord Curzon had something on his side when he complained later in the year that the Armenians had been on the point of extinction three months earlier if something was not done. Nothing had been done, apparently no damage had resulted, and the same sources were again prophesying extinction.[31]

It must also be borne in mind that to the delegates of the western powers the disposition of Turkey was of distinctly less importance than that of Germany and Austria. It may even be, as Harold Nicolson wrote later, that it was seen "not as an integral problem requiring solution in its own terms, but as the area of least resistance in which compensation could be found wherewith to bribe several esurient powers to relinquish their claims in Europe itself."[32] But one need not go as far as that to agree that the delegations thought of Turkey as secondary. During the spring of 1919 the conference was preoccupied with three problems: 1) the preparation of the treaty with Germany; 2) the drafting of the Covenant of the League of Nations, most important of all to President Wilson whose views could not be ignored; and 3) the break with the Italians over Fiume, which became so serious that the Italian delegation went home.

Moreover, the European plenipotentiaries believed the United States would assume the mandate when the time came. To the objection that Wilson had warned them repeatedly the Senate might not allow him to accept a mandate, the reply must be that Wilson's caveats may not have been so firm as they appear in the formal minutes of the

31 W. L. Woodward and Rohan Butler, eds., *Documents on British Foreign Policy 1919-1939* (London: Her Majesty's Stationery Office), hereafter cited as *DBFP*, 1st series, IV, 819.

32 Harold Nicolson, *Curzon: The Last Phase 1919-1925. A Study in Post-War Diplomacy* (Boston and New York: Houghton Mifflin Co., 1934), 75.

meetings. At least that is the impression produced by the notes made at the time by the official interpreter, Paul Mantoux, and not published until 1955.

> For example, Mantoux records the following exchange on May 13:
> M. CLEMENCEAU—Is it possible to predict what action the
> American Senate will take?
> PRESIDENT WILSON—I believe it will accept the responsibility.[33]

This contrasts rather strikingly with the official minutes in which Wilson merely warns that he will have to secure American approval.[34]

The minutes of the 11 A.M. meeting of May 21 deal thus with the question:

> It was difficult for her [the United States] to take a mandate
> even for Armenia, where she had permanent interests of long
> standing, and where a good deal of money had been spent by
> Americans for the relief of the Armenian people.[35]

Mantoux's notes record the President's remarks a bit differently: "She will take the Armenian mandate for humanitarian reasons."[36]

In each of these cases Wilson's statement as rendered into French by the official interpreter was more encouraging than what was allowed to appear in the official transcript.

A final consideration that should not be forgotten is that any peace settlement in the middle east had been rendered difficult by the contradictory promises made under stress of danger in the secret treaties and by the antagonism between the two chief Allies, which resulted from the continued occupation of Syria by British troops in defiance of the Sykes-Picot Agreement. The British leaders stated frequently that they had no intention of remaining permanently in

---

[33] Paul Mantoux, *Les Délibérations du Conseil des Quatre (24 mars-28 juin 1919). Notes de l'Officier Interprète*, 2 vols. (Paris: Editions du Centre National de la Recherche Scientifique, 1955), II, 58.

[34] *PPC*, V, 583.

[35] *Ibid.*, V, 765.

[36] Mantoux, *op. cit.*, II, 142.

Syria, but the sincerity of their assurances is hard to credit, even to the student who gets most of his information from British sources.

In view of these difficulties, it is unjust to assume that the great powers simply forgot their promises to the Armenians or that they sold them out at the behest of business interests or in pursuit of the aims of power politics. Nonetheless, when all allowances have been made for hampering circumstances, the fact remains that danger signs from Asia Minor abounded and that the conference not only paid too little attention to them but wantonly magnified the peril by its own actions.

Gerard cabled the American delegation on April 26 mentioning reports that the French had joined the Turks in persecuting Armenians in Cilicia and that French officers were openly pro-Turk.[37] He seems to have got his information from a memorandum by Miran Sevasly of the Armenian National Union of America.[38] It is only too probable that some of the French officers were pro-Turkish but if they were joining the Turks in persecuting Armenians in Cilicia it must have been on a localized scale. French military personnel was under British command in Cilicia until the agreement of October 1919.

Gerard, disturbed by these reports, was considering an appeal to Pichon. From this action he was apparently dissuaded by a cable of the same day from Acting Secretary of State Frank L. Polk:[39]

> I have given considerable attention to the Armenian question
> and I am glad to say that I think it is now in a condition that
> will satisfy them. I would therefore advise not sending the cable
> to Pichon at present.[40]

On May 4 *Le Temps* (Paris) warned of approaching danger in Turkey and called for the only solution—to impose mandates through-

[37] House Papers, dr. 8, f. 34.
[38] National Archives, Record Group 59, Files of the State Department, hereafter cited as NA, State Department, 860J.01/26.
[39] Polk was acting secretary in Lansing's absence. On July 28, 1919, he became Undersecretary of State and head of the American delegation in Paris after Wilson and Lansing had gone home.
[40] House Papers, dr. 8, f. 34.

out the empire and to train its people of all nationalities to govern themselves. The alternative, said the editors, was fanaticism and massacre. The British and French, as the two greatest Moslem powers, should face the situation and act together.[41] *Le Temps* was thought to express the views of the French administration.

On May 8, House cabled Gerard: "We have Armenian situation ever present with us and keeping closest touch with developments."[42] By the 19th, however, his confidence had begun to wane. On that date he wired:

> Since I am personally unable to give you authorization desired
> by American Armenian Committee, it might be well for the
> American Committee to send representatives to Paris to place
> their case before the conference.[43]

"Authorization" here seems to mean assurance of recognition for the Armenian state and relief for its people.

It is doubtful that the Armenian question had ever been in as good a position as House had previously believed, yet he had some reason to feel reassured about it in the middle of May since the Big Three, taking advantage of the absence of the Italians, were getting down to the middle eastern problem. On May 13, Lloyd George suggested:

> The United States should take a mandate for Armenia; France
> should take a mandate for northern Anatolia, Italy for southern
> Anatolia; and Greece should be dealt with as proposed by
> President Wilson [i.e., sovereignty for Smyrna and the adjacent
> district and a mandate for the rest of the territory claimed by
> Venizelos]. The United States, he earnestly hoped, would also
> take a mandate for Constantinople.[44]

Wilson demurred somewhat from this proposal, inasmuch as

... it had been represented to him that certain influential and

---

[41] *Le Temps*, May 4, 1919, 1.
[42] House Papers, dr. 8, f. 34.
[43] *Ibid.*
[44] *PPC*, V, 583.

important elements in Turkey were very anxious that Turkey should not be divided, but it must be subject to guidance. There should be a single mandate for the whole. . . . He felt there was much to be said for this proposal.[45]

Despite Wilson's hesitations two resolutions in the sense of Lloyd George's suggestions were agreed to by the Big Three on the following day as part of the proposals to be presented to the Italians on their imminent return to the conference. The first gave to the United States, subject to the consent of the Senate,

> . . . a mandate over the Province of Armenia as constituted
> within frontiers to be agreed upon between the United States,
> British, French and Italian delegations, whose recommendations,
> if unanimous, shall be accepted without further reference to
> the Council.[46]

It also provided in similar language for an American mandate over Constantinople and the Straits and a small contiguous territory whose boundaries were to be determined.

The second resolution disposed of the rest of Turkey by giving Greece "complete sovereignty" over the Smyrna region; Italy a mandate over the southern seaboard from west of Makri to the proposed Armenian boundary and inland to include Konia; France the remainder of Turkey in the form of a mandate.[47]

On May 16, A. J. Balfour put forward an alternative proposal which would have left the Turks, after the loss of European Turkey, Constantinople, and Armenia, with sovereignty over the purely Turkish parts of Anatolia, the Italians to be mollified with economic concessions rather than a mandate.[48] Lloyd George does not seem to have agreed with Balfour on May 16, but three days later he did. In the meanwhile, on the 17th, the conference had been informed of the concern for Turkey on the part of the Moslems of India; on the 19th

[45] *Ibid.*, V, 583.
[46] *Ibid.*, V, 622.
[47] *Ibid.*, V, 622-623.
[48] *Ibid.*, V, 672.

Lloyd George ". . . thought that it would be a mistake to tear up this purely Turkish province."[49]

Wilson again talked of Turkish sovereignty subject to "advice" on finance, economic matters, and foreign policy from France. "What he was suggesting was in effect to give a mandate to France without calling it a mandate."[50] Both men wanted the Italians out of Anatolia and hoped to compensate them elsewhere. Wilson didn't know where, but Lloyd George suggested Fiume. (He had previously favored giving them a part of Anatolia to keep them out of Fiume.)[51]

Two days later Lloyd George, after hearing more about Moslem opinion in India, was still less inclined to impose harsh terms on Turkey.[52] "The allies had no more right to split up Turkey than Germany, in former days, had had to split up Poland."[53] He continued to advocate taking away the Greek, Armenian, and Arab parts of the Empire, but he favored leaving purely Turkish areas for the Turks to govern. He thought such self-government might be subject to mandate and that America would be more acceptable to Moslems in that role than the other powers would be.[54] The Italians would have to be paid off somehow. He again suggested Fiume as compensation; Wilson still objected.[55] The President also warned that it was very doubtful the United States would take a mandate for the whole of Asia Minor.[56]

In balking on this point Wilson seems to have been entirely consistent. Although in favor of the Armenian mandate and at least willing to submit a similar proposal for Constantinople to the American people, he always discouraged the suggestion that the United

[49] *Ibid.*, V, 708.

[50] *Ibid.*, V, 709.

[51] *Ibid.*, V, 581-582.

[52] Wilson imputed Lloyd George's change of heart directly to Indian Moslem influence. See account of his interview with Magie and Westermann of the Intelligence Section on May 22, 1919. NA, State Department 185.5136/31.

[53] *PPC*, V, 756.

[54] *Ibid.*, V, 757.

[55] *Ibid.*, V, 758-759.

[56] *Ibid.*, V, 765.

States should be responsible for all of Asia Minor. He never altered this position even in the face of subsequent recommendations by both American commissions of inquiry.[57] It also seems clear that the other powers would not have been shunted aside from Anatolia to give the United States an inclusive mandate. It was not therefore at any time a serious possibility and perhaps should not have been so much discussed.

It was, nonetheless. In the middle of May the supporters of Armenia showed alarm at an attack from an unexpected source. On May 16 Nubar Pasha warned Colonel House that the Rev. Caleb F. Gates, president of Robert College, was advocating that Turkey and Armenia be kept together under an American mandate. Gates, he wrote, was "obsessed by the fear of massacres" which would result if the Turks, as a consequence of their "frightful crime," found themselves a majority in an Armenian state. Nubar protested vigorously that if the Allies, diverted by such misgivings, failed to impose terms on the "vanquished tyrannical powers" and to firmly proclaim the independence of Armenia within definite boundaries, all "possibility of the resurrection of the Armenian state will be lost forever and the enormous sacrifice of our people will remain without reward or result."[58]

Gates had expressed his opinion early in April after visiting southeastern Turkey "for relief purposes." His statement had been forwarded to the State Department from Constantinople on April 11. It read in part:

> The employment of armed Armenian soldiers in Cilicia created
> a very bad impression throughout the country. The Turks fear
> reprisals; they are fully armed and refuse to give up their wea-
> pons, believing that the Armenians will retaliate for injuries
> inflicted upon them. . . . It is to be feared that the creation of an
> Armenian kingdom will be the signal for serious trouble all over
> the country. I am strongly convinced that the wisest course will

[57] The King-Crane Commission (see Chapter VII) and the Harbord Mission (see Chapter VIII).

[58] House Papers, dr. 30, f. 22.

be to place an undivided Turkey under the control of some
Power that will administer it, giving equal justice to all races
and nationalities. . . . The long delay in deciding the fate of the
country is giving opportunities for increased tension and a spirit
of faction and intrigue. . . . The Turks are not at all disposed to
submit passively to unwelcome decisions which may be imposed
upon them.[59]

James W. Gerard was outraged by Gates's attitude and spoke his
mind in a cable to House, imputing a motive far less admirable than
the "fear of massacres."

> Am convinced he is more interested in Robert College and possi-
> bility converting Turks than welfare Armenia. . . . I told him . . .
> [I] was definitely convinced absolute impossibility to induce
> America to accept mandate for unspeakable Turks. *Times* and
> *World* brought out these facts editorially. *Tribune* strongly
> attacked proposed mandate for Turks, but favorable to Armenia.
> Even Lodge is strong advocate for Armenia, so are all churches.
> . . . Turks and their friends have no chance here so advised
> Gates accordingly.[60]

Gerard's charge that Gates was influenced by a desire to convert
Turks was groundless. Although he had gone to Turkey originally as
a missionary, his pastoral duties had been confined virtually from
the outset to eastern Christian congregations; and from the time of
his transfer to Euphrates College in Kharput in 1894 his work was
educational and administrative. From his own account it does not
appear that he ever converted a Turk to Christianity. It is true that
in his two decades at Robert College he had always sought to stimu-
late the "natural reverence" of his students—and had been praised by
Turks for doing so—but, although he remained all his days a convinced and practicing Christian, he seems to have ceased to care
long before 1919 whether the reverence of his students took Christian,

[59] NA, State Department, 860J.01/5.
[60] House Papers, dr. 8, f. 34.

Moslem, or Jewish form.[61] Gerard's attack would have come with greater grace had he risked his life to save Armenians from outraged Turkish mobs as Gates had.

Nor was Gates opposed to the creation of an Armenian state, although his position was not clarified until two months later.[62] What he objected to was not an Armenian state but rather to its establishment before peace, stability, and good government had been achieved. This could only be done in a united Anatolia under American supervision. While restoring order to the country the mandatory should aid Armenians who wanted to move into the Armenian area, and non-Armenians who wanted to move out of it to other parts of Turkey. When something like a "homogeneous Armenian population" had been created in Armenia it would be time to detach it from the Turkish state. Such a solution was the "only one that will give any hope of being permanent."

Even had this more conciliatory stand been made clear in May, it could not have satisfied Gerard and his committee, bent as they were on securing a much larger Armenia than Gates thought practical. Gerard cabled House again on May 21 to remind him the committee was standing by the maximum demand. "Please remember that the churches of America are deeply interested in this," he concluded.[63]

The Turks were not the only wrong hands the Armenians might fall into. Lord Bryce and presumably others in Great Britain feared some of the Allies might be in the running. On May 15 Bryce addressed to Lansing a "Confidential Memorandum on Questions before the Conference." With relation to Armenia he wrote:

> I need only say that her friends in this country would regret to
> see any part of Armenia or Cilicia delivered by way of mandate

---

[61] See Caleb F. Gates, *Not to Me Only* (Princeton: Princeton University Press, 1940).

[62] Louis Edgar Browne, "Turks and Armenians Want Aid of America," in *Chicago Daily News*, July 15, 1919, cited by Harry N. Howard, *The King-Crane Commission. An American Inquiry in the Middle East* (Beirut: Khayats', 1963), 188-189.

[63] House Papers, dr. 8, f. 34.

either to France or to Italy. Neither power could be trusted to administer the country with a sole view to the welfare of the inhabitants as America would do.[64]

In spite of these alarms the conference was so far from giving up its plan for an American mandate that Colonel House suggested to Herbert Hoover in May that he should become its governor.[65] Hoover was, then and always, against the mandate and said so. He later explained his position:

> It seemed to me certain that combined pressures of Russia and Turkey would necessitate our having to keep an American army of 150,000 in garrison, and that we would be at war with Turkey or Russia sooner or later.[66]

Hoover's opposition was shared by Lansing, more a conservative lawyer than a diplomat, who thought Armenia of no importance[67] and in addition regarded the whole mandate system as raising grave questions of international law.[68]

While alarmed appeals were coming in from various quarters and the conference, chiefly concerned with concluding peace with Germany, seemed to be barely inching its way toward a settlement in the middle east, the Government of the Republic of Armenia took a bold step. On May 28, the first anniversary of its separation from the other Caucasian states, it proclaimed its independence and its unity with Turkish Armenia.[69]

It may already have been too late. An act of the conference, which had nothing to do with Armenia, had dealt a severe, perhaps a fatal blow, to the Armenian aspirations. On May 15, with the concurrence of the Allies, Greek occupation troops had landed at Smyrna.

[64] NA, Peace Conference 185.2122/58b.
[65] Hoover, *The Ordeal of Woodrow Wilson*, 228.
[66] *The Memoirs of Herbert Hoover*, 3 vols. (New York: Macmillan Co., 1951), I, 455-456.
[67] *PPC*, XI, 116.
[68] Robert Lansing, *The Peace Negotiations: A Personal Narrative* (Boston and New York: Houghton-Mifflin Co., 1921), 151-153.
[69] NA, Peace Conference 867B.00/136.

6

Turkish Nationalism and the Occupation of Smyrna

FEARS FOR THE FUTURE of Armenia took two forms in the spring of 1919. The more common was that the peace conference would give Armenia back to the Turks; the other, that all or part of it would be awarded as a mandate to France or Italy, nations which would dominate and exploit it rather than guide it to self-reliant statehood. These fears may have diverted attention from the actual danger.

The student of the peace conference will seek in vain for a serious suggestion that any part of Armenia, except the portion assigned to France by the Sykes-Picot Agreement, should be given back to the Turks or to any power but the United States.[1] According to Colonel

---

[1] Outside of the conference the only suggestion of the sort that I have found was in an article by René Pinon, "La Liquidation de l'Empire Ottoman" in *Revue des Deux Mondes* LIII (September 1, 1919), 128-160. Pinon advocated a joint French-American mandate, a proposal hardly likely to meet with approval from French officialdom whose memory of the condominium in Egypt was still alive. Georges Picot, negotiator of the Sykes-Picot Agreement, told Captain William Yale the French people would not like an American mandate but would accept it. "Notes on conversation with M. Georges Picot," in Yale Papers.

House, Clemenceau even offered to surrender the French claims if America would take a mandate for the whole.[2] *L'Asie française,* bulletin of the influential *Comité de l'Asie française,* strongly urged an American mandate[3] and only suggested that France should assume the responsibility after it had become clear that the United States would not.[4] As for the British, not only did they first propose the American mandate to the peace conference but they clung to the project long after any likelihood of American acceptance had vanished.

While the extreme Armenian demands could hardly have been met—nor is it easy to understand how anyone who wished them well could have insisted on a scheme that would have made them a permanent and hopelessly outnumbered minority—the conference certainly intended to create an Armenian state under American mandate, including a sizeable portion of at least four vilayets, in addition to the Republic of Armenia and either the port of Trebizond or some other outlet to the Black Sea.

This could only be accomplished, however, if it was imposed on the Turks while the Allies were still sufficiently determined and sufficiently united to insist upon it and while the Turks could be induced, and if necessary compelled, to accept it. The enemy of Armenia, therefore, was not Turkey or France or Italy, but procrastination.

The will of the Allies could not be indefinitely relied on. France had the strongest of reasons not to offend the Turks. French investors had lost heavily in Russia and were not disposed to lose in Turkey.[5] Great Britain, moved primarily by the security of her empire, was sensitive to Moslem opinion, particularly in India.[6]

---

[2] House Diary, XV, 155 (Entry of April 14, 1919).

[3] *L'Asie française,* CLXXV, (February-July, 1919), 179.

[4] *Ibid.,* CLXXX (March, 1920), 91.

[5] *Ibid.,* CLXXV, 180, showed the importance of French interests in the following table:

Allied unity was equally unreliable. It was, in fact, especially vulnerable in the middle east, where a series of mutual irritations exacerbated the rifts likely to be produced in any case by divergent interests. The views of France and Italy with respect to Turkey were largely determined by commercial considerations,[7] Great Britain's by strategic. The claims of the Italians and Greeks overlapped in western Anatolia, while the French and British were increasingly at odds throughout the spring and summer of 1919 over the British refusal to yield Syria to the French as provided in the Sykes-Picot Agreement. Yet Great Britain and France were united in anger at Italy for the occupation of Adalia; in Smyrna they backed Greece against both Italy and Turkey, although the French adopted the

CAPITAL (in francs)

	France	England	Germany
Public debt	2,454,417,377	577,493,821	867,583,506
Private investment	830,856,000	235,818,675	575,903,000
Total	3,285,273,377	813,312,496	1,443,486,506

Thus France had 60% of that part of the public debt held by the three most interested powers and 50% of the private investment of the same three. England had less than 15% of either. The portion of both France and England should be somewhat higher because these are prewar figures. German investment declined during the war because the Germans were able to collect on their share of the public debt while the allied nations were not.

More detailed figures follow on pages 181-183 of the *Asie française* article. The editors made clear, however (179-180), that French interests were by no means entirely material. French culture was prized all over the empire, where the French language was universally known to educated people. Close relations had been maintained since the treaty between Francis I and Suleiman the Magnificent in the sixteenth century. There were over eighty French schools in Constantinople and Asia Minor with 24,000 students, "notre action . . . restant toujours dégagée de tout esprit confessionel." The French also maintained hospitals, orphanages, and homes for the aged.

A detailed paper prepared for Colonel House's Inquiry entitled "French Interests in Asiatic Turkey" bears out the claims of *L'Asie française* regarding the size of French investments.

[6] In addition to Lloyd George's tergiversations under Indian Moslem influence (see Chapter V), its importance is revealed frequently by diplomatic correspondence and questions in the House of Commons.

[7] In the case of Italy, perhaps the desire for an outlet for excess population was also a factor.

policy with less enthusiasm than the British and abandoned it sooner. Moreover, both popular and official feeling toward Greece in the west was largely admiration for Venizelos, which substantially diminished with a change in the Greek government.

Finally France, Italy, and Greece all had ambitions in Asia Minor in direct conflict with the Fourteen Points which President Wilson, at least, was still taking seriously.

Bad as this situation was, it could become worse with a change of government in virtually any one of the Allied countries. In fact, all of the regimes did fall, Orlando's in 1919, Clemenceau's and Venizelos' in 1920, Wilson's in 1921 after lasting for the period prescribed by the constitution, and Lloyd George's in 1922. Colonel House seems to have had this menace in mind but it failed to adequately impress most of the peacemakers—or most subsequent historians. Indeed, the American determination to cast Clemenceau in the role of villian has obscured the fact that a greater menace lay in those Frenchmen who were eager to replace him and who succeeded in doing so in January 1920.

There was, therefore, serious danger that the Allied will would weaken or that they would cease to have a united will at all. There was an equal danger that the Turkish will to resist would grow stronger. Ample evidence was available, particularly after May 1919, that just that was happening—and with the will, the means to carry it into effect.

The wisdom of hindsight, facilely displayed, is a loathsome thing, yet it is impossible not to wonder why no one ever thought of negotiating the Turkish treaty first, rather than last. The assumption was that Turkey could wait while Germany could not. But Turkey could not wait because the Allies had no such grip on Turkey as they had on the other central powers. The interior of Turkey was the only "conquered" territory over which they had virtually no control; Turkish resistance, once strong enough, could only be overcome by an investment of military force on a scale which none of the Allies was likely to make. In these circumstances, those who held the reins chose to postpone the Turkish settlement indefinitely.

They were urged repeatedly to do something quickly for Armenia.

The Armenian patriarch appealed personally to Admiral Mark Bristol, commander of the American naval forces at Constantinople, to protect his people.[8] President Gates, arriving in New York in June 3, told the *New York Times* that delay in acting on Armenia was having very serious consequences.

> While much could have been done last February, the situation has by this time grown tense. . . . The French, for instance, made a serious mistake in landing troops at Adana in Cilicia. They put Armenians in French uniforms and when the Turks saw this they naturally concluded that the Entente intended to use force against them, and consequently they began to arm.
>
> The plight of the Armenians at the present time is pitiable. . . . Unless they can be got back to their land immediately they will not be able to raise food, and so they will starve next winter. This should have been one of the first tasks of the Peace Conference. While they have been debating in Paris, a tragedy has been in the making in Turkey.[9]

Armenians in French uniforms were bad enough. When the Greeks appeared in the west, they were wearing their own.

Following the Armistice of Mudros, Allied naval units had entered the Bosphorus. Commissioners of the Allied nations were named to oversee the occupation. The Turks kept the framework of their previous government, purged by the Sultan of all C.U.P. elements, but Constantinople was controlled by the victors. Cilicia was occupied by British and French; other coastal areas were, of course, subject to control by the Allies whenever they chose to exercise it. The greater part of Turkey, however, in the center and the east, was left under the control of the Turks with a few Allied officers to supervise disarmament. Compliance with their orders depended upon the willingness of the Turks to cooperate. This willingness the Allies were able to secure at first, in part because the Turks had lost heart, in part because the Sultan, determined to restore absolutism,

[8] NA, Peace Conference 676.68/12.
[9] *New York Times*, June 4, 1919, 23.

was willing to accept foreign supervision, if necessary, rather than face constitutional demands from his subjects. The mood of the people was one of apathy mixed with despair. Turkey had probably suffered more than any other nation in the war.[10] She had been badly beaten and knew it. By the accounts of most observers, she was ready to accept a harsh peace. Admiral Calthorpe, the first British High Commissioner, believed so. "The Turks gradually came to realize their defeat and were prepared to (surrender?) great sections of their Empire . . ." he telegraphed to Lord Curzon on July 27, 1919.[11]

Bernard Lewis, one of the outstanding western historians now working in the Turkish field, takes the same view:

> Among the new leaders in the capital even the will to independent survival seemed to have failed and political discussion centered on the form which Turkish subjection was to take, and on the relative merits of an American or a British mandate. . . . The Turkish people, beaten and dispirited, seemed ready to accept almost anything that the victors chose to impose on them.[12]

The same impression arises from the recollections of Halide Edib,[13] Turkish Nationalist, reformer, and writer. She was the wife of Dr. Adnan (who later took the surname Adivar). Halide Edib's account of the events from the armistice to the triumph of the Nationalists is perhaps the most illuminating available in a western language because of her personal participation in most of the events she described. Even when the reader thinks she is a bit insensitive to the feelings of the other side, she probably represents supremely well the feelings of her own. Her honesty is attested by her frank expression of dislike for the Nationalist leader, Mustafa Kemal Pasha, in spite of her certainty that he was essential to the movement.[14]

---

[10] Evidence on this point is furnished by the report of Major-General Harbord, head of the American Military Mission to Armenia (see Chapter VIII).

[11] *BDFP*, 1st ser., IV, 703.

[12] Bernard Lewis, *The Emergence of Modern Turkey* (London: Oxford University Press, 1961), 236.

[13] Halide Edib, *The Turkish Ordeal* (New York: The Century Co., 1928).

[14] *Ibid., passim.*

Halide Edib's account opens with a description of her own condition, physical and moral, at the time of the Allied occupation. She believed it to be typical of the general feeling in the country.

> I felt stupefied, tired, and utterly sick of all that had happened since 1914. I was conscious that the Ottoman Empire had fallen with a crash, and that it was not only the responsible Unionist leaders who were buried beneath the crushing weight of it. . . .
> Even those who had believed in the moral superiority of the Allies in Turkey were not blind to the fact that the big talk of justice, right of peoples, etc., would not be applied to this country. Yet the Fourteen Points of President Wilson so ostentatiously announced, and the supreme war weariness of all the peoples, including the victors, made it advisable to leave the Turks alone in a land where they were in an incontestable majority.[15]

As the author was not particularly active in politics at the time, her account of the early months of the occupation is not an inside story of events in high places but a graphic description of everyday life as it appeared to the conquered Turks. She tells us that "insolence of the Greeks and the Armenians and the treatment of peaceful Turkish citizens in the streets became scandalous."[16] Senegalese soldiers were uncontrollable. Turks were continually arrested on any handy pretext by the Allied authorities. Houses were requisitioned and the owners not even allowed to take away their personal belongings. The attitude of the occupying forces toward the Turks was colored by that of their Greek and Armenian interpreters.[17] Turkish women were pushed out of streetcars; even Turkish children were cursed by Allied soldiers. Fezzes and veils were wantonly ripped.[18]

Colonel Heathcote-Smythe visited the Turkish prisons in Constanti-

---

[15] *Ibid.*, 3-4.

[16] *Ibid.*, 4.

[17] This may seem a trivial matter, but its importance is very well brought out by Arnold J. Toynbee, *The Western Question in Greece and Turkey: A Study in the Contact of Civilizations*, 2nd ed. (Boston and New York: Houghton-Mifflin Company, 1923), 32-33.

[18] Halide Edib, *op. cit.*, 4-5.

nople. These, or at least some of them, were horrible, Halide Edib admitted, "but there were no political prisoners in them, and a Turkish prisoner was exposed to the same hardship as a Christian." Colonel Heathcote-Smythe ordered all the Christians set free, although most of them were common murderers. Among them was an Armenian who had killed two members of his own family; Halide Edib heard accounts of the terror occasioned by the colonel's clemency among the surviving relatives.

A Greek had shot a quiet, inoffensive Turkish youth in front of Tokatlian's, a famous Armenian restaurant in Pera, the European quarter. He "had done it for the fun of shooting a Turk." As Turks were disarmed while Christians had armed themselves unimpeded by the occupying authorities, a series of murders "verging on massacre" took place in Turkish quarters.[19]

On streetcars and ferryboats Greek women purchased second-class tickets and rode first-class, rudely thrusting the Turks into the cheaper compartments or even off the cars. An old lady, called unmentionable indignities by a Greek woman, wept inconsolably at her disgrace, for which she could not even relieve herself by reacting normally for fear of hurting her son, a liaison officer with the French. He had told her the French were "nice people" and always asked her to "hold her tongue."[20]

Most wounding of all to Halide Edib was the favoritism shown to Armenian over Turkish children in orphanages and the attempt of the Armenians to claim any child who couldn't produce papers, even if the child's memories clearly showed him to be a Turk.

It is impossible to say how much credence should be given to these stories. Halide Edib did not perhaps sufficiently recognize that military occupations always produce disagreeable incidents and she certainly made no allowance for the natural desire of the Christians to settle some old scores. Nonetheless her account was probably veracious in general and in any case it was an example of the reaction of

[19] *Ibid.*, 5-6.
[20] *Ibid.*, 6-9.

a humane and educated Turk to the social reversal that had taken place.[21]

She does not suggest that these humiliations alone would have led to organized counter-violence on the part of the Turks. On the contrary, she writes that the numerous associations which were springing to life "were not as yet strictly revolutionary."[22] They were precipitated into intransigence by the landing of the Greeks at Smyrna on May 15, 1919.

The Greek landing was itself precipitated by that of the Italians at Adalia at the end of April.[23] From there they spread out over southwestern Anatolia, going ashore at such places as Budrum and Scala Nuova, and penetrating inland as far as Konia. Although the territory they occupied was part of that promised to them in the Treaty of St. Jean de Maurienne, the landings were made without consultation with, or even notification of, their allies. The British and French were understandably annoyed and, coming as it did at the same time as the dispute over Fiume, the Italian action produced what looked like a major rift in the Entente.

The Turks were not inflamed to the point of large-scale resistance against the Italians, who appear indeed to have behaved rather well. Halide Edib testified:

Although as foreigners people hated to see them in a country
which did not belong to them, still the behavior of the Italians
wherever they went during the occupation period was that
of a civilized people.[24]

Obviously this good lady did not see the Italians "wherever they went." Just as obviously she was making the strongest case she could against the Greeks and was not above using the Italians as a stick to

[21] President Gates agreed the occupation was unjust and inefficient and blamed its failure on the jealousy of the three occupying powers. Gates, *op. cit.*, 246.

[22] Halide Edib, *op. cit.*, 19.

[23] This of course does not mean that the project sprang to life without previous discussion of any sort. Venizelos had urged it before the Council of Ten on February 4 (*PPC*, III, 868-875) and it had been discussed in committee.

[24] Halide Edib., *op. cit.*, 19.

beat them with. Nonetheless, considering her unforgiving attitude toward other occupying forces and her deep sense of outrage that Turkish territory should be occupied at all, hers must be considered a fairly impressive testimony. Even if it had not been echoed elsewhere, it would be an index of the difference in Turkish reaction toward occupation by one of the great powers and occupation by Greece.

The disastrous effect of Italy's hasty action is not, therefore, to be sought in its reception by the Turks but in the response of her allies, as prompt as it was ill-advised. On May 5 the Council of Three approved the occupation of Smyrna by Greek forces and on May 15, it began.

The Allies were not without warning against the action they took. The American experts, for example, had written in their recommendations of January 21:

> Although an alternative Greek area is shown in the Smyrna region, it is not part of this recommendation that it be assigned to Greece. . . . To give her a foothold upon the mainland would be to invite immediate trouble.[25]

The recommendation of the British Foreign Office was similar:

> In return for obtaining Eastern Thrace, Greece should be induced to renounce her claims to Smyrna, and an interchange might be effected between Turkish inhabitants of Eastern Thrace and Greek inhabitants of Western Anatolia.[26]

It is true that the British members of the Committee on Greek Claims subsequently voted for the resolution to award the Smyrna district to Greece, as did the French, but there is reason to think that some of the British experts were never reconciled to the decision. Harold Nicolson and Arnold J. Toynbee clearly were not.[27]

---

[25] "Tentative Report and Recommendations," 1039.

[26] Memorandum presented to the British delegation on January 2, 1919, cited in Lloyd George, *op. cit.*, II, 1234.

[27] Professor William Yale has told me that at the time the question came before the committee the British members were against allowing the Greek occupation. He was not sure their views were presented at a committee meeting but was

The Americans on the committee, W. L. Westermann and Clive Day, voted against the resolution because they could not accept the Greeks' low estimate of the number of Turks resident in the area. They concluded that in all of the sanjaks, except that of Smyrna itself, the Greeks were in a minority.[28] David Hunter Miller recorded that the Americans also objected on economic ground to the separation of Turkey's chief port from the hinterland it served.[29]

The Italians refused to vote on the resolution or even discuss it, maintaining that no committee of the conference had a right to discuss the disposition of territory promised by treaty to Italy.[30]

The committee's resolution dealt with the ultimate disposition of Smyrna, not with the hastily improvised occupation of May 15. (Its report was not presented until May 30.) Whatever the merits of the case for permanent annexation, there could be no justification for attempting to settle it under the disguise of a temporary military occupation.

There is no mystery about the Allies' motives for sanctioning this disaster. Few aspects of the peace conference can show such unanimous testimony. Harold Nicolson recorded in his diary on May 2 that when the Italians sent two men of war to Smyrna, Lloyd George

> ... gave instructions that a British Dreadnought and a Greek Cruiser should also go there. The Italians, by trying to steal a march on the Asia Minor Coast, have helped the Greeks more than they know.[31]

positive that they assured Professor Westermann of their intention to vote against the proposal. This information, conveyed orally, was confirmed by Professor Yale in a letter of April 11, 1963. He remembers the circumstances clearly, recalling that "Westermann was quite indignant about their last-minute reversal."

[28] Conférence de la Paix, 1919-1920, Recueil des Actes de la Conférence (Paris: Imprimerie Nationale, 1923), Partie IV. Commissions de la Conférence. C. Questions Territoriales. (5) Commission chargée d'étudier les questions territoriales intéressant la Grèce, p. 39, in NA, State Department 763.72119/P94/19.

[29] Miller, op. cit., X, 291.

[30] Receuil des Actes de la Conférence, IV, C, v, 155.

[31] Nicolson, Peacemaking (Diary entry of May 2, 1919), 321-322.

On May 4 Lloyd George told the Council of Three:

The Greeks should be allowed to occupy Smyrna, since their compatriots were actually being massacred at the present time and there was no one to help them. . . . *He would like to settle the forces of occupation in Turkey before the Italians returned to Paris.* . . .

President Wilson said he could not do it so hastily.

Mr. Lloyd George said if they discussed it with the Italians, they would anticipate them.[32]

The following day the Big Three agreed on the Greek landings. To the objection that such an action was a violation of the pledge made to the Italians in the Treaty of St. Jean de Maurienne, Lloyd George replied that the pledge had been conditional upon Italian contributions to the war and upon the concurrence of Russia, which had never been obtained.[33]

Winston Churchill, Secretary of State for War in Lloyd George's coalition cabinet, agreed that the purpose of the landings was to forestall the Italians who had already seized Adalia, Budrum, Makri, and Alaya.[34] Sir Eyre Crowe, himself a member of the Committee on Greek Claims, was in a better position to be sure; he referred bluntly to the "consideration which primarily influenced that decision, namely the importance of preventing Italy from taking Smyrna."[35]

It must be admitted the Greeks had some ethnic claim to the area; the Italians never pretended to have any. The Greek claim, however, was limited to the sanjak of Smyrna itself. In Aidin, for example, they were not even a substantial minority. Nor can we take the ethnic argument too seriously if we reflect that it applied much more clearly to eastern Thrace. Needless to say, it was never raised with respect to

[32] *PPC*, V, 465-467; italics mine.

[33] *Ibid.*, V, 484.

[34] Winston Churchill, *The Aftermath* (New York: Charles Scribner's Sons, 1929), 386-387.

[35] Crowe to Kidston, December 1, 1919, *BDFP*, 1st ser., IV, 914.

Cyprus, which was held by the British, with a population that was eighty per cent Greek.

The argument that the Allies were committed by prior agreement to turn over a portion of the Ionian coast to Greece is even feebler. In January 1915 Sir Edward Grey, then Foreign Secretary, had offered "most important territorial compensations" to Greece on the coast of Asia Minor if the Greeks would declare themselves allies of the Serbs and participate in the war. He renewed the offer three months later, this time with the encouragement of the French and the Russians, but still it was made conditional upon Greek participation in the war against Turkey.[36]

The condition was not fulfilled. Owing to King Constantine's preference for the Central Powers—he was the Kaiser's brother-in-law and had received his own training in the German army—and perhaps to the natural reluctance of a small nation to be drawn into the conflict, the Greeks not only failed to aid the Serbs but even to defend themselves when the Bulgarians occupied Greek territory. Not until two years later was Venizelos able to bring the Greeks into the war on the side of the Entente. Surely a condition so spectacularly unfulfilled invalidated any promise.

The promise to the Italians was also conditional, but the condition had become irrelevant almost as soon as the treaty was signed. Russian approval was required because the Russians were one of the most powerful allies and the one with the most direct interest in Turkey. Following the Bolshevik revolution, however, they withdrew from the alliance and renounced any territorial claims based on the secret treaties. Moreover, the type of government and economic system which the Bolsheviks were introducing was regarded, rightly or wrongly, by the western nations as a menace to their own ultimate security. Their immediate security had already been jeopardized by the Russian abandonment of both the eastern and Caucasus fronts. Under these circumstances, Russian approval of a treaty between Great Britain, France, and Italy was not only irrelevant but absurd.

[36] Notes of January 23 and April 7, 1915, cited in Lloyd George, *op. cit.*, II, 1210-1212.

Lloyd George was at his most disingenuous in urging this "condition" against the Italian claim.[37]

Far more important than either legal or ethnic arguments was the effect of the Greek landings on Turkish willingness to accept the kind of peace the Allies wanted to make. Here the difference between Greeks and Italians was as between night and day. It was simply that the Turks had no such hatred for the Italians as for the Greeks, and the Italians had no similar hatred for the Turks. In all likelihood the Turks would have resisted an Italian occupation sooner or later, but in the conditions that then prevailed, there was all the difference in the world between sooner and later.

Yet the deed was done. Harold Nicolson records his feelings when asked to draft the resolution awarding the "Smyrna-Aivali zone and a mandate over most of the Vilayet of Aidin" to Greece, while at the same time Turkey was to be driven entirely out of Europe (with, presumably, much of the territory thus lost going to Greece): "It is immoral and impracticable. But I obey my orders. The Greeks are getting *too* much."[38]

The Allies had been warned by British and American experts. They were warned again by the reaction of the British cabinet. Nicolson recorded three days later: "The cabinet at home are showing signs of life. They have heard of the proposed partition of Turkey. Montagu, Sinha, Bikanir and even Curzon are threatening to resign."[39] On the next day Balfour too was threatening to resign.[40] On May 14 Nicolson had offered his evaluation of the decisions of the Big Three: "It is appalling that these ignorant and irresponsible men should be cutting

[37] I am aware that before the peace conference opened France and Great Britain had announced that they considered the Treaty of St. Jean de Maurienne invalid because of Russian failure to ratify, but I can't see that their attitude was any the less petty and opportunistic for that.

[38] Nicolson, *Peacemaking*, 335 (Diary entry of May 13, 1919); italics Nicolson's.

[39] *Ibid.*, 340 (Diary entry of May 16, 1919). Montagu, Sinha and Bikanir constituted India's delegation to the conference. They were, respectively, Secretary of State for India, Undersecretary of India, and Maharajah of Bikanir.

[40] *Ibid.*, 342 (Letter of May 17 to V.S.W.).

Asia Minor to bits as if they were dividing a cake."[41] He attributed the same sentiment to Balfour who added that the ignorant and irresponsible men had only a child to lead them. Nicolson concluded ruefully that he was the child.[42]

The stir in the cabinet was no tempest in a teapot. Most of the members crossed to Paris for a meeting on the 19th. Although their deliberations produced no change in policy, at least three members—Montagu, Lord Milner, and Winston Churchill—expressed themselves against the line Lloyd George was taking, according to Nicolson, who was separated from the meeting only by a glass partition and heard it all.[43] Winston Churchill later conceded that his attitude was to some extent influenced by the "consternation" the decision produced in the British General Staff, but:

> Making every allowance for the pro-Turk inclinations of the
> British military mind, it was impossible to excuse the imprudence
> of this violent act, which opened so many new perils when our
> resources were shrivelling. At the War Office we were not long
> in feeling its consequences. Our officers in twos and threes were
> all over Asia Minor supervising the surrender of armies and
> munitions as prescribed by the Armistice. They rode about freely
> and unarmed from place to place, and with their finger indi-
> cated what should be done. They were almost mechanically
> obeyed. . . . The Turks were under the spell of defeat. . . .

From the moment, however, that the Turks realized it was not Great Britain or Moslem troops from India they were to endure ". . . but Greece, the hated and despised foe of generations, to their eyes a revolted province, certainly a frequently defeated opponent; from that moment, Turkey became uncontrollable. . . .

"That Greeks should conquer Turks, was not a decree of Fate that any Turk would recognize."[44]

---

[41] *Ibid.*, 337 (Letter of May 14 to V.S.W.).
[42] *Ibid.*, 342 (Letter of May 17 to V.S.W.).
[43] *Ibid.*, 343 (Diary entry of May 19).
[44] Churchill, *op. cit.*, 388-390.

The author of the above passage is perhaps too much the literary man to be completely credible. He does not, however, stand alone. In 1921 Arnold J. Toynbee, investigating the Greco-Turkish war which began with the landing at Smyrna, talked to one of the British officers who had been engaged in disarming the Turks in the interior. This man was not "in twos and threes" but all alone except for a couple of orderlies and clerks. Yet he had been transmitting orders for disarmament to the Turkish authorities who had been obeying them without question until rumors of the landings began to arrive. At first incredulous—they knew the terms of the armistice and did not believe the Greeks would dare to defy the Allies—the Turks gradually became persuaded that the reports were true. By the time the English officer heard the news officially, after hearing it from every other possible source, they were no longer obeying him but rearming and drilling their men. He was lucky, Toynbee records, to escape detention.[45] Others, less lucky, were thrown into prison.

Nor is contemporary confirmation wanting. Admiral Richard Webb, the British Assistant Commissioner at Constantinople, wrote to Sir Ronald Graham of the Foreign Office on June 28, 1919:

> What I was going to write about was the increase of friction out here between Greeks and Turks. It has now become most serious, and of course it all dates back to the time of the occupation of Smyrna by the Greek troops. This occupation has led, not unnaturally, to much bloodshed, and now it is leading to trouble everywhere in Turkey.[46]

The same story was told by the High Commissioner in a telegram to Lord Curzon the following day. The Greek occupation had not been quiet but "ambitious"; the Turks were much afraid for the future.[47] On July 8 Calthorpe telegraphed even stronger misgivings to Balfour: "In my opinion this country is now confronted with possibil-

---

[45] Toynbee, *The Western Question in Greece and Turkey*, 186-187.
[46] *BDFP*, 1st ser., IV, 655.
[47] Calthorpe to Curzon, June 29, 1919. *Ibid.*, 1st ser., IV, 656.

ity of rapid disintegration of all authority and all security over wide areas."[48]

On August 17, 1919, Webb wrote to Sir Eyre Crowe:

> But one thing that is quite certain is that the worst day's work for his country Venizelos ever did was when he induced the Supreme Council to allow Greek troops into Smyrna to "pacify" the place. Apart from turning the whole district into a shambles . . . it has sown the seed of still more bitter animosity between Greek and Turk than existed before—an animosity that has to be seen to be realized.[49]

Lord Curzon's view of the matter was similar. "I myself thought," he wrote, "that this was the greatest mistake that had been made in Paris, and that it was the starting point of most of the troubles which have since ensued."[50]

Le Temps expressed a view that may have been that of the French government on July 7: "Since Greek troops landed at Smyrna there has been a real war between Greeks and Turks." Competent people, *Le Temps* complained, had not been consulted. M. Defrance, the French commissioner, had not even been informed.[51]

If *Le Temps* could be suspected of pro-Turkish leanings, no such suspicion could be entertained of *L'Asie française*, which had convoked the international conference of Armenians in November 1913. Its editors, however, reacted just as strongly against the policy:

> By detaching from Anatolia a small strip of territory around Smyrna we will be letting ourselves in for an artificial operation doomed by geography. . . . Since we cannot leave a foreign population at the mercy of the Turks, some kind of supervision must be imposed, but it would be equally inappropriate to

---

[48] *Ibid.*, 1st ser., IV, 666-667. See also Calthorpe's dispatch of July 27, 1919 (*Ibid.*, 1st ser., IV, 703).

[49] *Ibid.*, 1st ser., IV, 733.

[50] *Ibid.*, 1st ser., IV, 838.

[51] *Le Temps*, July 7, 1919, 1.

place Turkish elements under the control of a state having the same nationality as the minority to be protected.[52]

Equally strong condemnation came from Arnold J. Toynbee, of all contemporary westerners perhaps the most likely to be a "philhellene." His classical studies, his position as professor of Greek language and literature, both ancient and modern, at the University of London, and his several years in Greece as a young man before the war, all might well have disposed him to favor the Greek side of the controversy. Moreover, as editor of Lord Bryce's Blue Book on Armenian atrocities, he was in as good a position as any European to know all that could be said against the Turks. However, an eight months' tour of investigation in 1921 reinforced his earlier impression that, although there had been bad behavior (to put it mildly) on both sides, the original offense was against the Turks, an offense that continued so long as Greek troops remained in Anatolia. In the preface to the second edition of his book on the Greco-Turkish crisis, Toynbee wrote:

> I remain convinced that the crucial event in the tragedy was the landing of Greek troops at Smyrna on the 15th of May 1919.
> . . . That error set in motion the three formidable forces of Turkish patriotism, Anglo-French rivalry, and Anatolian military geography; and nothing, so far as I can see, could have prevented these forces from producing the resultant that they have actually produced. . . . The fact remains . . . that failure was predictable from the beginning.[53]

The warnings of the King-Crane Commission will be found in Chapter VII, but the reaction of General Harbord and his associates, whom President Wilson sent to Armenia on a mission of inquiry in the fall of 1919, may be anticipated here:

> The events at Smyrna have undoubtedly cheapened every Christian life in Turkey, the landing of the Greeks there being looked upon as deliberate violation by the allies of the terms of

---

[52] *L'Asie française*, CLXX, 222-223.

[53] Toynbee, *The Western Question in Greece and Turkey*, preface to second edition, xxxi.

the armistice and probable forerunner of further unwarranted aggression.[54]

The Near East, a London weekly by no means hostile to the British official position, summed up the landings as the "acme of callousness."[55]

Americans on the scene made similar judgments in the days following the landing. Gabriel Ravndal, a career diplomat of Norwegian birth who was the American Commissioner at Constantinople, telegraphed the peace conference on May 20: "The occupation of Smyrna by the Greeks has stirred the Moslems of Turkey to the core, and they are in a desperate mood."[56]

Admiral Bristol added his recommendation on May 29:

I earnestly recommend some statement regarding Greek occupation or else occupation of Turkey by the associated military forces. . . . Everyone here doing his utmost to control situation but most respectfully urge heeding warning regarding Greek occupation without concerted action military forces of other countries.[57]

Nor was the conference without warnings even before the action was taken. The American Minister to Greece, Garrett Droppers, a former professor of economics at Williams College, wrote as early as March 31, 1919, to express his misgivings about allowing Greece to annex substantial additional territory. He doubted the Greeks had the experience or political maturity to govern a larger area than they already had and was particularly skeptical about placing them in a position of authority over a non-Greek population. Furthermore, he argued, even if the annexation of Smyrna was right, it wouldn't settle anything. Greeks in other parts of Turkey would still clamor for lib-

[54] Major-General James G. Harbord, U.S. Army, *Conditions in the Near East.* Report of the American Military Mission to Armenia, hereafter referred to as Harbord Report, in *Senate Documents,* 66th Congress, 2nd Session (Washington: Government Printing Office, 1920), XV, Document No. 264, 11.

[55] *The Near East,* XVII (January 2, 1920), 14.

[56] NA, Peace Conference 867.01/32.

[57] *Ibid.,* 767.68/11.

eration.[58] The later agitation for a "Pontic" state on the Black Sea provided vindication for this view, if vindication were needed.

As a final testimony, General Tasker H. Bliss, one of the American peace commissioners, wrote in a memorandum dated November 10, 1919:

> Unfortunately, the United States has made her bed and must lie in it. Had we stood out against Greek occupation it would probably not have been made. The French were apparently not eager for it. At the meeting (at which I was present) when the occupation was decided on there was no Italian representation and it was held to be necessary to keep the movement secret from the Italians till the last moment. It appeared to be mainly pressed by Mr. Lloyd George in support of Mr. Venizelos. My impression is that the American representative was made to believe that it was necessary to prevent an impending massacre of Christians.
>
> Had Mr. Wilson any idea that a force of 70,000 or 80,000 men would be sent, he would have known that permanent conquest and not mere preservation of order was intended.[59]

This is, to be sure, one-sided testimony, but the diligent researcher will have difficulty finding anything on the other side except Lloyd George's misleading justification written some years later. Even observers who called attention to the deterioration in Turkey before the landings did not dispute their accelerating effect. Admiral Webb, for example, was quoted in the *New York Times* of April 18 as warning that brigandage, breakdown of order, and Allied loss of prestige were resulting from delay in settlement; he was later among the strongest in condemning the Smyrna decision as the pivotal episode in the collapse of the Allied position.

Harold Nicolson said at a later date that he had favored Greek occupation.[60] The diary he kept at the time fails rather spectacularly to bear this out:

58 *Ibid.*, 767.68/10.
59 Polk Papers, dr. 74, f. 35.
60 Nicolson, *Curzon: The Last Phase*, 94, note 1.

Toynbee and I plot together. . . . We agree . . . (2) That . . . we shall be unable to put the Greeks into Smyrna. I mean to keep them there. They can't hold it without allied support or unless the whole of Turkey behind them is split up among the allied powers . . . (3) We agree, therefore, to propose to cut the Gordian knot. Let the Turks have Anatolia as their own. Give the Greeks European Turkey only. . . .

Such a solution would at least have the merit of finality. All other solutions would entail trouble in the future. We put this down on paper; we sign it with our names; we send it in. It will not be considered.[61]

Nicolson's further argument that the "proportions of power obtaining at the time" were adequate to keep the Greeks at Smyrna[62] is a misleading half-truth, since it glosses over the fact that the occupation inevitably effected a drastic change in the "proportions of power," stimulating the Turks to violent resistance at the same time that it drove a sharp wedge between the Allies.

If Lloyd George were our only source of information, we would suppose that the occupation, whether right or wrong as a policy, was at least a tactical success. "Some difficulties," he wrote, "arose from time to time as to the limits of Greek occupation, but these were adjusted without any serious trouble."[63] This gives no hint that the adjustment took almost four years, that it cost a very large number of Greek and Turkish lives, or that it ended in complete failure for his policy.

Fortunately, we do not have to rely on Lloyd George. The peace conference appointed an Inter-Allied Commission of Inquiry on the Greek Occupation of Smyrna and Adjacent Territories which submitted a report on October 14, 1919. The commission consisted of Brigadier-General R. H. Hare (British), Brigadier-General Bunoust (French), Lt. General A. Dall'Olio (Italian) and Rear Admiral Mark Bristol (American).

[61] Nicolson, *Peacemaking*, 312 (Entry of April 14, 1919).
[62] Nicolson, *Curzon: The Last Phase*, 92.
[63] Lloyd George, *op. cit.*, II, 1250.

While by no means exonerating the Turks for the bloodshed and anarchy that followed the Greek landings—the Turkish authorities were blamed for having permitted the escape of numerous common-law prisoners before the Greeks arrived and for having no control over the Nationalist movement—the commission placed most of the blame for the ensuing violence on the Greeks:

> The international situation in the Vilayet did not call for the landing of Allied troops at Smyrna. On the contrary, since the Greek landing, the situation is troubled because of the state of war existing between the Greek troops and the Turkish irregulars.[64]
>   Their occupation, far from presenting itself as the carrying out of a civilizing mission, at once took the form of a conquest and a crusade.[65]

The Greeks were blamed specifically for allowing the circulation of armed Greek civilians and of occupying territory not covered by the agreement. Some of the resulting bloodshed was blamed on both parties, but some—for example, that at Menemen—on the Greeks alone.[66]

The report concluded by recommending the replacement of Greek by Allied forces.[67] Since the commission had previously stated that prior to the occupation there had been no need for foreign troops at all, it must be understood to have concurred in the view that the occupation itself was a substantial cause of the deterioration of the situation.

A different view, and one which puts the Greeks in a somewhat better light, was presented in a memorandum prepared in July 1919 by Lloyd George's secretary, Philip Kerr (later Lord Lothian) for Bal-

[64] PPC, IX, 47.

[65] Ibid., IX, 71-73.

[66] Ibid., IX, 69-70.

[67] Ibid., IX, 71-73. The report in its entirety, together with Greek objections and Italian reservations, is in PPC, IX, 44-73. General Dall'Olio's reservations related to the inclusion of any judgment of the wisdom of allowing the Greeks to occupy the region which, he maintained, went beyond the commission's instructions.

four's information.[68] Its effect was to absolve the Greeks of going beyond their instructions on the ground that they did so either to counter a serious military threat by the Turks or to forestall further occupation by the Italians. It did not, however, seriously attack the charges of atrocities committed by the Greeks, but merely maintained that their government would be better for the region in the future than that of the Turks, "our enemies."

In any case, an exact assessment of blame is not necessary, for the point to be emphasized is not that Greek behavior gave exceptional cause for Turkish anger, but that the mere presence of occupying Greek troops in their chief port was calculated to enrage the Turks.

If Lloyd George was, as all the evidence makes him appear, chiefly responsible for the blunder, why did he do it? Winston Churchill thought he had a kind of obsession about Greece. It was not devotion to classical Greece such as was commonly found among British statesmen who had attended Oxford and Cambridge. Philhellenes of that sort easily put Lloyd George's back up. It was not related to the past at all, but to the future. It was a conviction that Greece was the coming nation of the eastern Mediterranean and that it would serve Britain well to maintain a close connection. The Greeks numbered about six million, but the Prime Minister believed , according to Churchill, that in the next sixty years they would increase to twenty million.[69] If this was actually Lloyd George's opinion, it was a grievous miscalculation. Even with the addition of Cyprus, Greece has a population today of substantially less than twenty million; it is Turkey that has passed that mark.

Nicolson assigned five reasons for Lloyd George's attitude: 1) his devotion to the cause of those whom he considered oppressed; 2) his hatred of the Turks, "that human cancer," the only people who contributed nothing to enlightenment or progress; 3) his distrust of the

[68] *BDFP*, 1st ser., IV, 860-867.
[69] Churchill, *op. cit.*, 415. Lord Beaverbrook, who was close to Lloyd George in the postwar years, agrees with this analysis of the Prime Minister's point of view. Lord Beaverbrook, *The Decline and Fall of Lloyd George* (New York: Duell, Sloan and Pearce, 1963), 152.

kind of person who favored the Turks, in Great Britain likely to be either a military man or a member of the Conservative Party; 4) a "strange survival of feeling regarding the crescent and the cross"; and 5) his confidence in Venizelos. Almost as an afterthought Nicolson mentioned the desire for a strong British ally at both ends of a Smyrna-Piraeus line against the day when it would be no longer possible to keep the Russians from passing the Straits.[70]

None of these considerations, except perhaps the last, were of a sort to impress the kind of men who made French and Italian policy and who had the clamors of their own nationals to satisfy. As a consequence, Lloyd George's behavior was puzzling in the extreme to his allies. Nicolson admits that Greece became for them a symbol of British machinations, reinforcing their inclination to come to terms with Turkey.[71]

Halide Edib describes graphically the reaction of the Turkish people to the news of the Smyrna occupation. They were stunned, then angry, then fired with a determination that nothing could stop.[72]

Ahmed Emin Yalman, later editor of the daily *Vatan*, then a young man who had returned to Turkey after studying at Columbia University and had been banished from Constantinople because of his opposition to the government, gives a similar account:

> The sentiment in the country changed so suddenly and violently that the government felt obliged to let us political exiles return to the capital. Our reception in Istanbul by delegations with flowers and speeches turned into an antigovernment demonstration to the dismay of those in office.[73]

---

[70] Nicolson, *Curzon: The Last Phase*, 95-97. Note the similarity of this view to that of Arnold J. Toynbee, *The Western Question in Greece and Turkey*, 74.

[71] Nicolson, *Curzon: The Last Phase*, 104-107.

[72] Halide Edib, *op. cit.*, 24-25, *passim*.

[73] Ahmed Emin Yalman, *Turkey in My Time* (Norman: University of Oklahoma Press, 1956), 87-88. Yalman supplies convincing corroboration to Halide Edib because, although much less emotional, he tells the same story. He sees Turkey as completely crushed, its resurrection doubtful until the humiliation of the Greek occupation swept it with the gust of anger that could only be appeased by revolt.

A few days after the landing, speaking at an international gathering at the Girls' College (American), of which she was a graduate, Halide Edib fired her first gun. Without mentioning Smyrna, she "spoke of the futility and vanity of education unless it affected and bettered the behavior of men toward their fellow-men." As she tells the story, she never became any more "political" than that, but the "vision of the tortured and martyred on the quai of Smyrna" was always before her eyes. Her grief for her country must have been apparent in what she said or in her manner, for at the conclusion of the exercises the English General Long spoke to her with "genuine concern and manly trouble." When she had previously met General Long, he had assured her of British lack of interest in Turkey, remarking, "We have bitten off more than we can chew already." Something in her head kept "repeating and repeating: 'Turkey is certainly a big mouthful to swallow—England is making Greece bite off the awkward corners first.' "[74]

From that time forward her life was a succession of gatherings and demonstrations, with a deputation to the Sultan, culminating in the giant meeting in Sultan Ahmed Square on June 6. She does not tell us how many people attended—Turks were not then much interested in statistics—but her appeal to her "wronged and martyred nation" was heard by a "mass of humanity." She and her hearers alike were swayed by a profound, almost religious feeling, but the westerner should not be misled by the somewhat "oriental" expression of their emotion. What they were asking for was a western concept of justice, indeed the concept most in vogue in the west at the time, the "self-determination of peoples." Casually glancing at the typical banner draped over the rostrum while Halide Edib was speaking,[75] the westerner would probably suppose its inscription to be a verse from the Koran. What it said, however, was "Wilson's Twelfth Point."[76] The Turkish reaction to the occupation cannot be understood if we suppose that it meant nothing more to the Turks than a harsh imposi-

[74] Halide Edib, *op. cit.*, 24.
[75] *Ibid.*, photograph facing page 16.
[76] *Ibid.*, 30.

tion by a triumphant enemy. They saw it as a betrayal by the Allies of their own principles, principles which the Turks had accepted as an honest statement of intention.

The Turks could only conclude from this that they must work out their own salvation by whatever instruments were at hand. They were fortunate in that the chief instrument was already aboard a ship bound for Samsun where neither the Sultan's government nor the Allied high commissioners could exercize any real authority over him. This was Mustafa Kemal Pasha, the brilliant officer who had defended the Dardanelles against the British four years earlier.[77]

Born in Salonika in 1881, educated at the military academy in Monastir and the War College in Constantinople, Kemal early became opposed to the government of Abdul Hamid. He has sometimes been identified with the Young Turk movement, but his involvement in it was rather formal, the result of its absorption of the revolutionary organization in the army, *Vatan ve Hurriyet*, and he was usually at odds with the Young Turk leadership.[78] Equally misleading is the charge that under his leadership Turkish nationalism was pro-German.[79] He was not on good terms with the Germans and believed Turkey's entry into the war on the side of the Central Powers to be a mistake. Prior to 1919 his distinctions were military, not political.

He served on several fronts in the Italian and Balkan wars. In 1913 he was assigned to Sofia as military attaché, but when Turkey entered the world war he asked for active service. His request was granted and success at Gallipoli was the result. He later served against the Russians on the eastern front and was preparing the defense of Aleppo against the British and Arabs when the Armistice of Mudros was signed.[80]

---

[77] He later became "Atatürk" (Father of the Turks) by vote of the Grand National Assembly when all Turks were required to take surnames.

[78] On this point see E. E. Ramsaur, Jr., *The Young Turks. Prelude to the Revolution of 1908* (Princeton: Princeton University Press, 1957), 98-101, and Lord Kinross, *Ataturk* (New York: William Morrow and Company, 1965), *passim*.

[79] For example, in Paillarès, *op. cit.*, *passim*.

[80] Bernard Lewis, *op. cit.*, 238-240.

He found little to do in Constantinople. He later characteristically described the situation in the capital:

Those who had dragged the nation and the country into the Great War had thought only of saving their own lives and had fled abroad. Vahideddin, who occupied the position of Sultan and Caliph, was a degenerate who, by infamous means, sought only to guard his own person on the throne. The cabinet, headed by Damad Ferid Pasha, was weak, cowardly, and without dignity, subservient to the will of the Sultan, and ready to agree to anything that might protect him as well as their own persons.[81]

Since nothing could be accomplished in the capital, Mustafa Kemal cast about for ways of getting out where something could be done. Escape proved ridiculously simple. The Sultan appointed him inspector-general of the Ninth Army (renumbered the Third Army in June). Based on Samsun on the Black Sea coast, this army was well away from the restraints of Constantinople. Kemal's instructions were to restore order to the country and peace between Moslems and Christians, to disarm both regulars and irregulars, and in general to supervise demobilization of the Ottoman forces.

He arrived in Samsun three days after the Greek landings at Smyrna and set to work in a sense directly opposed to his orders. He established links between existing groups which were ready to resist the Allies, created new groups, and laid the groundwork for a Turkish army of liberation.[82] Soon after he arrived, the government, realizing its mistake, ordered him to return. He refused.[83]

Kemal lost no time in getting in touch with those authorities from whom he might expect collaboration, among them Kazim Karabekir Pasha, in command of the Fifteenth Army Corps at Erzerum. This terrible Turk was admired by Halide Edib for his endless kindness to children. At a later time he "adopted about two thousand Turkish

---

[81] A Speech Delivered by Ghazi Mustapha Kemal, President of the Turkish Republic, October 1927 (Leipzig: K. F. Koehler, 1929), 9.

[82] Bernard Lewis, op. cit., 240-241.

[83] Calthorpe to Curzon, July 8, 1919. BDFP, 1st ser., IV, 667.

orphans whose parents had been massacred in the Erzerum and Erzinjan regions."[84]

By the end of June, Kemal and Rauf Bey, former Minister of the Navy who had joined the Nationalists, had an army and a military government. They refused to recognize the regime at Constantinople although claiming to be loyal to the Sultan. They represented themselves as resisting "Greek infiltration." The cabinet in the capital was "lamentably weak" against them.[85]

Kemal had sent a coded telegram to a number of leaders, both civil and military, in which he declared that as a result of the impotence of the central government, the nation was regarded as "non-existent" and that only the "will and resolution of the nation can save the independence of the nation."[86] He asserted the rights of Turkey and called on the districts to send delegates to Sivas. Those of the eastern vilayets met from July 23 to August 17 at Erzerum; the Congress of Sivas, which convened on September 4, had representation from the entire country. Kemal chaired both meetings which drafted early versions of what came later to be known as the National Pact.[87]

When the Erzerum meeting was in session, Damad Ferid's government ordered the arrest of Kemal and Rauf. Kazim Karabekir refused to comply.[88]

---

[84] Halide Edib, *op. cit.*, 401. This may appear a very tall story designed to win sympathy for Turks, but it receives curious confirmation in the account of an American woman in charge of hospital work in Kars when the Turks conquered the city in October 1920. With the entire community trembling in terror at the approach of the victor, General Kazim Karabekir came to the hospital in person and assured himself the children were getting the best possible treatment. Throughout the occupation he supported the Americans in hospital, orphanage, and relief work. His men proved assiduous at finding wounded people who were trying to hide and bringing them to the attention of American medical authorities. Elizabeth Anderson, "Hunting Trouble in Armenia" in *The Atlantic Monthly*, CXXVII (May 1921), 695-707.

[85] Telegram from Ravndal, July 1, 1919.   NA Peace Conference 867.00/290.

[86] Bernard Lewis, *op. cit.*, 242.

[87] *Ibid.*, 242-243. The text (in English) of the Sivas Declaration is printed as Exhibit D to the Harbord Report in *Senate Documents*.

[88] Bernard Lewis, *op. cit.*, 243.

Admiral Calthorpe wrote to Curzon on August 1st:

The fact is that this country has now quite definitely reached the point at which every Turkish element in political life is dominated more by national sentiment and the desire to conserve at least the unoccupied remnant of the Empire as an undivided whole than by any other consideration.[89]

Such a state of mind inevitably strengthened the Nationalists as the party actively resisting the fragmentation of the country. They were not, however, hostile to all forms of foreign intervention in the summer and fall of 1919. On September 9 the National Congress at Sivas addressed a letter to the president of the United States Senate requesting that the Senate send a committee to visit all parts of the Ottoman Empire to see for themselves what conditions prevailed.[90] On October 15 a statement signed by Mustafa Kemal himself even suggested that they would welcome foreign supervision:

We make a special point of adding that the assistance of a powerful and impartial foreign nation will be of great value to us in saving us from the iniquitous oppression of which we are the victims and in hastening our development.[91]

Such feelers may not have been too seriously intended. There was, to be sure, Nationalist sentiment for varying degrees of foreign assistance. Some, including Halide Edib, felt that the weakness and backwardness of the country made help imperative. A nation whose total revenues were barely enough to pay the interest on its debt would have to go through a period of tutelage. Americans could provide sound administration and the kind of educational system that would lead to enlightened self-government.

Others who laid less stress on these positive aspects of American supervision advocated it as a defense against domination by European

[89] *BDFP*, 1st ser., IV, 712.

[90] NA, Peace Conference 184.02102/5. Exhibit F, Harbord Report.

[91] *Ibid.*, "Condensed memorandum concerning the organization and points of view of the League for the Defence of the Rights of Anatolia and Rumelia," Exhibit C, p. 8.

imperialists. This domination was sometimes thought of as a British mandate, sometimes as partition of the country by the European allies.[92] Kemal may have been temporarily of this point of view, but it is more likely that he regarded it as a bargaining position. By talking as if he wanted American supervision he could have hoped to keep the imperialists at bay until Turkey was strong enough to dispense with all foreign control. This interpretation of his attitude becomes more persuasive if we accept as true the report that he proposed to Georges Picot a French "economic mandate" over all of Turkey in return for relinquishment of French claims in Cilicia. Such a proposal, if he made it, can hardly have been other than a tactical move designed to gain time for strengthening Turkey's resistance to encroachment by the Greeks and British.[93]

In any case, these overtures met with no response. A situation from which something of value might have been retrieved was allowed to deteriorate further. Throughout August British despatches from Turkey had stressed the need for getting Greek and Italian troops out of the country as a first step toward making peace with the Turks. A word to the wise—how many thousand words to the foolish!

A number of pages have now been devoted to a quarrel between Turks and Greeks with a subplot involving another quarrel between the Italians and their allies—and scarcely a word about Armenia. If such apparent side issues were in fact the heart of the question, it was because the Armenians' aspirations were at all times at the mercy of events over which they had no control. The Greek landing at Smyrna was perhaps the most decisive of these.

Prior to May 15, 1919 the Turks were prepared to accept a harsh peace. An Armenian state in eastern Anatolia, even a small one, was not a disposition they could have welcomed, but had the Allies been firm enough, it could have been swallowed, if necessary forced down

---

92 Kemal, *op. cit.*, 77-100.

93 Roderic H. Davison, "Turkish Diplomacy from Mudros to Lausanne" in Gordon A. Craig and Felix Gilbert, eds., *The Diplomats 1919-1939* (Princeton: Princeton University Press, 1953), 178. For Kemal's conversation with Georges Picot, Professor Davison cites Roger de Gontaut-Biron and L. Le Révérend, *D'Angora à Lausanne* (Paris, 1924), 12, 204.

their throats. In a memorandum dated May 27, 1919 the American Vice-Consul Edelman suggested that liberal Turks would have accepted, although with scepticism as to its success, an independent Armenian state on the ground that "the sentiment of the world demands the creation of this new country." He added that the Turks, like other mideastern peoples, had great faith in the capacity and disinterestedness of America.[94]

The Greek occupation, in addition to setting the Allies against each other, stiffened the Turkish will and kindled the Turkish spirit to the point at which, unless the Allies were willing to back Greece to the limit or to launch a major military action themselves, the future of Turkey, including the Armenian vilayets, was up to the Turks.

While the Greeks, by urging this ill-advised policy on the peace conference, lost something for themselves (for, if they had been willing to stay out of Smyrna, they would almost certainly have been compensated by substantial gains in eastern Thrace), the most inevitable and serious losses were sustained by the Armenians. There was no territory elsewhere in the world with which to compensate them and their position was such that, except in Cilicia, there was no way the Allies could get help to them without a very large and difficult military operation which, quite aside from any other objections to it, their peoples would hardly have tolerated. It may therefore be said that the Smyrna blunder sealed the fate of Armenia, although it was only four years later at Lausanne that its end was made official.

One may well wonder whether the Allies could have done anything to make this horrifying situation worse. They did. Two events of mid-1919, both bordering on the grotesque, could have had no effect but to add to the despair of the Turks and to strengthen their resistance.

More than five months after the conference convened and just before the treaty with Germany was signed, the Turks were invited to send a delegation to Paris to discuss the peace settlement. On June 17 a party headed by the Grand Vizier, Damad Ferid Pasha, made its appearance before the Supreme Council.

Damad Ferid urged his nation's case by denying that either the

[94] NA Peace Conference 185.5136/33.

Turkish people or their present government had any responsibility for the war just ended. The Committee of Union and Progress had made secret arrangements with the Kaiser and then had used Russian designs on Constantinople to play upon the people's fears and whip them to a fighting pitch. (The Allies could hardly have made an effective reply to this, knowing as they did how far these fears were from being illusory.) The C.U.P. had been responsible for the persecution and slaughter of countless innocent persons, Moslem as well as Christian. Their atrocities had left Asia Minor desolate and many homeless. Damad Ferid appealed to the victors to balance centuries of Ottoman tradition against the horrible but brief period of Young Turk tyranny which put the state and its people in a very bad light. The nation, he said, would now devote itself to "intensive economic and intellectual culture in order thus to become a useful factor in the League of Nations."

The Grand Vizier asked for an end to the Allied occupation, referring to the deplorable excesses at Smyrna, and a virtual restoration of the empire to the *status quo ante bellum*. He alleged an identity of interests between Turks and Arabs despite their linguistic differences. He concluded by referring to a memorandum being drawn up by the delegation which would be presented to the conference in a few days.[95]

The memorandum, dated June 23, 1919, in addition to reiterating some of what had already been said, dealt with more specific questions such as boundaries and the relation of Turkey to its neighbors. The Armenian question was discussed under Points Two and Four.

The first of these made clear that the Turks accepted no Armenian claim to a state on former Ottoman territory. They regarded Turkey as extending to the Russian and Persian frontiers "as they were before the war." The fourth point indicated a willingness to recognize an Armenian state, if the Allies did so, but only in Transcaucasia.[96] There is no reference to the districts of Kars and Ardahan, ceded

[95] Damad Ferid's statement in *PPC*, IV, 509-511.
[96] *Ibid.*, VI, 693.

under duress to Russia after the war of 1877 and returned to Turkey by the Treaty of Brest-Litovsk in 1918. Presumably the Turks did not concede that they were part of the Armenian Republic. In any case it is clear that no part of pre-1914 Turkey was to be included in Armenia except, of course, as part of such boundary rectifications as might be made in the discussions which the Turks were willing to join. From the tone of the Grand Vizier's statement and the memorandum, it must be supposed that any concessions made by Turkey would be small ones.

The memorandum concludes with a claim to virtually the entire prewar empire, although the Turks were willing to discuss with Great Britain the status of Cyprus and Egypt.[97]

The Supreme Council responded to these appeals by agreeing, at its meeting on June 23, that

> ... the Turkish Delegation should be thanked for the statements they have made to the Peace Conference and that a suggestion should be conveyed to them that they might now return to their own country.[98]

It also asked Balfour to draft a reply to the Turks, a reply which would in no sense outline peace terms but merely tell the Turks that they couldn't have what they wanted and must wait until the Allies decided what they could have.

Balfour's reply, sometimes attributed to Clemenceau who merely read it to the Turks in his capacity as president of the conference, shows its author at his best and his worst. It was superbly lucid, incisive, even witty; it made all its points with a finality that must have dissuaded the Turks from any thought of dealing with it verbally. It was also unnecessarily wounding and humiliating to a beaten enemy.

The reply rejected the Turkish appeals in their entirety. The Allies, it said, were glad to admit the sincerity of the Turks in repudiating

[97] Turkish memorandum in *Ibid.*, VI, 691-694.
[98] *BDFP*, 1st ser., IV, 652.

the crimes committed under the Committee of Union and Progress, but

> ... a nation must be judged by the Government which rules it,
> which directs its foreign policy, which controls its armies; nor can
> Turkey claim any relief from the legitimate consequences
> of this doctrine because her affairs, at a most critical moment
> in her history, had fallen into the hands of men who, utterly
> devoid of principle or pity, could not even command success.[99]

However, it was clear from the Turkish statement that more than present revulsion toward the crimes of the preceding regime was being urged in vindication of Turkish claims. The conference had been asked to weigh the entire record of the Ottoman Empire against the reign of the Young Turks. The Allies were not impressed by that record. There was "no case to be found," Balfour wrote,

> either in Europe or Asia or Africa, in which the establishment of
> Turkish rule in any country has not been followed by a diminu-
> tion of material prosperity, and a fall in the level of culture;
> nor is there any case to be found in which the withdrawal of
> Turkish rule has not been followed by a growth in material
> prosperity and a rise in the level of culture. Neither among the
> Christians of Europe, nor among the Moslems of Syria, Arabia,
> and Africa, has the Turk done other than destroy wherever
> he has conquered; never has he shown himself able to develop
> in peace what he has won by war.[100]

Finally, there was the argument based on the feeling of Moslems all over the world. It does not figure either in Damad Ferid's statement nor in the Turkish memorandum, but it had figured in the delibera-tions of the Council of Four. In refuting it, Balfour's irony jabbed remorselessly:

> The Turkish Empire is, it seems, to be preserved unchanged,
> not so much because this would be to the advantage of either
> the Moslems or of the Christians within its borders, but because

[99] *Ibid.*, 1st ser., IV, 646.
[100] *Ibid.*

its maintenance is demanded by the religious sentiment of men
who never felt the Turkish yoke, or have forgotten how heavily
it weighs on those who are compelled to bear it.

But surely there never was a sentiment less justified by facts.
... What religious issue is raised by a struggle in which Protestant
Germany, Roman Catholic Austria, Orthodox Bulgaria and
Moslem Turkey banded together to plunder their neighbors?
The only flavor of deliberate fanaticism in these transactions
was the massacre of Christian Armenians by order of the Turkish
Government. But your Excellency has pointed out that, at the
very same time and by the very same authority unoffending
Moslems were being slaughtered in circumstances sufficiently
horrible, and in numbers sufficiently large, to mitigate, if not
wholly to remove, any suspicion of religious partiality. ...

To thinking Moslems throughout the world, the modern history
of the government enthroned at Constantinople can be no source
of pleasure or pride. ... In an impressive passage of your
Memorandum you declared it to be your country's mission to
devote itself to "an intensive economic and intellectual culture."
No change could be more startling and impressive; none could
be more beneficial.[101]

That a nation which had capped a career of unparalleled crime
with an overwhelming defeat should appeal for a return to the *status
quo* on the basis of religious sentiment outside its borders was preposterous enough. Here, if anywhere, Balfour's sarcasm might seem
to be justified. Yet here he was actually on his weakest ground. The
question of Moslem sentiment had been raised because France and
Great Britain, as great Moslem powers, were vulnerable to it.
Whether or not the Turks took the argument seriously, there were
many in the Allied camp who did—not the least of them, in some
of their moods, Balfour and his chief, Lloyd George.

The Turks, thus summarily dismissed, set out for home. Their trip
was a memorable one. The French government was in charge of all
arrangements and made virtually none. The liaison officer, Lieutenant
Le Révérend, joining the delegation at Lausanne where it had been

101 *Ibid.*, 1st ser., IV, 646-647.

allowed a few days to see to the repatriation of Turkish nationals marooned in Switzerland, did not even bring with him the passports they had surrendered upon arrival in France. The British liaison officer, Lieutenant Colonel W. F. Blaker, was obliged to travel to Berne to secure new passports from the Turkish embassy as well as to obtain British papers which would facilitate the operation. He had also to secure a sealed baggage car, as one of the Turkish princes had decided to join the party in Switzerland and had added to its luggage much valuable property. The French officials did not respect the sealed car, opening it to put in the baggage of a French party. The new passports did not arrive until two hours before the scheduled departure of the eastbound train.

Since the private cars promised the delegation had failed to materialize, the members had to be scattered throughout the train. Dining facilities had also been promised and were in fact provided as far as Trieste. From there to Bucharest, sustenance was to be had only by a stampede at each station. The one solid meal on this stage was obtained at a place two miles from the railroad. The older members of the party, including Damad Ferid and former Grand Vizier Tewfik Pasha, were not equal to a dash of that kind and survived on what their juniors could bring back to them.

At Bucharest the delegation was left in the waiting room of the main railroad station while an appeal was made to the French embassy. There the *chargé d'affaires*, Henri Cambon, son of the distinguished diplomat, Paul Cambon, found hotel accommodations. Apparently Cambon was the only Frenchman who was in any way helpful throughout the journey. Le Révérend, of little account at best, reached his nadir in Bucharest where he went off with friends and was not seen again by the delegation until the train was ready to pull out. Blaker and the Italian liaison officer, Captain Ferrari, were left to assist the Turks as best they could.

The French cruiser *Waldeck Rousseau* was to take the delegation on the last stage across the Black Sea from Constanza to Constantinople. When the party arrived in Constanza the *Waldeck Rousseau* had gone elsewhere. Three smaller French ships were pressed into

service. Several of the diplomats were seasick; it must be admitted
that the same fate might have overtaken them on the larger craft but
a cruiser would have given them more dignity when they disem-
barked at Constantinople. It might also have given them a kinder
feeling toward an adversary which had so recently talked of a peace
in which the time-honored motives of revenge and national aggran-
dizement were to have no place. As Blaker wrote in his report:

> They felt they had been unceremoniously bundled out, whilst
> the lack of arrangements for their journey must have created the
> impression that the French Government, once its unwelcome
> guests were beyond the French frontier, was only too glad to
> wash its hands of them. It was particularly unfortunate that the
> grand vizier and an old frail man like Tewfik Pasha were sub-
> jected to avoidable discomfort and that they were denied the
> consideration demanded both by their status and by the rules
> of ordinary courtesy.[102]

Another blow at cooperation took the form of action designed to
weaken the Nationalist movement through the agency of the Kurds.
Here the offenders were not French but British.

Representatives, or persons styling themselves representatives,
of Kurdish aspirations had addressed an appeal to the peace conference at an early date—February 6, 1919—in which they claimed most
of Armenia as "Kurdistan," putting themselves forward as a better
buffer against Bolshevism than the Armenians, who were themselves "strongly contaminated by these dangerous ideas." By virtue
of the antagonisms of their political parties and the rivalries of their
revolutionary committees, the Kurds further charged, the Armenians
could not provide adequate security to their neighbors.[103]

Probably this appeal made little serious impression on anyone.
While conclusive evidence on the point is lacking, the scarcity of
references to the Kurds in the literature of the conference is evidence
of a kind. It seems much more likely that they were welcomed as a

---

[102] *Ibid.*, 1st ser., IV, 703.
[103] *L'Asie française*, CLXXV, 192-193.

picturesque element but given even less attention than the Montenegrins and the Albanians who furnished the same kind of romance.

However, by a curious coincidence we begin running across the Kurds in British diplomatic correspondence just as the flowering of Turkish nationalism can no longer be disregarded. On July 10 Admiral Calthorpe wired Curzon: "Major Noel thinks great advantage might be gained from every point of view by assistance of Kurdish chiefs along Northern frontier of Mesopotamia."[104] Major Noel was Assistant to the British Political Resident in the Persian Gulf. He had just arrived in Constantinople, bringing with him an ardent enthusiasm for the Kurds. Thomas Hohler, Political Officer at Constantinople, described him in a letter of July 21, 1919 to Sir J. Tilley of the Foreign Office:

> My present trouble is Kurds. Noel has arrived here from
> Baghdad, and he is a nice fellow and an able one, but he is an-
> other fanatic. He is the apostle to the Kurds. There is no one like
> them, so good and noble and generous! The Turks and Armenians
> are equally worthless and despicable. Kurds never killed any
> Armenians, but saved thousands of them, on the contrary;
> though the Armenians killed lots of Kurds. In fact they never
> did any harm. I am afraid Noel may turn out a Kurdish Col.
> Lawrence.[105]

Hohler went on to relate that Noel's obsession with the Kurds had led him to such extremes as attending Kurdish meetings in uniform. He agreed that if British policy was to weaken Turkey in every way the Kurds were an instrument that could be used for that purpose. But it should be done delicately.

Unless Hohler was a very serpent, there is no reason to suppose he thought Noel other than an individual of odd enthusiasms. Nonetheless, rumors began to circulate about British propaganda in Kurdistan directed against the Turkish Nationalists. Michel Paillarès described the event that ensued:

[104] *BDFP*, 1st ser., IV, 678.
[105] *Ibid.*, 1st ser., IV, 693.

In August of this year while a Nationalist Congress was meeting
in Angora, Major Noel of the Intelligence Department in Syria
came from Aleppo to Diarbekir to try to raise the Kurds against
the Angora government. If I can believe the Young Turks, he
had even organized a plot to assassinate Mutafa Kemal. There
was a great outcry over the affair; we were told that documents
would be published which would embarrass the English,
but nothing appeared. Major Noel, repudiated by his superiors,
was recalled and that was the end of it.[106]

Paillarès was obviously wrong about the site of the conference. He
was also mistaken in supposing Noel to have been previously employed in Syria. Nor do other accounts mention an assassination
plot. With these exceptions—at least the first two may be merely
results of rushing his book through the press—his story agrees with
contemporary American reports. Nor can he be dismissed as ani-
mated by an anti-British bias. Many of his countrymen were, but he
was persuaded that the salvation of France lay in close cooperation
with the British.

The bulk of the story was confirmed in a telegram from Ravndal
to the State Department on September 12:

Reports from Sivas indicate a futile attempt on the part of
British agent Noel . . . to stir up the Kurds and with their aid
break up the so-called National Congress. These schemes are
supposed to have been encouraged from Constantinople and to
have matured at Malatia.[107]

Finally the American commission in Paris was informed by Constantinople on October 2: "General Harbord confirms British propaganda in Kurdistan and attempt to suppress Turkish Nationalist
Movement."[108]

Although this comic opera *coup d'état* ended with Noel's recall,
its effect on the Turks may be imagined.

[106] Paillarès, *op. cit.*, 66.
[107] NA, State Department 860J.01/84.
[108] NA, Peace Conference 184.02102/—.

7

The King-Crane Commission

*F*ROM THE OPENING OF THE peace conference the Americans relied on the device of sending commissions of inquiry to areas in dispute or to those which presented special problems.[1] It was believed that the reports of these missions furnished the delegation with reliable and current data which made it possible to take an informed stand on controversial points, perhaps also to counteract the prejudices or selfish demands of our allies.

A mission referred to variously as destined for Turkey, Syria, and the near east was discussed at a very early date. William C. Bullitt, who had returned from an assignment in Russia and was on hand at Paris for the conference, urged an impartial investigation in a memorandum to Secretary Lansing on January 29, 1919. The French, he

---

[1] On July 12, 1919, for example, the American Commissioners Plenipotentiary agreed to continue the Rhineland Commission, the Teschen Commission, the Klagenfurt Mission, the Halstead Mission, the Dyar Mission, the Summerall Mission, and the Polish Mission, and to discontinue the Mission to Southern Russia. It was reported at the same meeting that General Bliss was "revising" the Mission to the Baltic States. *PPC*, XI, 295.

said, were bent on enforcing the Sykes-Picot Agreement and the other secret treaties while the British wanted to abandon them. Our line should be that the treaties were no longer in force since our allies had accepted the Fourteen Points as a basis for peace.[2]

On February 1, perhaps as a result of Bullitt's suggestion, "Mr. Lansing gave to Mr. Herter a letter which he had addressed to the President and which had been approved by the President, suggesting that Dr. Barton serve with Mr. Frederic C. Howe on a commission to Turkey."[3]

Dr. James L. Barton, a former missionary who had been president of Euphrates College in Kharput, was secretary to the American Board of Commissioners for Foreign Missions (Congregational) and organizer of the Near East Relief.

Frederic Clemson Howe, a Cleveland lawyer and author of such works as *The City: the Hope of Democracy* and *The Modern City and its Problems*, had been named Commissioner of Immigration in 1914. He had known Wilson at Johns Hopkins, but had grown somewhat apart from the President because of his consistent opposition to the repressive wartime measures of the administration. He was still close enough, however, to be invited to the peace conference.

Howe recorded in his autobiography that shortly after his arrival in Paris, Colonel House told him the President

> ... planned to send a mission to Syria to ascertain the wishes
> of the Syrians themselves in regard to a mandatory. He desired
> me to familiarize myself with all the treaties and engagements
> of the allied powers relating to the Near East, and to hold myself
> in readiness to leave for Syria at a moment's notice. Doctor Barton,
> of the Armenian Relief Fund, was to be my associate on the
> mission.[4]

[2] NA, Peace Conference, 184.017/1.

[3] *PPC*, XI, 8. Christian A. Herter, later Governor of Massachusetts and Secretary of State under President Eisenhower, was Secretary of Transport Questions in the American Commission.

[4] Frederic C. Howe, *The Confessions of a Reformer* (New York: Charles Scribner's Sons, 1925), 291.

The choice of Howe led to one of the oddest episodes of the peace conference. Some time in February he started for Rome where he believed he was to meet Dr. Barton. From there they would travel to Brindisi to be met by a destroyer which would take them to Constantinople. The unheated train was packed. Some passengers stood in the corridors throughout the thirty-six hour trip from Paris to Rome. Unable to find Barton in Rome, Howe went on to Brindisi hoping to make connections there. When he got off the train, it was raining and bitter cold. As the hotels were jammed, a cab driver found him a place to sleep in a scabrous establishment crowded with humanity of every sort. Howe would have none of it and took to the streets again. It was hours before he found a place for the night and by the time he got to bed he had evidently come down with a fever. Overnight the visions he had cherished for several years of a Syria restored to its ancient glory (a curious dream for a Progressive from beyond the Alleghenies, but he tells us it was his) went into the discard. Convinced that America was wanted in the east only to pull England's chestnuts out of the fire and that to become involved would embroil us forever in European affairs, a familiar American nightmare, he returned to Paris and told Colonel House that any American effort in the area should be on an "imposing scale" and very well prepared. He later persuaded himself that the King-Crane Commission answered to that description.[5]

Howe was back in Paris by February 20. The commissioners expressed surprise at his action, along with some doubt as to whether expenses should be paid for his useless journey. Henry White said, apparently a bit ruefully, that he "was afraid" they should be, and the others concurred.[6]

And so they should, for Barton had telegraphed on February 3: "Am leaving this week for Constantinople. Will meet Mr. Howe there unless otherwise directed."[7] On February 18 he telegraphed again: "I understand F. C. Howe is not coming to join me. Can I

[5] *Ibid.*, 300-302.
[6] *PPC*, XI, 61.
[7] NA, Peace Conference 184.017/6.

consider this releases me and can I proceed with my present relief work?"[8] To this the commissioners replied that he was released and that they would keep in touch with him.[9] Barton subsequently undertook a tour of several thousand miles reporting his observations and recommendations to Paris.

On February 21 William M. Buckler, a career diplomat and archeologist who was Henry White's half-brother, was suggested as a replacement for Howe. Leon Dominian was already on his way to Paris and might join Buckler.[10]

Dominian, a Constantinople-born geographer who had taught at the New Mexico School of Mines, was the author of *The Frontiers of Language and Nationality in Europe* (1917) and a member of the Inquiry. Upon arrival in Paris he was asked to head the new commission and by March 4 was able to present his plans for it to Joseph C. Grew, Secretary-General of the American Commission.[11] However, at the February 24 meeting a new method of investigation was suggested by Allan Dulles, Technical Advisor on Political and Diplomatic Questions, who recommended bringing George Stewart, the treasurer of Beirut Protestant College [*sic*] to Paris to talk to the commissioners.[12] The idea was accepted but it was considered preferable to ask for the college's president, Howard Bliss,[13] who was already in Paris where he had appeared on February 13 before the Council of Ten to plead that Syria be allowed an "untrammeled" choice of a mandatory power.[14]

On February 26 Dr. Bliss told the American commissioners that the people of Syria were relying on the Fourteen Points. He urged that an interallied commission be sent to investigate, or, if an in-

[8] *Ibid.*, 184.017/15.

[9] *Ibid.*

[10] *PPC*, XI, 63-64.

[11] NA, Peace Conference, 185.91/29.

[12] The proper name of the institution was "Syrian Protestant College"; it later became the "American University of Beirut."

[13] *PPC*, XI, 66-67.

[14] *Ibid.*, III, 1015-1021.

terallied commission was out of the question, an American commission "which could talk freely to all classes of Syrians." He saw no point in asking Syrians to come to Paris because of the difficulty of getting a representative opinion in that way.[15] This seems to be the origin of the French charge that Dr. Bliss was behind the King-Crane Commission.[16]

On March 13 the American delegates were still discussing the dispatch of a commission under Dominian, which by this time was real enough to be getting too big and costly. The geographer Isaiah Bowman, another member of the Inquiry, was present to explain the need for a large operation. When he referred to the problem of fixing the boundaries of Georgia and Armenia,

> Mr. Lansing observed that he was not in favor of studying the boundary question of these districts . . . and that he was not particularly interested in the districts mentioned. He felt that the three great questions in the Near East which required decisions were (1) Mandatories, (2) Syria, and (3) Greek claims in Asia Minor. He felt that on these questions we should receive as much information as possible, but he understood that both Dr. Barton and Mr. Glazebrook were or would be reporting to the Commission on these matters.[17]

Because of the objections of Lansing and his colleagues the proposed commission was cut down to five officials. By March 18 its expenses had been estimated satisfactorily and it was virtually ready to leave.[18] So matters stood on March 20 when President Wilson, taking up Dr. Bliss's suggestion, proposed sending an interallied commission to Syria. A falling out between the British and French over Britain's conflicting promises to France and to King Hussein of the Hejaz gave him his chance.

---

[15] *Ibid.*, XI, 76-77.

[16] See, for example, Comte R. de Gontaut-Biron, *Comment la France s'est installée en Syrie* (Paris: Plon-Nourrit, 1924), 248.

[17] *PPC*, XI, 116. Glazebrook was the American Consul at Jerusalem.

[18] NA, Peace Conference 181.91/47.

The meeting of the Council of Four that convened in Lloyd George's apartment on March 20[19] was confronted by a large map prepared by the French and colored to show the areas disposed of in the Sykes-Picot Agreement. Using this map to illustrate his points, Pichon detailed the difference that had arisen. After relating the conversations between Lloyd George and Clemenceau in London during the preceding December, he courteously accused the British of welshing on the agreement. He made it clear that France was advancing no new territorial claims nor was it objecting to the system of mandates: "If a mandate were granted by the League of Nations over these territories, all that he asked was that France should have that part put aside for her." When Lloyd George objected that this would be a violation of the convention with King Hussein, Pichon replied that France had no convention with King Hussein and that he had seen the text for the first time a few weeks previously when Sir Maurice Hankey, Secretary of the British delegation, had showed him a copy.[20]

Lloyd George countered by reminding the meeting that the British had done most of the fighting in the middle east and had needed Arab help. General Allenby, who was present, testified the help he had received had been "invaluable." Lloyd George followed this up by pointing out that France had in effect recognized the agreement with Hussein by excluding Damascus, Homs, Hama, and Aleppo from the zone of direct French administration and placing them in the proposed Arab state. Pichon replied that there was no argument on that point, reiterating that France could not be bound "by an agreement the very existence of which was unknown to her at the time when the 1916 agreement was signed." At this point President Wilson entered the discussion:

> [He] said that he would now seek to establish his place in
> the Conference. Up to the present he had had none . . .
> The only idea from the United States point of view was as to

[19] *PPC*, V, 1-14.
[20] *Ibid.*, V, 7.

whether France would be agreeable to the Syrians. The same
applied as to whether Great Britain would be agreeable to the
inhabitants of Mesopotamia. It might not be his business, but
if the question was made his business, owing to the fact that
it was brought before the Conference, the only way to deal with
it was to discover the desires of the populations of these
regions. . . .

President Wilson suggested that the fittest men that could be
obtained should be selected to form an Inter-Allied Commission
to go to Syria, extending their inquiries, if they led them, beyond the confines of Syria. Their object should be to elucidate
the state of opinion and the soil to be worked on by any mandatory. . . . If we were to send a commission of men with no previous
contact with Syria, it would, at any rate, convince the world
that the Conference had tried to do all it could to find the most
scientific basis possible for a settlement. The Commission should
be composed of an equal number of French, British, Italian,
and American representatives.[21]

Clemenceau agreed on condition the commission should not confine
its inquiry to Syria but should cover all Turkish territory.[22] Lloyd
George said the British would have no objection to the commission's
operating in Palestine and Mesopotamia, which constituted their
principal interests. He added that there would be no objection about
Armenia either, in which they had less interest.[23]

Ray Stannard Baker, director of the American Press Bureau who
was close to Wilson during the conference, believed that the March
20th meeting was the first time the President had heard of the
Sykes-Picot and St. Jean de Maurienne Treaties. "I remember," he
wrote later, "his speaking to me with great disgust of this Sykes-
Picot Treaty; said it sounded like the name of a tea; called it 'a fine
example of the old diplomacy.' "[24]

21 *Ibid.*, V, 8, 12.

22 *Ibid.*, V, 12-13.

23 *Ibid.*, V, 13.

24 Ray Stannard Baker, *Woodrow Wilson and World Settlement*, 3 vols. (New
York: Doubleday, Page & Co., 1922), I, 74.

Baker also recalled that in spite of the rather ambiguous statements of Clemenceau and Lloyd George,

> ... the President considered his suggestion accepted. I saw him shortly afterward, and he told me with enthusiasm about his plan: 'I want to put the two ablest Americans now in Europe on that commission.'
>
> He asked me if I could make any suggestions as to possible appointees. I suggested President Henry Churchill King of Oberlin College, a man of sound judgment and high ideals. The President immediately asked me to get in touch with President King and he was appointed, with Charles R. Crane, as a member of the commission.[25]

Henry Churchill King, author of several theological works, was on a leave of absence from his position as president of Oberlin and serving as chairman of the Committee on the War and the Religious Outlook, a private American venture. He was in Germany when word reached him that Colonel House would like to see him in Paris. When he learned what House wanted, he was at first uncertain whether he should stay away from Oberlin as long as the commission assignment would require. He was reassured by a most opportune visit from H. H. Johnson, a trustee of the college, who asserted positively that he must take the job.[26]

Charles R. Crane, a personal friend of President Wilson, who was appointed a few days later, was a former president of the Crane Company, a manufacturer of valves and fittings. He had traveled to the mideast as a young man, acquiring an interest in the remote places of the world which never left him. In 1914 he retired from the Crane Company selling his interest to his brother Richard. In 1917 he was a member of a special commission of inquiry in Russia, headed by Elihu Root. The King-Crane Commission was thus his second assignment of this type from President Wilson.

---

[25] *Ibid.*, I, 77.

[26] King's Diary, cited in Donald M. Love, *Henry Churchill King of Oberlin* (New Haven: Yale University Press, 1956), 282.

It might be expected that with the announcement of Wilson's determination to name American representatives to an interallied commission, preparations for Dominian's expedition would be halted. Unfortunately, the American delegation didn't work that way. Wilson confided in Baker but not in his fellow-commissioners. On March 26 Dominian informed them of his decision to withdraw because "a man of Armenian origin on a mission would be interpreted by both Mohammadans and Christians as an indication of policy which it was certainly not the commissioners' intent to convey."[27] There was no suggestion, however, that his party be disbanded. On March 29 the commissioners decided to hold up action on its departure because a rumor of the new investigation had reached them,[28] but on March 31 an order for the commission (without Dominian) to proceed via Rome to Smyrna was requested.[29] Finally, on April 2, Major Tyler, who had assisted in organizing it, realizing that it was being superseded, called attention to the difficulties the King-Crane Commission might be expected to encounter and suggested that it could achieve better results if it used the services of four officers already appointed by Dominian—Pier, Yale, Hoskins, and D. King.[30]

It was apparently Wilson's expectation that the proposed Interallied Commission on Mandates in Turkey would be formed quickly and leave soon for the middle east. However, the matter dragged on for two months, the members alternately preparing to leave and falling into discouragement about their mission.[31] The delay was not a mere matter of administrative red tape; the enterprise from the start faced active opposition. None of the Allies were enthusiastic, but the British and Italians would probably have gone along but

[27] NA, Peace Conference 181.91/58½.

[28] *PPC*, XI, 140.

[29] NA, Peace Conference, 181.91/67.

[30] *Ibid.*, 181.91/71½. Only Yale was named to the King-Crane Commission.

[31] For an account of the alternating anticipations and frustrations experienced by the American members of the Commission until they finally left Paris at the end of May see King's diary in Love, *op. cit.*, 281-287; for the events and transactions in Paris which caused the delay see Howard, *op. cit.*, 31-86.

for the determined opposition of France. French motives are clear enough; the authoritative British history of the peace conference states categorically: "The French government, indeed, conscious that the result of such an inquiry would be against their Syrian claims, used every effort to prevent the investigation."[32]

At the same time the French had an argument which appealed to some of the experts in the American delegation. *Le Temps* protested as early as March 25 that there was no need for a junket to the east since all ethnic groups of Asiatic Turkey were represented in Paris along with competent scholars from the Allied countries. The editors "would be very much surprised if this was not the opinion of the best British and American specialists as well as that of their French colleagues."[33]

William Yale, who served the King-Crane Commission as Technical Advisor for the Arabic-speaking areas, thought *Le Temps* was right:

President Wilson acted in direct opposition to the advice of
the American advisors and the head of the Section of Western
Asia of the American Delegation to Negotiate Peace, whose
opinion it was that, as all the necessary data relative to the political situation, ethnical and boundary problems, the desires of
the communities concerned, and so forth, were available in Paris,
a decision should be reached at Paris without further delay.[34]

The Zionists were equally opposed. On May 8 Felix Frankfurter, writing on the stationery of the *Organisation Sioniste,* told the Presi-

---

[32] Temperley, *op. cit.,* VI, 148.

[33] *Le Temps,* March 25, 1919, 1.

[34] William Yale, "An Analysis of the Syrian-Palestine Situation in 1919: The American Point of View", unpublished master's thesis, University of New Hampshire, 1928, introduction, no page number. Professor Yale has told me he still believes the sending of the Commission to have been a mistake and reiterates that President Wilson acted against the opinion of his advisors, although he concedes that Professor Westermann changed his mind following receipt of General Allenby's cable from Cairo to Balfour on May 30 (*BDFP,* 1st ser., IV, 256). Allenby warned that Prince Feisal was determined to raise the Arabs against the British and French if the Commission wasn't sent. However, by May 30 the Commission had already left Paris.

dent the project had "brought the deepest disquietude to the representatives of the Jewry of the world."[35]

The tug-of-war was finally ended on May 21 when Wilson brought
the matter to a head at a meeting of the Council of Four:

> He then adverted to the commission for Syria. The Delegates
> whom he had nominated were men of such standing that he could
> not keep them waiting any longer in Paris, consequently he had
> instructed them to leave for Syria on Monday and to wait there
> for their colleagues on the Commission.

Lloyd George thought he would give the same orders to the British
members. He probably counted on French opposition to save him
from doing so and Clemenceau did not disappoint him. So long as
British promises to withdraw from Syria and allow French troops to
occupy it had not been kept, France could not cooperate in the
investigation.[36] Lloyd George "said he could not send Commissioners if the French would not send any, but the American Commissioners could go alone."[37]

They did. On May 25 Charles R. Crane left for Constantinople, to be
followed shortly by the remainder of the Commission, now offiicially
known as the American Section, Interallied Commission on Mandates in Turkey, and unofficially ever since as the King-Crane Commission. On May 30 the British, French, and Italian delegations, without quite saying so, bowed out for good.[38]

Although the President had asked for the "two ablest Americans
now in Europe" as commissioners, Crane had little claim to expertise
on the Ottoman Empire, and King none at all. They were fortunate in
obtaining the services of three technical advisors who could make
such a claim. Professor Albert H. Lybyer was appointed General
Technical Advisor, with Dr. George R. Montgomery as Technical
Advisor for the Northern (Turkish-speaking) Regions and Captain

[35] *BDFP*, 1st ser., IV, 260.
[36] *PPC*, V, 760.
[37] *Ibid.*, V, 812.
[38] *Ibid.*, VI, 132-133.

William Yale as Technical Advisor for the Southern (Arabic-speaking) Regions.

Professor Lybyer, an ordained Presbyterian minister, had taught mathematics at Robert College in Turkey, and history at Harvard, Oberlin, and the University of Illinois. He was a member of Colonel House's Inquiry and went to Paris as assistant in the Balkan Division of the American Commission to Negotiate Peace.

George R. Montgomery, who was born in Turkey, was, like President King, a Congregationalist minister. During the Greco-Turkish war he had been correspondent for the *London Standard*. He served as special assistant to the ambassador in Constantinople in 1917. He later became director of the Armenia-America Society and attended the Lausanne conference in that role.

Captain Yale was a member of the American Commission to Negotiate Peace. Previously he had lived in the middle east, first as a representative of the Standard Oil Company of New York, later as a special agent of the Department of State. He had filed a number of reports on the state of affairs in the Arab countries during 1917 and 1918. In June 1918 he was commissioned as a captain and assigned to Allenby's headquarters as American Military Advisor, remaining in that capacity until January 1919, when he went to Paris to serve on Professor Westermann's staff.

It will be noted that three of the five policy-making members of the Commission were Protestant clergymen. There is no reason to suppose this was by design nor, in the light of American interests in the middle east at the time, is it surprising. It may be wondered, however, if such a lineup did not lay itself open to charges of bias from some of our allies, from the numerous sects, Christian and other, of the middle east, and from the Zionists.[39]

Arriving in Jaffa on June 10, the Commission almost immediately found two aspects of the situuation of sufficient urgency to prompt

[39] Such charges were in fact made. For a French view see Gontaut-Biron, *op. cit.*, and E. Brémond, *Le Hedjaz dans la Guerre Mondiale* (Paris: Payot et cie, 1931). A Zionist viewpoint will be found in Frank E. Manuel, *The Realities of American-Palestine Relations* (Washington: Public Affairs Press, 1949).

communication to Paris. On June 20 a telegram was sent from Jerusalem for President Wilson's attention, pointing out that the "careless descent" of the Greeks at Smyrna had "produced distress reacting all over this coast" and that Moslems and Christians in Palestine were hostile to large Jewish immigration or "any effort to establish Jewish sovereignty over them."[40]

A second telegram from Beirut on July 10 foreshadowed much of the Commission's report on Syria. It concluded with a request which provides the incomparable commentary on the fate of the high ideals proclaimed by the Allies—"that political rights be not less than under Turkey."[41]

The report is divided into three parts, dealing respectively with Syria, Mesopotamia, and the non-Arabic-speaking portions of the Ottoman Empire. There was in addition a confidential appendix for the use of the American delegation only; it dealt solely with Syria.

The method employed in ascertaining the wishes of the Syrian people was that of traveling about the country, inviting individuals and groups to consult with the Commission and to submit statements and petitions. The Syrian portion of the report thus probably represents the first large-scale opinion sampling in the world's history. Although more than one judgment may be possible on the wisdom with which the commissioners assessed the material at their disposal, there can be little doubt that the coverage was good. It resulted in the recommendation of an American mandate for the whole of Syria, including Lebanon, Palestine, and part of what is now Jordan, with Great Britain as second choice. The mandate should be for a limited term and devoted to the well-being of the Syrian people. It should have a "strong and vital educational emphasis," should assure complete religious toleration, and aim at preparing the Syrians to govern themselves. A modification of the Zionist program was asked in order to restrict, not eliminate, Jewish immigration and reject any proposal for a Jewish state. Recognizing the United States might not accept a mandate, or if it did, that such a responsibility would be

[40] *PPC*, XII, 748.
[41] *Ibid.*, 749-750.

"more natural and important" in Asia Minor than in Syria, the commissioners believed they must follow their instructions which, as they interpreted them, obliged them to recommend the United States as the mandatory since that was the wish of the local population.[42]

The report on Mesopotamia, produced without benefit of a visit to the country, was understandably brief. Its recommendations repeated four points of the Syrian report—for a mandate, unity of the territory, a single mandatory, and a constitutional monarchy. Since there was evidence of a favorable attitude toward Great Britain, a British mandate was recommended.[43]

From the vantage point of fifty years' distance, it seems certain that the failure to visit Mesopotamia was a principle weakness of the report. The fault lay less in the loss of information that might have been gleaned in an investigation than in the inevitable inference, drawn by both French and Arabs, that the Americans were acting in collusion with the British. Yale later declared that the decision not to visit Mesopotamia was made by Charles R. Crane:

It was clear that Mr. Crane had no intention of permitting the commission to go to Iraq. It seems likely that Mr. Crane got his

[42] The text of the Syrian report is in *PPC*, XII, 751-799. Two members filed minority reports on Syria. Yale and Montgomery believed the Commission had no authority to recommend against the Zionist program since our government had already been committed to it by President Wilson. Montgomery believed further that in any case the future of Palestine could not be settled solely by consulting the wishes of the existing inhabitants, but that the feelings and interests of world Jewry would also have to be taken into account. Yale's more important dissent from the majority arose from his skepticism regarding the grounds for the creation of a Syrian state in 1919. What the others interpreted as Syrian nationalism appeared to him a kind of pan-Islamism under which Syria would be drawn to the neighboring states of Iraq and Arabia and into a Moslem community. Knowing Syria as the others did not, he feared the effect of such a policy on the Christian population. See "Recommendations as to the future disposition of Palestine, Syria, and Mount Lebanon" prepared by Captain William Yale, Technical Advisor to the American Section of the International Commission on Mandates in Turkey; Howard, *op. cit.*, 101-102, 195-197. Additional information is contained in a personal letter from Professor Yale to the author dated November 11, 1960.

[43] *PPC*, XII, 799-802.

idea that the Iraqi favored the British control of Mesopotamia from leading Britishers at Paris.[44]

If Great Britain was assumed to be the choice of the Iraqis because the British said so, French anger at the Commission is all too comprehensible. The same criterion applied to Syria would have awarded it to France.

Following completion of the Syrian itinerary, the Commission traveled by ship from Mersina to Constantinople, arriving on the evening of July 23. In the old Ottoman capital they set to work to prepare their report on Syria; the majority opinion was largely entrusted to Professor Lybyer, while Captain Yale, described as "very pessimistic," worked on his dissent. At the same time they began to formulate recommendations for the problems of Constantinople, Anatolia, and Armenia. This territory, comprising roughly the present Turkish Republic, is called in the report "the non-Arabic-speaking portions of the Ottoman Empire."[45]

The Commission now faced a different problem than that with which it had been confronted in Syria. There they had dealt with a rather well-defined area, already virtually cut off from the Ottoman Empire, in which it was possible to travel about, get in touch with representatives of the people, and find out what they wanted.

No such situation existed in Turkey. Although there was substantial agreement that an Armenian state should be created in the east, there were sharply differing views of what should be included in it. Even if agreement were reached on boundaries, no purpose would be served by interviewing the inhabitants concerning their wishes, since the bulk of the Armenian residents had been driven from their homes and had not been repatriated. In the case of the "Constantinopolitan state" there was equally little point in sampling resident opinion, since the creation of the state would be prompted by international, rather than local, needs. The heavy concentration of officials would make a local sampling misleading in any case.

[44] William Yale, *The Near East: A Modern History* (Ann Arbor: University of Michigan Press, 1958), 315-316.

[45] For this portion of the Report see *PPC*, XII, 802-848.

As for the remainder of Turkey, the Commission had no such authorization to determine the view of the population as in the case of Syria, for it was assumed that Turkey's fate would be determined by the Allies rather than by the Turks. They could not even be consulted officially on the choice of a mandatory, as the Syrians had been, because the peace conference had not decided that Turkey was to be placed under a mandate.

Furthermore, there was serious doubt that a free expression of opinion could be obtained even if it had been wanted. The military government of the Allies was far more repressive in Turkey than in Syria and, as the people were unsure that the Americans would accept a mandate, they would hardly venture to express a preference for America for fear of retaliation on the part of another mandatory.

Finally, further travel was discouraged by the growing conviction of the need for a quick settlement for all parts of Turkey. The commissioners believed haste was essential, nor did they feel obliged to apologize for it because all of the materials for decision were at hand. Starting with the papers prepared for the Inquiry and information brought out at the peace conference, they solicited opinions from as many sources as possible.

Again we must conclude their coverage was good. Its most obvious weakness lay in the absence of direct testimony from the group destined ultimately to play the greatest role in the Turkish settlement, the Nationalists. If this was a fault, it was a natural one. In the summer of 1919 none saw clearly and few saw partially the importance of Kemal's movement. Moreover, the views of the organizations that were heard were, on balance, very close to those of the Nationalists. Turks in Constantinople were perhaps more generally willing to accept American supervision than those in the east. Many of them also appeared ready to cede some land in the east to the Armenian Republic. But these differences should not be exaggerated. As late as September of the same year Kemal was talking, however deceptively, about the need for American assistance, while the amount of territory the Constantinople petitioners were willing to cede to Armenia was so small as to approximate the intransigence of the Nationalists who insisted they would cede none.

Although immobilization in the capital made contact with the Nationalists impossible, the Commission was able to obtain a thorough presentation of other Turkish views. Among those who appeared before it were representatives of the National Liberal Party, the Committee for the Protection of Smyrna, the Peace and Safety Party, the Entente Libérale, the Ottoman League of National Unity, the National Congress, the Committee for the Protection of Thrace, the Committee for the Protection of the Six Vilayets, and the Ottoman Press Association. In addition memoranda were filed by a group of Turkish women and an unnamed coalition representing a synthesis of Turkish opinion. The latter group appears to have been in touch with Mustafa Kemal.

In more normal times these parties and associations would have represented a broad spectrum of political opinion. In the shadow of impending dissolution of their country their differences became minor. All feared the division of Turkey into spheres of European influence and demanded the preservation of the Turkish nation in areas where Turks formed the majority. None was seriously opposed to some kind of foreign help but all wanted it compatible with Turkish sovereignty. The United States was overwhelmingly chosen for the role of foreign guide but some thought Great Britain would be acceptable. All spoke for equal rights for minorities but few were ready to accept the cession of any territory for the creation of a non-Turkish state. In the case of Armenia the majority conceded the possibility of a boundary rectification to enlarge the domain of the existing Republic, but the impression arises from their testimony that they did not expect such rectification to be of significant extent. Only Ahmed Emin (Yalman), the editor of *Vakit*, suggested the size of the Armenian state should be proportional to the prewar Armenian population. The petition of the National Congress asserted that "the six vilayets are much more Turkish than Alsace-Lorraine is French."[46] Although Halide Edib, who served as interpreter for two of the dele-

[46] Howard, *op. cit.*, 167.

gations, thought the Commission "unsympathetic,"[47] some of the groups praised it for its impartiality, a quality they had not found in Europeans.

Following the Turks various minority groups were heard. The Kurdish Democratic Party demanded a Kurdish government in a large part of Turkey and Iraq. In the eastern vilayets their claims conflicted almost entirely with those of both Turks and Armenians. It was only in the Hakkiari district and in the Iraqi province of Mosul that Kurdish aspirations had any chance of being taken seriously. A variety of Greek pleas was also heard. Smyrna was the principal object of their efforts, but Thrace was also demanded. Some Greek statements claimed other coastal areas of Asia Minor, while a committee from the Black Sea littoral wanted a Greek state created in the old province of Pontus. Some demands were geographically vague, insisting only that the Greeks of Asia Minor wanted to be free of Turkish control. Bulgarian representatives asked for Thrace, the Assyro-Chaldeans wanted a state of their own under a mandate, and the Georgians came petitioning merely for economic assistance and the assurance they could remain separate from Russia.

The Armenians appeared early in August. All of the chief religious divisions—Gregorian, Catholic, and Protestant—were represented as were both Turkish and Russian Armenia and various political parties. They were in agreement in their desire for a united Armenian state, wishing to be governed by neither Turkey or Russia. There was less unanimity on the size of the state they wanted and the type of organization to which it should conform. Turkish Armenians demanded the maximum, claiming ports on both the Mediterranean and the Black Sea; those representing the Republic were less specific. Russian Armenians were, as they had been for some time, more radical than their Turkish fellows in social philosophy. While some of the Marxist *Hunchaks* had turned to a more nationalist outlook, others had stuck to their earlier convictions. The *Dashnaks*, actually in control of the Republic, were more moderate than the extreme *Hunchaks*, but told the

---

[47] Halide Edib, *op. cit.*, 60. She modified her opinion later as she became personally acquainted with the members of the Commission.

Commission three-fourths of their people favored a program of gradual socialization, both in industry and in agriculture.

On the question of a mandate, the delegates of the Republic did not oppose it but do not appear to have stressed it as the Turkish Armenians did. Although church representatives appeared first, they did not plead Armenia's case on religious grounds. It remained for Professor K. K. Krikorian, who testified toward the end of the Armenian hearings, to raise the religious issue. Asking for a large Armenian state, he defended it as "the only important oasis in the Moslem desert and in the future struggle of western civilization with the Moslem militarism."

Appearing with the Armenians was Mary Graffam, an American missionary from Sivas who told the Commission it was no longer possible for Turks and Armenians to live under the same government. She asked for the creation of an Armenian state, thus placing herself in opposition to such Americans as Admiral Bristol, President Gates, and Mary Mills Patrick, former president of Constantinople Women's College. Miss Graffam was supported by other American religious personnel in Turkey, including James L. Barton, William W. Peet, Treasurer of the American Board of Foreign Missions, and George E. White, President of Anatolia College at Marsovan. White went further than the others in believing the Turks could not be trusted with even a "shred of independence." Consul-General Ravndal called for an American mandate over Anatolia and Armenia with internationalization of Constantinople and the Straits.

The most eccentric testimony came on the Commission's last day in Constantinople in the form of a letter to Montgomery from H. E. Pears, a son of Sir Edwin Pears. An an official of the Smyrna-Aidin Railway, Pears was familiar with the Smyrna area. His plea for a Greek state in that area was not unnatural. Nor perhaps was his advocacy of "other Christian states" in Anatolia. The reason for his stand was, however, quite unlike anything else brought to the Commission's attention. The Turks, he thought, were rapidly dying out and under Christian rule would soon become extinct. In his view, the sooner the better. When there were no longer any Turks in Anatolia, the Greeks, secure in person and property, would conquer the whole country by "peaceful penetration." This curious variant of the doctrine of self-determination did not impress the Commission.[48]

The interviews came to an end around the middle of August. They were then subjected to sifting and evaluation from which the report emerged.

The Commission believed itself bound by its instructions and by the resolutions adopted by the Council of Ten on January 30, 1919 to which the instructions made special reference. These committed the conference to permanent separation from the Turkish Empire of "Armenia, Cilicia and perhaps additional areas in Asia Minor" and to dealing with these areas under the mandatory rather than the colonial system. It was further stated that the administration of the mandates should be in the spirit of the joint British-French Declaration of November 9, 1918.[49]

A conviction of urgency is attested by the emphasis the report gave to the danger of the kind of settlement the commissioners believed our Allies were disposed to force on the Turks (and which in the subsequent Treaty of Sèvres they did attempt to force on them). It was pointed out that a mere division of the spoils among the French, British, Italians, and Greeks would make impossible any cordial relations with the Turks (Turkish reaction to the Greek occupation of Smyrna was cited as "illustrative"), demand enormous military expenditures, in all likelihood provoke retaliation against local Christians (Smyrna was again cited), alienate American opinion, create dissension among the Allies, and convince men of independent moral judgment all over the world that the Allies' purposes were no better than the Germans'. If the aims for which America had entered the war were not to vanish in a morass of cynicism, there was need for a

---

[48] For a detailed summary of the Constantinople hearings see Howard, op. cit., 161-194. Professor Howard's very full account is based largely on the papers and diaries of King and Lybyer and a 31-page "Memorandum on the King-Crane Commission" by Captain Donald M. Brodie, the Commission's Secretary and Treasurer.

[49] PPC, XII, 804-806.

clear demonstration that they had not been forgotten and Turkey was a good place to make the demonstration.[50]

Although it had been pretty clear from the first days of the peace conference that a separate Armenia would be created, the Commission felt obliged to justify it. It found its reason for an Armenian state in the unfitness of the Turks to rule even themselves, the bad treatment accorded by Turkish governments to the Turkish people and their much worse treatment of subject peoples. However, the "great and primary" reason for breaking up Turkey was the massacre of the Armenians. The only way in which Armenians could be protected in a Turkish state would be to establish a permanent mandate, while the League of Nations mandates were to be temporary. Since nothing less would guarantee the Armenians' safety or satisfy the world's conscience, a separate mandate for Armenia was imperative.[51]

Compelling as the argument of "historical misgovernment" was, it was buttressed by that of "the utter unfitness [of Turkey] for the strategic world position in which she is placed." The conjunction of unfitness to rule and the possession of "territory of critical significance to the world" made Turkey a menace to other nations and rendered necessary a restriction of her sovereignty.

In calling for this restriction the Commission was free of the consideration that motivated some of Turkey's critics, a desire to drive back the spirit of "orientalism" and to westernize Turkey. Conceding the desirability of eradicating some characteristics of the orient—"we will be done with Oriental domination in Turkey . . . when we get states which know in their citizens no privileged and unprivileged classes but only equals before the law"—the report nonetheless saw values in the east and hoped that Turkey, protected against its own weaknesses, would again be a "bridge-land" between east and west.[52]

The reasons for a "Constantinopolitan" state were no less cogent. The strategic importance of the Turkish Straits and the growing be-

[50] *Ibid.,* XII, 808-810.
[51] *Ibid.,* XII, 814.
[52] *Ibid.,* XII, 815-818.

lief that they had been the chief bone of contention among the European powers for almost a century and perhaps even the primary cause of the war just ended called for internationalization of the area with a single power acting as mandatory in the interests of the international community.

Having thus justified "a righteous division of the Turkish portion of the former Ottoman Empire," the Commission addressed itself to the problems involved. These were considered under five heads: a separate Armenia, an international Constantinopolitan state, a continued Turkish state, the Greeks, and other minority races.[53]

In creating a separate Armenia, it was not proposed to

> ... establish the rule of a minority of Armenians over a majority of other peoples. ... But such a separated state should furnish a definite area into which Armenians could go with the complete assurance that they would never be put under the rule of the Turks. It should also be a region in which Armenians could gradually concentrate, and from which the Turkish population might increasingly tend to withdraw; though no compulsion should be put on any people.[54]

If the maximum territory demanded by the Armenians were to be utilized for the creation of a new state, the result would be "the folly of setting an Armenian minority to rule a Turkish majority."[55] The state thus formed would hardly be Armenian at all, but rather a mixed Turkish, Kurdish, and Armenian state, incapable of defending itself or of maintaining internal order. It would be a disappointment both to the Armenians, who could never control the government, and the mandatory power which could never leave the country.

However, if the state were restricted to an area more nearly equivalent to ancient Armenia, if as many Armenians as possible were repatriated to that area, and if the movement of Armenians from other

[53] *Ibid.*, XII, 819.

[54] *Ibid.*, XII, 819-820.

[55] As pointed out in Chapter I, Turks alone did not have a majority in Armenia as a whole but Moslems outnumbered Christians there.

parts of Turkey were facilitated while those Turks who wanted to move out were helped to do so, there existed a strong possibility that by 1925 a small Armenian majority would have been created.[56] That purpose would be advanced by incorporating the Republic of Armenia into the new state.

Because an Armenian majority would not exist at the outset and because even when a majority was created, it would be a small one, a short-term mandate would not serve the purpose. A mandate of longer term was therefore recommended with the United States as mandatory power. An American mandate was desired by the Armenians, approved by the Allies, and even preferred by the Turks, if there had to be a mandate.[57]

The new international state to consist of Constantinople, European Turkey, the Straits and the Sea of Marmora, and enough of Asiatic Turkey to make it viable also called for a different kind of mandate. The Commission proposed a permanent mandatory subject to removal by the League of Nations.

> The mandatory . . . should be a real mandatory for the League . . . not a power using its position to advance its own national interests. To this end, the mandatory should be territorially and strategically disinterested.[58]

Since the European powers had been territorially and strategically interested in the Straits for a century, it is easy to see which power was to be recommended as mandatory.

The report called for a Constantinopolitan state free to all people for any legitimate interest. It pointed out that Constantinople would continue to be a natural location for religious and educational foundations. It should, therefore, be administered with every consideration for Moslem feelings; it was even suggested that the Sultan could continue to reside there if desired. The city, however, would no longer be

[56] For population estimates, see *PPC*, XII, 825-827.
[57] *Ibid.*, XII, 819-820.
[58] *Ibid.*, XII, 828.

under Turkish control and, of course, no longer the capital of Turkey.[59]

When Armenia had been surrendered in justice to the Armenians and Constantinople and the Straits to "just and imperative world interest," Turkey would be left with an area larger than France and a population of ten million, of whom eight million would be Moslems (seven million of these Turks) and one and a half million Greeks.

> If the principles of national unity and of self-determination
> are to be truly applied to the Turkish people, Anatolia, the bulk
> of Asia Minor remaining, with ample outlets to the sea, should
> be left for a Turkish state, but under such conditions as may
> sacredly guard the rights of all minorities, whether racial or
> religious.[60]

The Turkish state, like the others, should be under a mandate, not only to safeguard the right of minorities but for the good of the Turks themselves. Although it was no part of the Commission's assignment to recommend a mandate for the Turkish state, that was the only way in which Turkey could be rehabilitated.

> The Turks if left to themselves in a condition of poverty, igno-
> rance, and general exhaustion, with a feeling that they had been
> unjustly treated and then abandoned by all the world, could
> not fail to be a source of trouble and disturbance until another
> crisis, with perhaps another great war, would necessitate some
> such solution as is now suggested, but under conditions less
> favorable to success.[61]

Again the United States was recommended as the mandatory, since it was the choice of the Turkish people and was in the best position to give Turkey what it needed.[62]

Although various minorities claimed a separate national existence, the Commission concluded that nowhere within the truncated state

[59] *Ibid.*, XII, 829.
[60] *Ibid.*, XII, 833.
[61] *Ibid.*, XII, 839.
[62] *Ibid.*, XII, 844.

were conditions such as to justify further partition, although limited autonomy might be granted to the Kurds in the mountains north of the Iraqi border and to the Greeks in those portions of the sanjak of Smyrna in which they constituted a clear majority. The Italian claim to Southwest Turkey "rests upon nothing that is compatible with the principles of the Commission's instructions." It was emphasized throughout that assurance of equal treatment to minorities would be a responsibility of the mandatory power.[63]

The Commission's deliberations had led it to recommend three mandated states with a boundary commission to fix the limits of each and with a single mandatory to administer all three. A single mandatory was justified on both political and economic grounds. On the political side were the close ties of centuries, the "delicate adjustment of which can best be accomplished under one power," policies of repatriation and exchange of populations, adjustment of the public debt, police control, repression of brigandage, and the avoidance of friction between mandatories.

Economically, the report pointed to the value of uniform systems of coinage, weights, and measures, similar commercial laws, and the co-ordination of road and railway networks.[64]

There was need, however, not only to justify a single mandatory but to show that the United States was uniquely qualified to fill the role. In addition to the reasons already adduced for each mandate, there were a number of general reasons for the choice of America to guide Asia Minor and indeed all of the middle east toward modern statehood. Perhaps nothing in the report, or indeed in all the literature of the peace conference, shows so clearly the view Americans had of themselves, and that some other peoples had of them, or accounts so well for the mixture of hope and exasperation our people brought to the world at that time. The commissioners wrote in full consciousness of the hope; perhaps the events of subsequent years brought them a better understanding of our allies' exasperation.

First, the Syrian and Turkish peoples alike had seen in Americans

63 *Ibid.*, XII, 836-838.
64 *Ibid.*, XII, 839.

"a passion for peace and the possibility of its attainment." They believed that America had entered the war in the interests of a "righteous peace." They believed further that Americans had "a passion for democracy, for the common man everywhere, in spite of inconsistencies at home and abroad, and could treat men of all races with a genuine respect born of some insight into their own individual gifts." Along with this went the American faith in "universal education, as possible for the rank and file of every nation, and as absolutely essential to a democracy."[65]

They also believed that America had a "certain idealistic international faith," a stubborn belief in the League of Nations and in the possibilities of its mandatory system, "when honestly carried out." They believed in her unselfish aims in the war and that "she was now seeking for no share in the spoils of the war" and "was not involved in any joint plan for an exploiting division of either Syria or Turkey." The high quality of our relief and educational services in the region were alluded to. America, the Commission affirmed, had a duty to assume these mandates to check the tide of cynicism and disillusionment that was threatening to destroy every positive gain that had been expected to follow from the defeat of the Central Powers.[66]

Finally, America had ample resources to carry out the purposes of the mandate. Large amounts of capital would be needed for the rehabilitation of Turkey with little hope of return for some time. After an interval of development, the country might well become an attractive field for investment, but even if it did not,

> America might well spend millions to insure relations of peace
> and good will among nations, rather than the billions required
> for another war, sure to come if the present cynical national
> selfishness and lack of good will are not checked.[67]

Against the possible charge that in accepting control over so much land and so many people, America was showing itself to be just an-

65 *Ibid.*, XII, 844-845.
66 *Ibid.*, XII, 845-846.
67 *Ibid.*, XII, 847.

other imperialistic power, the Commission replied that the United States was not seeking the mandates and perhaps would prove unwilling to accept them. It was the Commission's duty to call attention to the need for American action so that the Peace Conference could put the issue squarely up to the American peeople. Whatever the wisdom of this attitude, its sincerity is attested by the conditions the Commission considered prerequisite to American acceptance of the mandates:

> ... that she is really wanted by the Turkish people; that Turkey should give evidence that she is ready to do justice to the Armenians, not only by the allotment of the territory within her borders, recommended for the Armenian state, but also by encouraging the repatriation of Armenians, and by seeing that all possible just reparation is made to them as they return to their homes; that Turkey should also give evidence that she is ready to become a modern constitutional state, and to abolish military conscription; that Russia should be ready to renounce all claims upon Russian Armenia; that the Allies should cordially welcome America's help in the difficult situation in Turkey; and especially that all plans for cutting up Turkey, for the benefit of outside peoples, into spheres of influence and exploitation areas should be abandoned. These conditions are necessary to a successful solution of the Turkish problem. Unless they are fulfilled, America ought not to take the mandate for Asia Minor. And the Commissioners do not recommend that the mandate be given to America if these conditions cannot be substantially met.[68]

The report of the King-Crane Commission was completed late in August 1919. On the 28th the full text was delivered to the peace conference in Paris. President Wilson was advised of its recommendations on the 31st but the full report did not reach the White House until September 27. It was, therefore, not available to the President until after the physical collapse which caused the cancellation of his

[68] *Ibid.*, XII, 847-848.

nation-wide speaking tour in support of the Covenant of the League of Nations.

From the time of its presentation to the peace conference, the report, to all intents and purposes, simply disappeared. The mere fact that it was not published does not, of course, mean that it was, as some have charged, "suppressed." There is no rule governing the publication of state papers and many are never published. Nonetheless, in view of the circumstances—disagreement between the United States and its allies over a peace which we were equally involved in negotiating, apparent defection of our allies from their agreement with our principles, appointment of a commission to look into the situation with a view to recommending a solution on the basis of those principles, a very sharp report echoing and amplifying them and warning against the tendency of our allies to overlook them, finally the disappearance of the report and a shroud of complete silence around it—a mere failure to publish comes to look like suppression.

At least one of the American commissioners plenipotentiary, Henry White, always thought so.[69] Harry N. Howard so regarded it as late as 1931 when the passions of the moment might be expected to have cooled.[70] W.J.M. Childs, writing in the Royal Institute of International Affairs history of the peace conference, called it "suppressed, perhaps as being too plain spoken and likely to embarrass both the American Government and the peace conference if published."[71]

Significantly, the British representatives at the peace conference read the report. At a meeting of the American commissioners on September 24, 1919, Buckler asked for a copy for the British. Frank L. Polk, Undersecretary of State who had headed the American delega-

---

[69] "White . . . always strongly condemned the temporary suppression of the King-Crane report on Syria under pressure from France." Allan Nevins, *Henry White: Thirty Years of American Diplomacy* (New York: Harper and Brothers, 1930), 458.

[70] "Its findings were of such a character that even the American government saw fit to suppress them, to avoid 'embarrassing' the peace conference in general—and France in particular." Harry N. Howard, *The Partition of Turkey 1913-1923* (Norman: University of Oklahoma Press, 1931), 238.

[71] Temperley, *op. cit.*, VI, 149.

tion since July, denied the request but admitted that the British had already read the report, adding: "I don't doubt that they made copious notes of it."[72] As a matter of fact, Colonel French, the British Acting Political Officer in Cairo, had predicted the recommendations with remarkable accuracy as early as July 19.[73]

Whether or not French officialdom had seen the report, they were having none of it. The quasi-official *Le Temps* maintained the tone of hostility it had assumed from the first. In a despatch from Constantinople, printed on August 23, its correspondent François Psalty wrote: "A great deal of commotion with very little accomplished—that is the balance sheet of the mission of inquiry which will be, in any case, soon forgotten."[74]

However we describe it, the disappearance of the King-Crane Report can only be accounted a misfortune for the Armenians. It could have done them no harm; it might have done them some good. The similarity of its findings to those of the Harbord Mission would surely have lent some weight to the argument for the mandate. Ironically, its unavailability was entirely unrelated to its discussion of Armenia or of Asia Minor generally. This is demonstrated by the prominence achieved by the Harbord Report, which was cited by virtually every member of the Senate who participated in the debate on the mandate. That the work of King and Crane and their associates should stand or fall by its Syrian section may be justice of a kind, since it was the British-French disagreement on Syria that gave President Wilson his chance to send them to the middle east; nonetheless, it was another setback for the Armenians.

The report was still unknown to Americans, except a few to whom King and Crane had sent personal copies, when Ray Stannard Baker published a series of articles on the peace conference in August 1922.

---

[72] *PPC*, XI, 432-433.

[73] In a despatch to Lord Curzon, *BDFP*, 1st ser., IV, 315.

[74] *Le Temps*, August 23, 1919, 1. Psalty differed from most French commentators of the time in making no pretense that there was an overwhelming demand for the French in the middle east. He wrote (*Ibid.*, September 2, 1919, 2): "La vérité est qu'on nous boude légèrement."

The Commission was the subject of the article of August 20. On the same day the *Times* commented editorially:

> If this exhumed report could have been given to the public
> when it was submitted or soon after, it might have helped to
> prevent the inauguration or continuance of three policies that
> go counter to the Commission's findings: a divided Syria, a
> Zionistic program in Palestine, and the control of upper Syria
> by a power that was persona non grata to a large part of the
> population.[75]

On December 2, 1922 the full text of the report was published by the periodical *Editor and Publisher* which prefaced it with a vigorous introduction of several pages praising its honesty and objectivity and denouncing the diplomacy which had set it aside to rely on the old imperialist aims and methods in making peace. The editors called it "one of the great suppressed documents of the peace-making period," adding

> ... if it had been published promptly, as intended, it would
> completely have altered the current of events in Turkey; and
> possibly have changed the whole American attitude toward post-
> war responsibilities. Certainly it would have freed us from a
> flood of unfounded propaganda; and it might easily have saved
> the lives of possibly a million persons, needlessly sacrificed
> since the war.[76]

On the following day, December 3, the report was reprinted by the *New York Times*. There is no evidence that either printing aroused widespread interest among readers, but it was noticed in the White House, where

> ... there was no hesitancy on the part of the present adminis-
> tration in saying that every day it rejoiced that the government

---

[75] *New York Times*, August 20, 1919, Section II, 4.

[76] *Editor and Publisher*, LV, No. 27, Second Section, II. One can sympathize with the strong position of the editors in this preface without agreeing that the report was "rigorously concealed by a then spineless State Department." It was a presidential, rather than a State Department, paper.

had not undertaken the responsibility of mandatory for any Turkish territory. . . . As time passed, it was said, the conviction became stronger than ever that the traditional policy of the United States was "pretty wise." This government, according to the statement made, would not take on responsibility for the affairs of the rest of the world.[77]

This may be a good time to return to Dr. James L. Barton before even the most attentive reader has forgotten who he was. Having failed to make contact with Frederic C. Howe, Barton set out on his own investigation of the Ottoman Empire. On February 26 he cabled from Constantinople:

> Political, social, economic and moral condition of this country in critical state and becoming steadily worse. Immediate steps should be taken to put a single mandate over entire country . . . This expresses the judgment of my colleagues and leading Englishmen, Americans, Turks, Armenians and Greecians[sic] . . .[78]

On March 27, having covered a good deal of country, he cabled again, this time from Cairo:

> Have itinerated Eski-Shehir, Afion-Karahissar, Konia, Adana, Tarsus, Aleppo and other places conversing with leaders of many nationalities and observing conditions. Situation in interior worse than at Capitol [sic] and not improving. All classes desire early peace conference putting responsibility pacification and organization entire country under one responsible power.[79]

On April 9, Barton, still in Cairo, cabled again to report: "Feeling is universal that Peace commission must deal soon and thoroughly with Turkish question, including Armenia, if a much more complicated situation would be avoided." Noting that one hundred thousand Armenian refugees in Aleppo and Damascus alone were unable to return to Turkey because there was no order in areas not under foreign occupation, he continued:

[77] *New York Times*, December 6, 1919, 3.
[78] House Papers, dr. 2, f. 28.
[79] *Ibid.*

All classes, including Turks, urge early action in Paris removing suspense and guaranteeing safety. Large majority all populations prefer America as mandatory for entire country, while Armenians seem unanimous and Syrians three-quarters favorable.[80]

Finally, while the King-Crane Commission was touring Syria, Dr. Barton again sent word of the urgency of the situation to the Americans in Paris. He stressed the desperation of the Armenian's plight and the implacable Turkish attitude toward them which threatened to "precipitate fresh and startling atrocities since Turks are armed and panic-stricken, scattered Armenians unprotected."[81] It was reports of this sort from Barton and others that determined the creation of an American military mission of inquiry which should visit Armenia and inform the President of the situation there and of the problems that would confront a mandatory power.

[80] *Ibid.*
[81] *Ibid.*

8

The Harbord Mission

By MIDSUMMER the state of affairs in Armenia was causing serious concern to the American delegates in Paris. In the absence of any effective Allied occupation, Turkish troops, usually irregulars, were all that were available to maintain order on the Turkish side of the border. There was testimony that, at least after the Smyrna landings, they were less concerned to maintain order than to disturb it. In such circumstances it was easy to believe that those Armenians who had survived the deportations and massacres were again in danger. Urgent appeals for aid arrived frequently at the peace conference. Alarming enough in themselves, they became more so when considered in conjunction with reports on the growing strength of Turkish nationalism.

In addition to danger from the Turks there was trouble between the Republic of Armenia and its Transcaucasian neighbors, Georgia and Azerbaijan; worst of all there was famine in the Republic whose population had been virtually doubled by refugees.

Two Americans, Major Joseph Green and Colonel William N. Haskell, both of whom had previously been stationed in Rumania, did

168

their best to alleviate the hardships of the Armenians. Major Green was sent to the Caucasus in May 1919 by Relief Administrator Hoover who subsequently received from him the most pitiable descriptions of the state of affairs.[1]

To meet these perils Hoover wrote Wilson on June 28 asking for a single Allied high commissioner for Armenia. On July 3 he proposed Colonel Haskell for the post.[2] Two days later Haskell was appointed by the Council of Heads of Delegations.[3] Throughout the summer of 1919 Haskell and Green were the chief sources of information on Armenia; both reflected the bleakest possible view of the situation.

In the meantime the campaign had not let up in the United States. Gerard's committee cabled to the President on June 22, 1919, asking for immediate help to "Caucasus Armenia" in the form of

> ... requisite food, munitions, and supplies for fifty thousand
> men and such other help as they may require to enable the
> Armenians to occupy the non-occupied parts of Armenia within
> the boundaries defined in the memorandum of the delegation
> of integral Armenia.[4]

The signers included three prominent Republicans—Charles Evans Hughes, Elihu Root, and Senator Henry Cabot Lodge—and two prominent Democrats—Senator John Sharp Williams and Governor Alfred E. Smith.

On July 16 Hoover told the Supreme Economic Council of starvation in Armenia:

> The only method of access to this area is over a railway from
> Batoum and this railway is in the territory of the so-called
> Georgian government. . . . The Georgian authorities have con-
> stantly interfered with the movement, have repeatedly demanded

---

[1] Hoover, *The Ordeal of Woodrow Wilson*, 142-143.

[2] *Ibid.*, 144.

[3] *PPC*, VII, 28. The Council of Heads of Delegations had succeeded the Supreme Council and the Council of Four as the chief organ of the peace conference, although the Supreme Council did not officially pass out of existence until the following January.

[4] House Papers, dr. 30, f. 30.

that they should be given a portion of the foodstuffs, and have
latterly stopped the movement of the traffic four or five days
at a time, despite the protests of all the local allied officials.
It is impossible to depict the situation in Armenia, for, until
the last sixty days, the population has been eating the dead.[5]

Major Green cabled three times at the end of July to warn that the
Turks were advancing into Armenia and to call for military protection
from the Allies to avoid "disaster . . . more terrible than massacres of
1915" with the "Armenian nation crushed to everlasting shame of Allied powers."[6]

To make matters worse the British were scheduled to withdraw
their troops from Batum on August 15. Hoover, kept in touch with developments through Haskell and his associates, wrote Polk on July 30:

Unless British forces already in the Caucasus can be retained
and unless they can be reinforced to probably double the
number, we are faced with a practical extermination of the
Armenians.[7]

Dr. Barton visited the Caucasus and was equally alarmed at the
prospect of British withdrawal.[8] Although the troops were apparently
never reinforced, the British did delay their withdrawal from the Caucasus; whether or not this averted extermination of the Armenians is
impossible to say. There were some who thought fears of Turkish invasion exaggerated. Among these was probably Lord Curzon and certainly Admiral Bristol, who had succeeded Ravndal as American High
Commissioner.

This was the kind of picture of Armenia that was reaching the peace
conference and the American leaders. It may have been exaggerated
but there was no way of knowing in Washington or Paris whether it
was or not. President Wilson was not likely to be unmoved by such
reports from any part of the globe; these dealt with a people who had

[5] *PPC*, X, 482.
[6] *Ibid.*, X, 532.
[7] Polk Papers, dr. 78, f. 57.
[8] NA, State Department 860J.01/62.

made a real contribution to winning the war, who had received, or so
it was believed, the most solemn assurances that they would be given
their independence, a people in whom America had for some time
taken a special interest and whom it was the united desire of our allies
to place under our tutelage. It appeared imperative to find out what
their situation was as well as to explore the problems connected with
an American mandate. The President, acting on the suggestion of
Hoover and former Ambassador Morgenthau, telegraphed the American Mission in Paris on August 1st to authorize the despatch of a mission of inquiry to Armenia with Major-General James G. Harbord at
its head.[9]

Harbord, then in his fifties, had been an army man all his adult life.
He had headed the Philippine constabulary and commanded American troops at Soissons and Chateau-Thierry. Chief of Staff in 1917-
1918, he had recently (May 26, 1919) been reappointed to that post.
He was held in the highest esteem by Secretary of War Newton D.
Baker who would have advanced him to commander-in-chief if a replacement for Pershing had been necessary.[10]

Harbord welcomed the assignment. He told later of his astonish-
ment at finding how little first-hand knowledge there was of a country
so much discussed as Armenia. He was particularly impressed, not to
say staggered, to learn that Boghos Nubar, the head of the Armenian
delegation at the peace conference, had never been to Armenia.[11]

Even before he reached Turkey he was made aware of the power already attained by the Nationalist movement. Although in the summer
of 1919 the United States was conducting its business with Damad
Ferid's government through the Swedish embassy, the General found

---

[9] Ibid., 860J.01/29. The events leading to Harbord's appointment are recorded
in detail in John Philip Richardson, The American Military Mission to Armenia,
unpublished master's thesis, George Washington University, 1964, Chapter II.
See also Hoover, Memoirs, I, 455-456; Henry Morgenthau, All in a Lifetime
(Garden City: Doubleday, Page & Co., 1922), 336-339.

[10] Baker to H. J. Reilly, October 31, 1928, cited in C. H. Cramer, Newton D. Baker
(Cleveland and New York: World Publishing Co., 1961), 292.

[11] James G. Harbord, "Investigating Turkey and Transcaucasia," in World's Work,
XL (May, June, July, 1920), 36.

it necessary to appeal to Mustafa Kemal's party for permission to travel in the eastern regions.[12]

The mission left Constantinople early in September. It consisted of a group of army officers, including two brigadier-generals, Frank R. McCoy and George Van Horn Moseley, and Capt. Stanley K. Hornbeck, who had been serving as Chief of the Far Eastern Division of the American Commission to Negotiate Peace. Professor W. W. Cumberland of the University of Wisconsin, who had been the American Commission's economic advisor in Paris, was a member, as was Trade Commissioner Eliot Grinnell Mears, who took ninety-four photographs of the country and its people.[13] Hussein Bay, professor of Turkish at Robert College, went along as Turkish interpreter, while Major Shekerjian and Lieutenant Kachadoorian served as Armenian interpreters.

The mission was instructed to "investigate and report on political, military, geographical, administrative, economic and other considerations involved in possible American interests and responsibilities in that region."[14] Traveling by ship, railway, car, "carriage," and on horseback, General Harbord and his associates visited virtually all the important cities of Turkish Armenia and Transcaucasia as well as many villages. Their tour took them into all three of the Transcaucasian republics and all of the vilayets of Turkish Armenia except Van and Bitlis, which were inaccessible to motor travel. However, Captain Niles of the U. S. Army had visited both of them on horseback in August. His "report corroborates our observations in the neighboring regions."[15] A visit was paid to the catholicos at Etchmiadzin where "His Holiness spoke of his hopes for an American mandate in Ar-

---

[12] *Ibid.*, 38.

[13] Other members were Col. Henry Beeuwkes, Medical Corps; Lt.-Col. John Price Jackson, Eng.; Lt.-Col. Jasper Y. Brinton, JA; Lt.-Col. Edward Bowditch, Jr., Inf.; Commander W. W. Bertholf, U. S. Navy; Major Lawrence Martin, General Staff; Major Harold Clark, Inf.; William B. Poland, Chief of the American Relief Commission for Belgium and Northern France.

[14] Harbord Report, 3.

[15] *Ibid.*, 4.

menia, expressing his belief that America in her disinterestedness is unique among the great nations."[16]

Mustafa Kemal and other Nationalist officers conferred with the mission at Sivas where they made a favorable impression and reassured General Harbord that their movement was not antagonistic to Armenians. At the same time they made it clear there was to be no compromise on the right of Turkey to govern itself in its own way. General Harbord tried without success to moderate their self-confidence.

> I pointed out that nations as well as individuals could commit
> suicide, and reminded them that if they could not win with
> Germany and Austria on their side, they had little prospect of
> surviving a contest undertaken alone against the Allies.[17]

The Nationalists' reply is not recorded but what was in their minds may be conjectured. The Turks had had considerable success in staving off western domination so long as they had not been associated with Germany and Austria. Once allied to those powers, they had been severely beaten and were on the verge of losing everything. Could it be that their salvation lay in getting free of their European associates, which defeat gave them the opportunity to do, and relying on themselves again? An element of strength was their relative weakness, since it produced European indifference. While many Europeans had been deeply concerned about Ottoman minorities, their concern had never led to effective intervention in Turkey until the Turks became allied to two powers which threatened to destroy the balance of power in Europe. That the Turks saw this clearly while westerners couldn't may mean the Turks were more cynical—or it may mean their minds were less stultified by moralizing cant unbacked by any real will to act.

The mission interviewed representatives of every government exercizing sovereignty in the region as well as numerous private persons of such diverse provenance as "Turks, Armenians, Greeks, Kurds,

16 *World's Work*, XL, 272.
17 *Ibid.*, XL, 187.

Tartars, Georgians, Russians, Persians, Jews, Arabs, British and French, including Americans long domiciled in the country."[18] Conferences with the various delegations before leaving Paris provided additional resources. Reports from American relief organizations, the account of Benjamin P. Moore, who had been sent to Transcaucasia by the peace conference, and "the very complete library on the region, its geography, history, and governments loaned by the Library of Congress, the American Mission to Negotiate Peace, and others"[19] were also useful. The mission heard a number of eye-witness accounts of the atrocities of 1915.

Visits and interviews, travel observations, and study of the materials available in Paris served as a basis for eleven specialized reports on such aspects of Armenia as politics, government, finance, commerce and industry, population, and natural resources. Together with a bibliography they made up the twelve appendices to General Harbord's Report.[20]

[18] Harbord Report, 4.

[19] *Ibid.*

[20] The appendices with their respective authors are as follows:

A—Political Factors and Problems, by Capt. Stanley K. Hornbeck, Ordinance Dept., USA.

B—Government of Turkey and the Transcaucasus, by Lt.-Col. Jasper Y. Brinton, JA, USA.

C—Public and Private Finance of Turkey and the Transcaucasus, by Prof. W. W. Cumberland.

D—Commerce and Industry in Turkey and Transcaucasia, by Trade Commissioner Eliot Grinnell Mears.

E—Public Health and Sanitation of Turkey and Transcaucasia, by Col. Henry Beeuwkes, Medical Corps, USA.

F—Peoples of Turkey in Europe, Asia Minor and the Transcaucasus, by Lt.-Col. John Price Jackson, Eng., USA.

G—Climate, Natural Resources, Animal Industry and Agriculture of Turkey and the Transcaucasus, by Lt.-Col. E. Bowditch, Jr., USA.

H—Geography, Mining and Boundaries, by Maj. Lawrence Martin, Gen. Staff, USA.

I—The Press of Turkey and Transcaucasia, by Maj. Harold W. Clark, Inf., USA.

J—The Military Problem of a Mandatory, by Brig.-Gen. George Van Horn Moseley, Gen. Staff, USA.

K—Transport and Communications in Asia Minor and the Transcaucasus, by William B. Poland.

The report echoed the testimony of Bryce, Lepsius, Mandelstam and others regarding the atrocities and emphasized that some of them were still continuing. (For example, abducted Armenian girls were still forced to live with their captors.) The general's sympathy and that of his associates is too feelingly expressed to be doubted. They nonetheless stressed the very limited sense in which the region could be called "Armenian."

> Even before the war the Armenians were far from being in a majority in the region claimed as Turkish Armenia, excepting in a few places. Today we doubt if they would be a majority in a single community even when the last survivors of the massacres and deportations have returned to the soil, though the great losses of the Turkish population to some extent offset the difference brought about by slaughter. . . . We estimate a total of perhaps half a million refugee Armenians as available to eventually begin life anew in a region about the size of New York, Pennsylvania, and Ohio, to which would be added those, not refugees, who might return from other lands.[21]

Nor was the population likely to be able to accomplish much in the immediate future, since there was an immense rebuilding job to be done and no crop could be harvested before August of the next year. The situation of the refugees, estimated at 300,000, in the Armenian Republic was pictured as pitiable in the extreme, although improving somewhat as Colonel Haskell's organization was attempting to settle them in refugee camps, where they could be provided for on a more regular basis. With winter coming on even greater suffering might be anticipated, for "the winters there are extremely severe, fuel is scarce, and shelter inadequate."[22]

Across the border in Turkey things were equally horrible. Return-

---

L—Bibliography, by Maj.-Gen. James G. Harbord, USA.
Appendices, together with the full text of the Report itself in NA, Peace Conference, 184.02102/5. Citations of the Report in the present work refer to the slightly shortened version published in *Senate Documents*.

[21] Harbord Report, 8.

[22] *Ibid.*

ing Armenians had in some cases recovered their property, even occasionally received rent for it, but in many more they found it in ruins. The Turks were in no better state:

> They were practically serfs, equally destitute, and equally defenseless against the winter. No doctors or medicines are to be had. Villages are in ruins, some having been destroyed when the Armenians fled or were deported; some during the Russian advance; some on the retreat of the Armenian irregulars and Russians after the fall of the Empire. Not over 20 per cent of the Turkish peasants who went to war have returned. The absence of men between the ages of 20 and 30 is very noticeable. Six hundred thousand Turkish soldiers died of typhus alone, it is stated, and insufficient hospital service and absolute poverty of supply swelled the death lists.[23]

Not all of the devastation was the fault of the Turks.

> In the territory untouched by war from which Armenians were deported the ruined villages were undoubtedly due to Turkish deviltry, but where Armenians advanced and retired with the Russians their retaliatory cruelties rivalled the Turks in their inhumanity.[24]

In fact, the Turks were keeping better order in their areas of authority than the three Transcaucasian republics were keeping in theirs:

> Our mission was fired upon by Kurds in Russian Armenia and several motorcars were struck by bullets, and over half of the party were kept prisoners one night by Moslems who claimed to have been driven from their villages by Armenians.[25]

One of the most arresting features of the report, curiously relegated to the "Conclusions," was its denial of charges that Turkish troops were massing on the Transcaucasian border. Covering the frontier from the Black Sea to Persia, the mission found nothing to substanti-

[23] *Ibid.*
[24] *Ibid.*, 9.
[25] *Ibid.*, 24.

ate these stories. Turkish units were not at the frontier; they had, in fact, been reduced to skeleton organizations in a country whose most noticeable aspect was its depopulation.[26]

On this point Haskell expressed vigorous disagreement. Admiral deRobeck, Calthorpe's successor as British commissioner at Constantinople, relayed the colonel's opinion to Sir Eyre Crowe by telegram on October 23, 1919:

> He informs me that General Harbord appears to have gathered totally erroneous impression of state of things in Anatolia and Transcaucasia especially as regards present state of security and well-being of Armenians. . . .
>
> Colonel Haskell has derived an entirely different impression . . . namely that situation is extremely precarious, that presence of Allied troops will be indispensable before repatriation of Armenians can commence.[27]

Because there is so much testimony on the other side it is impossible not to wonder if General Harbord was completely deceived about the danger represented by the Turks. In his defense is the fact that Armenia held out through 1919 and a part of 1920 and when it fell, the opinion of the prejudiced Admiral Bristol that the Armenians had provoked attack[28] is echoed at least in part by an Armenian leader and a most sympathetic historian.[29] More important than Armenian provocation was the growing cooperation between the Turkish Nationalists

---

[26] *Ibid.*

[27] *BDFP*, 1st ser., IV, 844.

[28] NA, State Department, 860J.00/4.

[29] Vahan M. Kurkjian, *A History of Armenia* (New York: Armenian General Benevolent Union of America, 1959). The author quotes Simeon Vratzian: "We did not do anything to avoid this war; on the contrary, we were the immediate cause of it." (484) Kurkjian himself agrees with Admiral Bristol that the Armenian seizure of the coal mines at Olti in June 1920, while the Turks were fighting the French in Cilicia and the Greeks in the west, brought on the Turkish attack (483). This cannot be easily dismissed as an example of the disposition of some Armenians to blame everything on the *Dashnaks*. Kurkjian's political affiliation, if he has one, is unknown to me, but Vratzian was the leader of the briefly successful *Dashnak* revolt against the Bolsheviks in the spring of 1921.

and the Bolsheviks, a development made inevitable by shortsighted Allied policy.

In any case, the opinions of Haskell and Harbord were not as far apart as they might seem at first glance. No one who has read the report would imagine Harbord to have said the Armenians were in no trouble. He stressed that they were suffering great privation, that they could expect no crops for another year, and that they were in danger of attack which they had not the arms to resist. He merely made the reservation that they were not in danger from organized Turkish intervention. They were subject to raids by Tatars and Kurds, as they had always been, but they were not on the point of attack by a Turkish army. To say, as Haskell and others did, that Armenians would have to be protected from Turkish attack if they tried to go back to Turkish Armenia is quite different from saying the Turks would attack them in Transcaucasia. Harbord also conceded that the fear of Turkish invasion, in his judgment unfounded, was quite genuine in the Republic.[30]

Their differences did not prevent Harbord from paying high tribute to Haskell's relief work. It had made the name of America honored throughout the region as it had never been before. There was widespread knowledge of the Fourteen Points among nomadic Arabs, Daghestan mountaineers, Turkish Nationalist leaders, Transcaucasian governments, and the "Kurds who ten minutes before had fired at our party thinking us to be Armenians."[31] At Erzinjan the mission was met with a banner across the steps of a public building identified as a "courthouse." Its message was "Vive l'Art. 12 des Principes de Wilson." Two days later at Erzerum they encountered a similar banner with the same message in Turkish.[32]

General Harbord believed "there was much to show that, left to themselves, the Turk and Armenian . . . have hitherto been able to live together in peace." The aged vali of Erzerum told them that in his

---

[30] *World's Work*, XL, 273.

[31] Harbord Report, 10.

[32] Photographs accompanying the Harbord Report. NA, Peace Conference 184. 02102/5.

youth there had been no massacres. Persecution began only with Abdul Hamid. "Testimony is universal that the massacres have always been ordered from Constantinople."[33]

[33] Harbord Report, 10. Improbable as this seems, there is evidence to support it. Some of it—the statements of Enver and Talaat to Ambassador Morgenthau— has been presented in Chapter III. General Harbord was impressed with the testimony of American missionaries that some officials refused to carry out the deportation orders, testimony that was worthy of credence not only because of the character of the missionaries, but because they were able to name the officials. Later, when Dr. Johannes Lepsius had collected and published the relevant German documents, corroboration came from the perceptive consular official in Erzerum, von Scheubner-Richter, who reported on July 28, 1915 with reference to the deportations as a "solution" to the "Armenian problem."

Diese Lösung der Armenierfrage scheint den Anhängern der schroffen Richtung, zu der fast alle Militär-und Regierungsbeamte gehören, eine ideale zusein. Das türkische Volk selbst ist mit dieser Lösung der Armenierfrage keineswegs einverstanden und empfindet schon jetzt schwer die infolge der Vertreibung der Armenier über das Land hier hereinbrechende wirtschaftliche Not. (Lepsius, *Deutschland und Armenien*, 113).

Von Scheubner-Richter added that even in official circles the government's policy was not universally admired. He mentioned the kindness of the Third Army commander, Mahmud Kamil Pasha, and the vali, Tahsin Bey, unavailing though it was against the orders of the government.

The most impressive confirmation, however, was to be brought to public notice in 1921. On March 15 of that year an Armenian, Solomon Teilirian, assassinated Talaat Pasha in a Berlin street. He immediately surrendered to the police and demanded a trial, which took place on June 2 and 3.

Clearly the only defense for a deed of this sort consisted in the statelessness of the Armenian people. Crimes of the ghastliest description had been committed against them by the Turks. Yet they could bring no criminal actions against the offenders since they had no instruments of law enforcement of their own and were the chosen victims of the government to whom they ought to have been able to appeal for protection. In such circumstances, individual action against their tormentors was their only resource.

This was the defense that Teilirian adopted. To aid him his lawyers called on Dr. Lepsius who presented documentary evidence in the form of code messages from Constantinople to provincial officials. The documents had been furnished by a Turkish official in Aleppo; their authenticity was never challenged. They established beyond a doubt that the crimes against the Armenians were committed under the direct orders of the government and not on the initiative of fanatical local authorities. On the contrary, pity for the plight of the Armenians on the part of local authorities kept the slaughter from being even greater than it was. The evidence, which secured Teilirian's acquittal, was summarized by George R. Montgomery in *Current History*, XIV (July, 1921), 551-555.

Although taking into account the sins of the Armenians and the sufferings of other peoples, Harbord and his associates were certain the Armenians constituted a special case. They had made substantial contributions to the Allied cause, for which they had received encouragement from the Allies, only to find themselves in a position more defenseless than that of any of their neighbors.

> The moral responsibility for present unrest throughout Turkey
> is very heavy on foreign powers. Meantime, the Armenian, unarmed at the time of the deportations and massacres, a brave
> soldier by the thousands in the armies of Russia, France, and
> America during the war is still unarmed in a land where every
> man but himself carries a rifle.[34]

What could be done about it? General Harbord dismissed the suggestion that things could be left to "reform" on the part of the Turks. Their record was just too bad. Skilled at war but totally unsuited for any of the pursuits of peace and able to do nothing with their conquests but destroy them, they had to be ruled out—and ruled over.

Furthermore, any solution had to include the Armenians in Transcaucasia who were in an utterly hopeless plight, worse than that of their Georgian and Azerbaijani neighbors. The Georgians, through control of the railroad at Batum, could cut off traffic throughout the area while the Azerbaijanis held the oil at Baku. Armenia "alone of the three has nothing with which to exert leverage."[35] The governments of the three republics were all completely beyond the pale and their people would welcome a mandate. It should therefore be quite feasible to unite the Armenian Republic with Turkish Armenia under a mandatory power, which would also hold a mandate for the other two Caucasian republics. The report pointed out that a nation holding a mandate for Armenia would be in a helpless position if it did not at the same time control Anatolia and Constantinople. The impossibility of building an adequate railroad system without extending it into western Anatolia was cited as an example of the need to keep Asia Mi-

[34] Harbord Report, 11.
[35] Ibid., 13.

nor united. Whereas the King-Crane Commission had recommended a single mandatory for three separate states, Harbord went further to declare flatly for a single state and to make it a condition for accepting responsibility in Armenia at all.

Many Armenians, he conceded, would object to a completely unitary state, but some in responsible positions saw the need for it.

> The Armenian patriarch, the head of the Armenian Protestants, and others at Constantinople, on our return from Armenia, called and volunteered the belief that the Armenian question could not be settled within the boundaries of that country . . .[36]

A single state under an American mandate would be acceptable to the Turks.

> A party of distinguished Turks . . . stated that as between the independence of Turkey as it existed in 1914, and a mandate for the Empire given to the United States they greatly preferred the latter, and believed that they spoke for the educated classes of all Turkey.[37]

In further support of the view that the country should not be partitioned, the mission cited the mood of distrust toward the Allies which the occupation of Smyrna and the propaganda of certain European powers had created among the Turks. An announcement that a separate Armenia was to be carved out of Turkey might be a signal for massacres of Christians all over the country.

There was also something to be said for the Turk, who had a majority in the vilayets under discussion, had had it in 1914, and would have it when all the refugees had returned to their homes.[38] The Armenians

---

36 *Ibid.*, 16.

37 *Ibid.*, 16-17.

38 This is not strictly true if we accept the figures cited in Chapter I as the most nearly accurate we can find. Turks were not a majority in the vilayets under discussion. They were in fact less numerous than Armenians before the war. It was true, however, that Moslems of all kinds had outnumbered Armenians before the war and outnumbered them much more in 1919.

therefore would have a hard time to stand alone, made harder by what we should now call their "image" in the eyes of their neighbors.

> Notwithstanding his many estimable qualities, his culture, and his tenacity of race and religion, the Armenian generally does not endear himself to those of other races with whom he comes in contact. . . . He incurs the penalty which attaches among backward races to the banker, the middleman, and the creditor. Even the American missionary, who in so many instances has risked his life for his Armenian charges, does not as a rule personally like the Armenian as well as he does the more genial but indolent and pleasure-loving Turk. The Armenian is not guiltless of blood himself; his memory is long and reprisals are due, and will doubtless be made if opportunity offers. . . . Kurds appealed to this mission with tears in their eyes to protect them from Armenians who had driven them from their villages . . . The Kurds claim that many of their people were massacred under the most cruel circumstances by Armenian irregulars accompanying the Russian Bolshevists when the Russian army went to pieces . . .[39]

The report cited other claims of a similar sort against the Armenians. Not all of them were subject to verification but some were, including the destruction of forty-three villages which, according to the British consul in Batum, had been substantiated by a commission of inquiry on which the Armenians were represented. In the light of such occurrences, "the possibility of an Armenian minority being given authority over a Moslem majority against whom their hearts are filled with rancor for centuries of tyranny, may well justify apprehension."[40]

The question was even raised whether the best of the Armenian people had either perished or at least settled outside of their homeland. In the latter case, they might return and they might not.

> It is doubted if many wealthy and influential Armenians long domiciled in happier lands will return to their somewhat

[39] Harbord Report, 18.
[40] *Ibid.*

primitive homes, even though such absentees have raised their voices most loudly for an autonomous Armenia.[41]

The discussion makes it clear that the mission, although sympathetic to the Armenians, was not swept away by the kind of unreflective enthusiasm that affected many Americans back home. It was persuaded that serious handicaps existed in an effort to re-establish the Armenians in Armenia, some of them, or so the mission believed, arising from the unfortunate, although by no means incomprehensible, feelings of the Armenians themselves. The creation in such an atmosphere of a boundary between Armenia and Anatolia would oblige the mandatory powers to

... inaugurate government by placing a cordon of trustworthy foreign soldiers from the Black Sea to the Mediterranean. With a single power in control of both peoples and boundaries unannounced except as they have hitherto existed, such difficulties would not arise.[42]

It would be natural to have some intermediary authorities between the central government and the villages. For this purpose, Rumelia, Constantinople, Anatolia, Armenia, and Transcaucasia would be obvious units, but they would be administrative subdivisions, not independent nations.

To the obvious objection that the Turk

... at the end of his tutelage will still be the Turk, bloodthirsty, unregenerate, and revengeful, and that it is unthinkable that Armenia shall ever again form part of a country which may be governed by him,

the reply was that the Armenians would have other resources. They could submit their case to the League of Nations and if, in the meantime, they had shown they could govern themselves and others, the great powers could call for a plebiscite "and the mandatory could at any time be terminated by detachment of [Armenian] territory from

[41] *Ibid.*, 18.
[42] *Ibid.*, 19.

Anatolia as well as now and with much greater safety to [the Armenians] and convenience to [their] benefactors."[43]

It was therefore recommended that all of European and Asiatic Turkey should be governed by a single mandatory along with Transcaucasia. It was even suggested that the mandate should properly cover the entire Ottoman Empire, thus going even further than the King-Crane Commission which had been willing to leave Mesopotamia to the British. The mission believed, however, that the Arabic-speaking areas were "excluded from our considerations" and in any case not necessary to the solution of the Armenian problem.

Such a mandate would call for rare qualities in the nation which accepted it. There would have to be continuity in a policy beyond partisanship. There would have to be altruism and devotion to an "international duty to the peace of the world." The task could only be undertaken "at the unanimous wish of other parties to the Covenant of the League of Nations," and would have to be carried on under a fierce glare of publicity. No nation taking it up could afford to put it down, nor to fail.

The United States would be in a somewhat better position to assume the hazards of such an enterprise than any of the European powers:

Distance, our time-honored detachment from the affairs of the Old World, our innocence from participation in the intrigues which have hitherto characterized intercourse with the Turk, our freedom from bias through the necessity of considering Moslem public opinion in other parts of the world, and the fact that we have no financial interest in the great foreign debt of the Ottoman Empire, give America a viewpoint and an advantage in approaching the situation that are enjoyed by no other power.[44]

A great part of the work of the mission, therefore, had been devoted to assessing the situation as it would affect the United States if invited to assume a mandate.

[43] *Ibid.*, 19.
[44] *Ibid.*, 20.

A substantial number of troops, the report contended, would have to be furnished by the mandatory power to suppress disorders and help to organize and train a constabulary, to maintain order until the constabulary was ready to do so, and to "constitute a reserve for moral effect." In view of the lawlessness of some elements of the population and the urge for reprisals in some of the rest, such a reserve would have to be maintained for some time. Inasmuch as the other powers would probably welcome an American mandate, no problem of external defense was anticipated. General Harbord put the number of men required at 59,000.[45] (It should be borne in mind that this was written on the assumption of a mandate for all of Asia Minor. If the mandate was accepted for Armenia only, it is unlikely that the mission, aware of the attitudes and growing strength of Kemal's Nationalist movement, would have ruled out the possibility of defending the country from external attack.)

The area in which the United States Army had most recently faced topographical conditions similar to those of Anatolia was Mexico and the type of force recommended was admittedly influenced by Mexican experience. A regiment of railway engineers would be a necessity and in the earlier stages extra sanitary troops. It was estimated that the military expense would come to $88,500,000 in the first year, $59,000,000 in the second year, and $44,250,000 in the third. This would be to a considerable extent offset by local revenues.[46]

Naval expenses for ships at Constantinople, Smyrna, Mersina, Batum, and Baku, a transport capable of carrying a regiment, four to six destroyers, and a few additional smaller items would amount to relatively little, since men and ships could be drawn from the existing establishment, supplemented by some Turkish vessels. Because of the nature and history of the country and its comparative ignorance of the United States, the mission considered it of the greatest importance to start with the proper military and naval forces.[47]

[45] *Ibid.*, 23.
[46] *Ibid.*
[47] *Ibid.*, 24.

A mandate should not be assumed unless certain conditions were met. Among these were the complete control of Turkish foreign policy, authority over foreign concessions, including the right to cancel, with compensation, any already granted, and the unification of all Turkish finances. (The last, which may appear harmless or even routine, was perhaps the most difficult of acceptance, since it meant the end of foreign administration of the Ottoman public debt and of earmarking revenues for debt service. Creditors who had had access to a special fund might object to relying only on the state treasury for repayment.) Nations receiving territory at the expense of the Ottoman Empire, such as Syria and Mesopotamia, were to assume their share of responsibility for paper currency, foreign obligations, and, if necessary, reparations.[48]

The mission disclaimed any intention of recommending acceptance or rejection of a mandate by the United States. Nonetheless, General Harbord asked his colleagues to submit their opinions in writing. The memoranda submitted, attesting to the quality of the mission's personnel, make impressive reading today.[49] Since most of them gave reasons both favorable and unfavorable, it is not possible to say whether more were in favor or more against. Only Eliot Grinnell Mears expressed himself as flatly opposed, arguing that to accept authority in the middle east would make the Monroe Doctrine a "sham." Since Europeans were more imperialistic than ever, he believed we would be in for endless trouble as a mandatory. Professor W. W. Cumberland agreed that Europeans, at least the British, had become more imperialistic during the war, but for him that was the reason for assuming the mandate. It was precisely the Americans' devotion to "humanitarianism and idealism" that made us the people to extend a helping hand to the Armenians. He thought that there was in the United States "a fervor for service that is without parallel." He was not, however, unmindful of reasons against the mandate.

Lieutenant Colonel Jasper Y. Brinton, who is better described as "a lawyer from Philadelphia" than "a Philadelphia lawyer," since he

---

48 *Ibid.*, 25.
49 NA, Peace Conference 184.021/329.

had a humanity and breadth not usually associated with the latter phrase, argued that the Armenians couldn't survive as a nation without outside help which could only come from the United States; acceptance was therefore our obligation to civilization. He was "not aware of any convincing reasons why America should not accept the mandate."

Lieutenant Colonel John Price Jackson put the case from two points of view. That for acceptance represented the point of view of one who listened to the "demands of the heart," who was sensitive to "questions of honor" and set store by "standing by your friends." "I am personally inclined to sympathize with him," Jackson wrote. The contrary point of view was held by the "hard-headed business man who . . . reasons on the premises of dollars and cents. His arguments are certainly convincing when considered from his point of view."

Colonel Henry Beeuwkes thought a mandate desirable and that we should take it if Great Britain didn't. Apparently he hoped Great Britain would. Lieutenant Colonel Edward Bowditch was strongly in favor of acceptance. William B. Poland saw the mandate as a great inconvenience but also as a great opportunity.

Objective but leaning to the negative side was the mission's political expert, Stanley K. Hornbeck. Setting up the arguments for and against in parallel columns on the same page, a form later utilized by General Harbord, Hornbeck summarized briefly what could be said on both sides. At the bottom he listed the strongest reason for and the strongest against acceptance. Armenia, he said, represented a great humanitarian problem. The United States was better disposed and better qualified to deal with such problems than any other nation. On the other side, however, a mandated territory needs assurance of a continuity of policy on the part of the mandatory. Because of our Congressional system, it is hard to achieve such a continuity in foreign policy. There could be no assurance of it. With all his objectivity and fairness, Hornbeck left little doubt that he was disinclined to accept the mandate.[50] If, however, his answer is weighed with those of his

[50] He was still persuaded that rejection was the right answer when he talked to the author in 1964.

colleagues, the consensus that emerges might be expressed as "Proceed with caution—but proceed."

The same impression arises from General Harbord's conclusion. Although he used Hornbeck's formula, matching "reasons for" and "reasons against," he applied to it a unique twist which gave his arguments the force of a recommendation. Thirteen reasons for taking the mandate are balanced against thirteen for refusing it. For example, an appeal to accept obligations placed on us by the League of Nations is offset by "domestic problems growing out of the war"; the claim that America was the only hope of the Armenians was met by a reminder that other powers had shown an interest in Armenia, that the British were more experienced in such things than we, and that the United States, by the nature of its Congressional system, was incapable of continuity of policy; if American missions and colleges were important to the area, they had always been respected even by the Turks and certainly would be by another mandatory; that men are their brothers' keepers drew the reply that we had people nearer home to keep and the cost of maintenance of our brothers in Armenia would be high.

Nothing could be more even-handed than this scheme of balancing pros and cons. However, when we reach the fourteenth reason we find nothing at all on the negative side of the page. It is simply an argument for acceptance, in these terms:

> Here is a man's job that the world says can be better done by Americans than by any other. America can afford the money; she has the men; no duty to her own people would suffer; her traditional policy of isolation did not keep her from successful participation in the Great War. Shall it be said that our country lacks the courage to take up new and difficult duties?[51]

The report concluded with an exhortation:

> If we refuse to assume it, for no matter what reasons satisfactory to ourselves, we shall be considered by many millions of people as having left unfinished the task for which we entered the war, and as having betrayed their hopes.[52]

[51] Harbord Report, 25-28.
[52] Ibid., 29.

The Harbord Report, completed on board the *U.S.S. Martha Washington* and forwarded to the President on October 16, 1919, had a very different reception from that of King and Crane. On November 1st Polk wired Lansing:

> General Harbord has presented a remarkable report on Armenian situation. Strongly urge that you give him all the time you can when he arrives and if the President is well enough, arrange an interview as I feel sure he will be impressed.[53]

When the mandate question was debated by the Senate in May 1920, virtually every speaker referred to the Harbord Report. However, like the King-Crane document, it might never have been written for all the good it did the Armenians.

Although opinions have differed on General Harbord's personal position, it is hard to read his conclusion without being persuaded that he was making an almost passionate appeal to his government to grasp the nettle, to act boldly and unselfishly, to use the power, resources, and ideals of the American people in the service of their less fortunate fellows. Chief among those who took the opposite position was Herbert Hoover, who wrote as if the general had recommended flatly against any official assumption of responsibility.[54] As one of the two men who engineered Harbord's appointment, Hoover might be expected to be as well informed as anyone about the outcome of his efforts.[55] On the other hand, Ambassador Morgenthau, equally responsible for placing Harbord at the head of the mission, was equally positive the general favored the mandate.[56] The ambassador, moreover, expressed his view within a week of the mission's return. Hoover's was recorded thirty-two years later.[57]

---

[53] NA, State Department, 860J.01/126.

[54] Hoover, *Memoirs*, I, 455-456.

[55] Or he might have found it difficult to believe the man he had recommended had arrived at a position directly opposed to his own.

[56] "Mr. Morgenthau thinks after the Senate has ratified the treaty it may be possible for him with help of General Harbord to create wave of idealism in favor of mandate for Constantinople and Armenia." Grey to Curzon, October 23, 1919. *BDFP*, 1st ser., IV, 843.

[57] Morgenthau himself had favored American mandates for Armenia, Anatolia,

Since Harbord had recommended a mandate for all of Asia Minor, maintaining that Armenia could not be adequately administered without it, some critics may well have argued that, inasmuch as the mandate under discussion was not the one he believed necessary, his recommendation was, in effect, negative. They could go a step further by supposing that when the impossibility of a mandate for Asia Minor was made clear, Harbord himself was opposed to the lesser one.

The inference is a dubious one. The general didn't say so. Obviously he would have preferred the larger mandate to the smaller. Does this mean that, if he had been convinced the larger was out of the question, he would have opposed the smaller? Such a conclusion hardly appears justified nor does it gain in credence from reiteration by those who were opposed to any mandate. We could only be sure if the alternative had been put before Harbord in specific terms: "The more inclusive mandate which you recommended, and which you considered necessary for adequate administration of Armenia, is impossible. Must we therefore abandon Armenia or should we try, in the face of the difficulties which your report makes clear, to accept this 'man's job that the world says can be better done by Americans than any other,' and make it work?" As far as we know, this alternative was never offered to him. We are reduced to speculating on the nature of an unmade reply to an unasked question.

The view of the present writer, perhaps influenced by a wish that we had assumed the mandate, is that General Harbord would have answered in favor of Armenia and in favor of American assumption of a fair share of responsibility for the postwar world. Certainly Ambassador Morgenthau thought so for he spoke with confidence of Harbord's willingness to "create [a] wave of idealism in favor of mandate for Constantinople and Armenia"[58] with no reference at all to the rest of Asia Minor.

and Constantinople. His recommendations, drawn up in conjunction with Professor Phillip M. Brown and William M. Buckler in May 1919 and forwarded to the President in June, may be found in a slightly shortened version in Morgenthau, *All in a Lifetime*, 434-436.

[58] *BDFP*, 1st ser., IV, 843.

If further evidence is needed, General Harbord appears to have gone out of his way to provide it. In the magazine account of the mission which he wrote in the following year, he summed up the impression their Armenian journey had made upon himself and his associates:

> When the final decision is made that we as a nation will take
> no part in solving the problems of this region . . . there will be
> no member of our American Military Mission who will seek the
> duty of explaining our attitude to a wondering world. Someone
> who has not seen the horror of starvation and the abomination
> of desolation in this war-torn region can more satisfactorily
> present the virtue of our adherence to the non-entangling advice
> of George Washington, and inquire as did Cain in the same
> neighborhood—"Am I my brother's keeper?"[59]

[59] *World's Work*, XL, 192.

9

From Versailles to San Remo

$\mathcal{F}$OLLOWING THE SMYRNA INCIDENT, the fate of Armenia may be summed up in three propositions: 1) the position of Armenia grew weaker as that of Turkey grew stronger; 2) the Allies would do nothing about Armenia until they could find out what the United States would do; and 3) as all the best-informed observers constantly reiterated, the United States would do nothing.

Viewed from an interval of almost fifty years it now appears plain that the situation was rapidly deteriorating for the Armenians before the Versailles Treaty was signed (June 28, 1919) and that if anything was to be done, it had to be done quickly. Obviously, it could not have looked that way to some contemporaries, for the American mission adopted the opposite view. To them it seemed that anything done for Armenia would have to be done later. In a despatch to the Secretary of State on May 26, 1919, they warned:

> Campaign for mandate over Armenia appears still premature and unwise. Accordingly intimation has been discreetly conveyed

to Nubar and Pasdermadjian who have agreed to cable Sevasly instructing him to abstain from propaganda.[1]

How this struck the energetic Sevasly is unknown, but to the reader of the archives in the 1960's it looks like a sentence of death.

A different view was taken by those who were alarmed about Armenia. Gerard, for example, kept up his complaints that the Armenians were menaced by Turks and Tatars; by August he was asking about American troops.[2]

Two British officers, Colonel Rawlinson and Captain Farrell, were interviewed for an American intelligence report in July. Both knew the interior of Turkey; Rawlinson also knew the interior of the prison at Erzerum where he had been interned after the Smyrna episode. They were both convinced that if Turkish Armenians were to be repatriated, it would have to be with the protection of foreign troops. They questioned the wisdom of putting any part of Turkish territory under Armenian control.[3]

A conference of American officials held at Tiflis on July 23, 1919 forwarded a telegram to Major Tyler, Director of the Military Intelligence Bureau in Washington, as well as to the Department of State, to Henry Morgenthau and Herbert Hoover. They warned that the "Armenian Republic is approaching crisis," adding that Turks and Tatars were preventing relief in parts of Armenia. They also echoed Hoover's complaint that the Georgians were impeding the flow of supplies from Batum into Armenia. Finally they called attention to "lack of information in regard to intentions and decisions of Peace Conference" which was "intensifying disorders and undesirable political activities throughout Caucasus."[4]

The same irritation was expressed by American Consul-General Horton at Smyrna to the American ambassador in Paris. Dated July 11, Horton's report advised: "The Turks should be given to under-

---

[1] NA, Peace Conference 867.01/33. Pasdermadjian represented the Armenian Republic.
[2] *Ibid.*, 867B.00/197.
[3] *Ibid.*, 867B.00/178.
[4] *Ibid.*, 867B.00/175.

stand that they have a united Entente with which to deal, since they do not believe it now and are becoming more dangerous daily."[5]

The Turks did not believe they had a united Entente to deal with because they hadn't. The French had never been as determined to repress them as some of the other Allies but might have accepted the imposition of a harsh peace had it been put through the conference soon after it convened. They would probably have agreed to it readily enough in return for the kind of security they were asking in Europe. But their British and American associates had refused to separate the left bank of the Rhine from Germany, and the French were not in a tractable mood. They had had as many exasperations as the others during the long deliberations. They had also taken the measure of their colleagues. They knew there were strong elements in Great Britain that did not see eye to eye with Lloyd George on middle eastern policy. They also knew that President Wilson had lost much of his standing with the American people and could be largely discounted.

These may be mere speculations; what is certain is that French reluctance to force a harsh peace on the Turks began to break through the veils of diplomatic reticence in the summer of 1919. On August 19 *Le Temps* reminded its readers:

> The Turks have arms and leadership, they have their mountains, and they are accustomed from time immemorial to living as warriors. If we insist that some of them be governed by Christian minorities, they will fight; and the first victims of the fighting will naturally be the very Christians we intended to protect.[6]

A stronger statement appeared over the signature of "Pertinax" in *L'Echo de Paris*. The journalist who later fought the Nazis and their collaborators with his articles in *L'Europe Nouvelle* called for peace with Turkey without waiting for an American decision on the mandate. He also asked for the integrity of Turkey, without the Arabic-speaking areas but otherwise intact, and under the international

[5] *Ibid.*, 867.00/307.
[6] *Le Temps*, August 19, 1919, 1.

supervision of the League of Nations.[7] William M. Buckler of the American delegation, while by no means endorsing the article's recommendations, agreed with its diagnosis:

> What 'Pertinax' says today would appear to be true, i.e., that the chief causes of this Turkish Nationalist movement are the 'projets de partage'.[8]

The impending schism among the Allies as well as the desperate position of the Armenians was summed up by Clemenceau at a meeting of the Heads of Delegations on August 25, 1919:

> As to saving the Armenians, he did not know what could be done. There were no American troops. British troops were employed elsewhere. The French were not allowed by the British to play any part in Asia Minor. The Italians, it was true, had gone to Asia Minor in spite of the British, but they declined to replace the British in the Caucasus. As to the Turks, they were themselves powerless, as they could not control their own troops. He did not see from what quarter the Armenians could expect any assistance.
> M. Tittoni said that was one of the inevitable consequences of delaying peace with Turkey.
> *M. Clemenceau said that even when peace had been made, it was not likely that the Armenians would be better off.*[9]

As the French began to move toward an accommodation with the Turks, the British sat tight and insisted the next step was up to the Americans. Lloyd George told the House of Commons on August 18: "The Peace with Turkey has not been signed, not because of any delay on our part, but because we are waiting for the decision of America."[10]

On October 22 Harmsworth, Undersecretary of State for Foreign

---

[7] Pertinax's article is summarized in *BDFP*, 1st ser., IV, 816.

[8] *Ibid.*, 1st ser., IV, 817.

[9] *PPC*, VII, 839. Italics mine.

[10] *The Parliamentary Debates*. Official Report (London: His Majesty's Stationery Office, 1919), 5th ser., CIX, 2016.

Affairs, replying to a question in the House, said: "As regards the Turkish Treaty, its further consideration has been delayed in order to enable the United States Government to state their intentions."[11]

Between Lloyd George's statement and Harmsworth's the Turkish government had fallen. Damad Ferid, who had tried under the most adverse circumstances to cooperate with the Allies, had appealed on August 24 to both Calthorpe and Clemenceau to end the unnatural delay in making peace which was placing such a heavy burden on his government.[12] His plea brought no notice. With each day the delay became longer, the burden heavier. On October 1st he gave up. On the 3rd a new government was formed which was much more sympathetic to the Nationalists than its predecessors.[13] On the 10th Admiral deRobeck reported to Curzon:

> There can be little doubt that an army of occupation would now be needed to impose terms which would have been regarded as merciful in the hours of ruin and dejection following the Armistice . . . Armenian lives may be safe between Samsoun and Erzerum, but they are safe by the good will and pleasure of Mustafa Kemal and his associates.[14]

The change of government in Constantinople obviously worsened the chance of making the kind of peace the Allies wanted to make, but no hint that anything so unfortunate was taking place ruffled the calm of ministers answering questions in the House of Commons.

The action of the British government can hardly be excused on the ground that it honestly believed America was going to accept a man-date—any mandate. One expert British observer after another reported that it wasn't so. On August 18 Balfour, still in Paris, relayed the impressions he had gained from Polk:

> From various somewhat obscure hints let fall by Mr. Polk in private conversation I have gathered impression that he con-

---

11 *Ibid.*, 5th ser., CXX, 16.
12 *BDFP*, 1st ser., IV, 739-740.
13 Robeck to Curzon, *Ibid.*, 1st ser., IV, 787.
14 *Ibid.*, 1st ser., IV, 806-807.

siders it unlikely United States Government will ratify Treaty with Germany before end of September at earliest, and that probability of American Congress and Senate agreeing to United States accepting mandate for any part of former Turkish Empire is diminishing.[15]

The Washington correspondent of the *Times* (London) was not dealing with "obscure hints" when he wrote on August 26:

In view of continued intimations from London and Paris that we are still flirting with the idea that the United States will take over mandates for Asia Minor, it must be repeated that nobody here believes that the Senate will authorize anything of the kind.[16]

Four days later the same correspondent quoted the *New York Sun* of August 27 as expressing indignation that "we, who have asked for nothing, should be saddled with the plague-spots of the world."[17]

In reply to a question from Curzon on the possibility of America taking mandates, R. C. Lindsay, *chargé d'affaires* in Washington, wrote on August 16 that "from general impressions consider acceptance most unlikely," that it was favored only by "inconsiderable trade interests and missionaries."[18]

In September President Wilson had undertaken his swing around the country to take the German peace treaty and the League of Nations to the people.[19] It was a magnificently tragic effort, the last great work of a failing man. Surely no statesman ever sang a more beautiful swan song—nor a more futile one. Wilson acted as if he imagined himself to be the prime minister of a parliamentary government who could go to the country on an important issue and call for an election to settle it. Thus he never accepted that the Senate, not

[15] *Ibid.*, 1st ser., IV, 734.
[16] *The Times* (London), August 26, 1919, 11.
[17] *Ibid.*, August 30, 1919, 10.
[18] *BDFP*, 1st ser., IV, 730.
[19] Wilson's speeches in his swing around the country are in *Public Papers of Woodrow Wilson*, V, 590-645; VI, 1-416.

the people, would decide and that the people, far from punishing
those senators who opposed him, would almost certainly be more interested in some other issue when the next elections were held
more than a year later.

The trip ended in collapse at Pueblo, Colorado. While Wilson was
still recovering his strength in Washington, he was felled by another
blow, this one a stroke which, while leaving his mind clear, crip-
pled his body and ended his career. British observers who had
seen no likelihood of the Senate's accepting a mandate when Wilson
was able to fight for it certainly saw no greater chance when the
leader lay helpless. Lord Grey of Fallodon, the former foreign minister who was on a special mission in Washington, telegraphed on
October 10:

> Chance of Senate accepting mandates for America in Europe
> or Asia Minor was never good. It is now rendered more than
> ever remote by President's illness; indeed it seems to be alto-
> gether out of the question.[20]

Three days later Grey had what must be described as a "brain-
storm." In a telegram to Lord Curzon he advised:

> Anti-Wilson and party feeling renders it out of the question that
> any mandate will be conceded by Senate to present adminis-
> tration. It is, however, possible that General Leonard Wood
> may be selected as Republican candidate for Presidency at next
> election.
>   Republican success is expected. General Wood takes a broad
> view of foreign politics and in his first year of office might ask
> and be authorized to accept an American mandate for Con-
> stantinople, etc.[21]

If Lord Curzon reflected that General Wood's first year of office
would begin on March 4, 1921, he had no need to evoke the specter
of other possible Republican candidates to resist nibbling at this bait.

---

[20] *BDFP*, IV, 1st ser., 797, note 3.
[21] *Ibid.*, 1st ser., IV, 815.

Grey himself must have realized its fatuity for he cabled on October 22:

> I spoke to the Secretary of State and he entirely confirmed impression I had already conveyed to your Excellency that there is no chance whatever of Congress authorizing acceptance of mandates for Constantinople, etc.[22]

The Senate had already given some indication of what could be expected of it. Three resolutions dealing with Armenia had been introduced in the current session. Not one of them referred to the possibility of a mandate. John Sharp Williams of Mississippi and William King of Utah (in SJR 106 and SR 147 respectively) had urged protection of the Armenians against the violence of their neighbors. Henry Cabot Lodge of Massachusetts, the Republican leader, had affirmed a desire for the independence of an Armenian state including the six vilayets, Cilicia, Russian Armenia and some of Azerbaijan and Persia, with no suggestion at all as to how such a state was to be created and maintained (SR 38). Even these modest expressions of good will had not got out of the Committee on Foreign Relations.

If the Senate was generally indisposed to do anything for Armenia, what of the public? In the absence of any kind of referendum it is impossible to say what the consensus was, or even if there was a consensus. Yet no one who has looked at magazine and newspaper accounts, including letters to the editor, or the mail reaching the State Department can doubt there was still a large reservoir of concern about Armenia. The *New Republic* expressed more bluntly than most what was surely the prevailing journalistic opinion:

> It is impossible to admit that there can be honest differences of opinion as to the end to be realized, the final termination of the insane regime of Turkish brutality.... It must stop.... If we fail at this juncture to vindicate Armenia's right to freedom we shall never again persuade the world that our moral sentiments are anything but empty rhetoric playing over a gulf of selfishness and sloth.[23]

[22] *Ibid.*, 1st ser., IV, 842-843.
[23] *New Republic*, XX (September 10, 1919), 163-164.

Unfortunately, selfishness is always to the fore in the years immediately following a war. The American people in 1919 and 1920 could hardly be accused of sloth, but their energies were more directed to the pursuit of personal objectives than to large national and international purposes. It may be that the prevailing opinion was still sympathetic to Armenia and willing to do something to help but not to the extent of favoring any serious assumption of responsibility.[24] Against a wide but rather tepid sympathy was the much firmer resolve of those who were determined that the United States should not depart from its traditional policy of non-involvement.

An equally determined foe of the Armenians, although probably with a much different motive, was the High Commissioner, Admiral Mark Bristol. Bristol's mind was a strange mixture of prejudice and sense; the sense told him the Allies were being unnecessarily hostile to the Turks while the prejudice condemned the Armenians. When Armenian religious leaders—Gregorian, Catholic, and Protestant—appealed to the peace conference on August 18, 1919, alleging that their people were in grave danger,[25] they ran counter to the Admiral's view. In a cablegram received on August 17 he had charged that American relief workers, the British, and selfish Armenian interests were all pressuring for an independent Armenia under American mandate. The trouble in the Caucasus, he maintained, was coming from Azerbaijan rather than from Turkey, and the Armenians had done their share in stirring it up. The Turks were naturally susceptible to pressure to join Azerbaijan since they were afraid of losing more of their country. A minority of five million, the Admiral allowed, had suffered badly but so had the majority of Turks:

Therefore the main issue is the whole twenty-five million people that should be given peace in the quickest and best way possible, followed by good government, freedom of religious belief, universal education, efficient law courts and self-determination

[24] A position of this sort was taken by Charles Evans Hughes, who had been Wilson's opponent in the 1916 election, in response to an inquiry by James W. Gerard in August, 1919. Woodrow Wilson Papers, File VI, b. 365, f.635.

[25] NA, Peace Conference 867B.00/238.

when the people are educated to determine for themselves.
... I recommend America take the lead and open the fight for
one *mandatory* for the whole of Turkey and withdraw the
Greeks from Smyrna and stop all agitation for any separate
Armenia or any other partition of this country.[26]

Here Bristol appears not so much an enemy of the Armenians as
merely opposed to an impractical partition of Turkey. In other despatches his feeling toward the Armenians is undisguised. On August
30 he cabled Joseph C. Grew, Secretary-General of the American
Commission in Paris, that Colonel Rawlinson had investigated atrocities in the Olti district and pronounced them the work of Armenian
bands.[27] On October 1st he wrote to Polk to ask: "Why should we,
who were never at war with Turkey or with Russia, send troops
against these people? Look at what happened in Smyrna! Are we
to do the same thing in Armenia as was done in Smyrna?"[28] Inconsist-
ency shows up in this letter in which he claimed that the American
relief people, so recently part of the cabal for an independent Armenia, agreed with him.

On October 15 he wrote Polk again to "confess that I am trying
to influence [General Harbord] to take my view in regard to advocating the whole of the old Turkish Empire under one control or
mandate."[29]

Polk was becoming drawn to the same opinion. He had written
Bristol on the 14th:

I must say that I think there has been a tremendous amount of
hysteria about this Armenia situation and we stand a good
chance of being stampeded into doing something foolish. After
seeing the way the British, French, Italians and Greeks are
trying to carve up the Turkish Empire and present us with
the claws I am more and more of the opinion that we should
try to keep the Empire intact under some sort of mandate.[30]

[26] *Ibid.*, 867B.00/238A.
[27] *Ibid.*, 867B.00/255.
[28] Polk Papers, dr. 78, f. 69.
[29] *Ibid.*
[30] *Ibid.*

Polk, however, did not maintain this stand consistently. Bristol did. On January 15, 1920 he wrote to Polk: "I certainly hope that under no circumstances will our government recognize Armenia, even as a de facto government."[31]

Because of his steadfast opposition to Greek and Armenian aspirations Bristol is sometimes thought of as a good friend of Turkey. Ahmed Emin Yalman believes the Turks should recognize him as "one of the heroes of their national struggle."[32] There is a hospital today in Istanbul which bears his name.

The truth is that he didn't think much of the Turks either. On October 21 he inveighed against the disposition of the Allies to restore something like the status quo in Turkey. The French effort to insinuate themselves into the situation for selfish ends aroused his ire particularly. He pointed out that this meant not only the exclusion of American commercial interests but "the re-establishment of the rottenest government the world has ever known."[33] The point was made in a more personal way on December 4:

> If things go on as they are going now I see France and England
> re-establishing the Turkish rule, at least over some part of this
> country. I have no use for the Turk, and above all I never
> want to see the Turkish rule established again. I cannot con-
> ceive any worse crime.[34]

There is no contradiction here. Bristol believed all the peoples of the middle east to be equally incapable of self-government. Polk always replied diplomatically; it sometimes appears that he shared Bristol's views, but it cannot be affirmed with certainty. In any case he was more aware than Bristol that the United States, because of the opposition to Wilson in the Senate, was in a weak position to exert pressure for the kind of treaty we preferred. We were not only most unlikely to take a mandate of any kind but we might well

[31] *Ibid.*, dr. 78, f. 71.
[32] Yalman, *op. cit.*, 79.
[33] Polk Papers, dr. 78, f. 71.
[34] *Ibid.*

reject the German treaty. As he wrote to Bristol on November 18: "If the Senate rejects the Treaty, as looks more than likely, then we have no excuse for mixing up in the Turkish business."[35] On the following day the Senate rejected the treaty. Polk wrote again on December 9: "There is nothing we can say or do as to the situation in Turkey in view of the fact that we have not ratified."[36]

Prejudiced though Bristol may have been toward the Armenians, he was right in assessing British and French tendencies to move away from a radical settlement in Turkey. *Le Temps* served as bellwether as early as October 8 when it recognized that the change of government in Turkey made it necessary for the Allies to make peace with the Turkish Nationalists under Mustafa Kemal. The editors said nothing about restoring the Arabic-speaking areas to Turkish sovereignty and they appeared to be excluding Cilicia from it. They also called for international control of the Straits. Otherwise they were ready to restore everything to the Turks.[37]

The rest of the French press took a similar tone which Lord Robert Cecil told the House of Commons could "only be described as Turkophile."[38]

The British were wavering. Although they were not moving as decisively as the French toward abandonment of the Armenian cause, their diplomatic correspondence makes the same trend manifest. A despatch from Lieutenant Colonel Ian Smith in Constantinople quoted the warning of a highly placed Turk, friendly toward Mustafa Kemal, that the English were harming themselves by their suspicion of the Nationalists.

> The more we abstained and gave the impression of wishing to subdue the Nationalist movement, the more power we gave to the old C.U.P. and the more grounds we gave for anti-English feeling among the general run of Turks.[39]

[35] *Ibid.*, dr. 78, f. 70.
[36] *Ibid.*, dr. 78, f. 71.
[37] *Le Temps*, October 8, 1919, 1.
[38] *Parliamentary Debates*, 5th ser., CXXIII, 730.
[39] *BDFP*, 1st ser., IV, 794.

This type of comment might be expected to find ready acceptance among the military in Great Britain who had always leaned toward the Turks. Sir Eyre Crowe, writing to George Kidston in November, charged:

> The War Office makes no attempt to conceal part of that policy which, we know, they would like the Turkish peace terms to reflect, i.e., an independent Turkey as large as possible and continuing its rule over subject races whether they be Greeks, Kurds, or Armenians.[40]

In return Kidston told Crowe that not only the War Office but the India Office as well was pro-Turkish.[41] Sir Edwin Montagu, Secretary of State for India, was in fact throughout the period of the peace settlements a strong voice for Moslem opinion. Moslem opinion, however ill-advised, was highly sensitive to any offense to Turkey. It exerted a powerful influence in the British Isles. On September 10 and again on December 24, 1919, the *Times* printed letters to Lloyd George signed by about forty prominent persons asking for no interference with Turkish rights.[42] Although both letters stressed the importance to the empire of not estranging Indian Moslems, the second introduced an additional argument that would be of interest in the future. The British position in Asia, the signers said, had always been menaced from the north. A friendly Turkey would be a valuable bulwark against Bolshevism.

Kidston felt that an Armenian state of the size originally contemplated had become a dream. "The idea . . ." he wrote, "that it will ever be possible now . . . to join up Cilicia with Erivan in a single Armenian state is to me almost inconceivable."[43]

The Armenian cause looked very gloomy to him.

> We must cut our coat according to our cloth, and, unless the Americans or someone else have conscience enough to come in at

---

[40] *Ibid.*, 1st ser., IV, 894.
[41] Kidston to Crowe, November 28, 1919. *Ibid.*, 1st ser., IV, 909.
[42] *The Times* (London), September 10, 1919 and December 24, 1919, 9.
[43] *BDFP*, 1st ser., IV, 908.

the last moment to help, I fear that it may be very difficult to impose on the Turks the terms of the Supreme Council's reply to them of last June . . . If the terms had only been communicated to them immediately after the conclusion of the Armistice instead of in June, how different everything might have been.[44]

Lloyd George naturally reflected none of the misgivings that assailed lesser officials. Asked in Parliament by the indefatigable T. P. O'Connor

> . . . whether, in settling the terms of peace with Turkey, his pledges still held good that none of the Christian communities shall be again put under the yoke of a Power that has periodically butchered and plundered them, . . .

the Prime Minister replied: "That will certainly be the purpose with which the British delegation will enter the Conference."[45]

The conference referred to was a series of talks between British and French representatives to be held in London late in December. The subject was to be the settlement with Turkey. Clemenceau and Curzon had already had a preliminary meeting on December 11. There was to be no more waiting for the United States.

The first session took place on December 22 in the office of Lord Curzon, the new Secretary of State for Foreign Affairs. It opened with the presentation of a French note on peace with Turkey and British comments on it. There was a rather lengthy discussion of the powers to be represented on a commission to administer the Turkish Straits but significantly no discussion at all on whether or not such a commission was to be created. Although there still was disagreement on the question of ending Turkish rule in Constantinople, it was taken for granted that, whether they went or stayed, they were no longer to control the Straits.

On the question of expelling the Turks from their capital, Philippe Berthelot of the Ministry of Foreign Affairs, who represented France, pointed out at the request of Clemenceau that the French had not

[44] *Ibid.*, 1st ser., IV, 910.
[45] *Parliamentary Debates*, 5th ser., CXXII, 676.

originally favored it but had "deferred to the superior arguments of the British Government." Lord Curzon replied that the British government had made no final decision in the matter. Balfour, Lloyd George, and Curzon himself favored expulsion but "any decisions reached at the present conferences with M. Berthelot were subject to revision or confirmation by both the French and British governments."[46]

The future of the Turks in Constantinople has sometimes been treated as a tug-of-war between the French and British positions with the French winning out. Had it been as simple as that, the British would have won, for the French surrendered their position following the talk between Clemenceau and Curzon. Disagreement in the British cabinet kept the issue alive until the original French view prevailed. Before the first meeting of December 22 had adjourned, Armitage Smith of the British Treasury was viewing with alarm the consequences of a too precipitate expulsion of the Turkish government while Berthelot was reassuring him that it could be accomplished by stages.[47]

The French note proposed an Armenian state to include the Lake Van region, the plains of Bitlis and Mush, and the Republic of Armenia with the Armenians given all the territory disputed between them and Georgia and Azerbaijan. It excluded all the western part of the vilayet of Erzerum and the city of Erzerum itself, recognized to be preponderantly Turkish, but conceded the eastern part of the vilayet to the Armenians. The British objected to the exclusion of a city they believed essential to the safety of an Armenian state. Erzerum was not only a firm fortress in a vital valley but the head from which a railroad ran into the heart of Armenia.[48]

At a second meeting on the same day the removal of the Turks from their capital seemed closer to actuality with the agreement that an international regime there should be guaranteed by the League of Nations.[49] It was made clear that the French expected some status

[46] BDFP, 1st ser., IV, 938-940.
[47] Ibid., 1st ser., IV, 942.
[48] Ibid., 1st ser., IV, 952-956.
[49] Ibid., 1st ser., IV, 960.

for themselves in Cilicia under nominal Turkish sovereignty. They proved willing to yield on Erzerum, however, suggesting that the actual boundaries of the new state be worked out by an Allied commission. They also agreed to join the British in an appeal to the League of Nations for men and money to aid Armenia if necessary. Finally, they conceded the need for a free state around Batum to facilitate Armenian access to the sea.[50]

A memorandum by Colonel Chardigny, Head of the French Military Mission in the Caucasus, appears as an appendix to the minutes of the second meeting. It emphasized the difficulty of creating an Armenian state. The Armenians in the Caucasus, Chardigny wrote, were nowhere compact, but lived among hostile populations. In Turkish Armenia there were virtually no Armenians left. If they were to be resettled there, it would be among unwilling neighbors. The Turkish Nationalist movement was determined not to surrender "an inch of the soil of the six vilayets" (this from the pronunciamiento of the Erzerum Congress); hence a substantial military force would be needed, which Chardigny put at 20,000 men.[51]

At a third meeting on December 23 agreement was reached on an independent area for the Kurds who would be expected to come to terms with the Armenians. Lord Curzon assured his colleagues that they were ready to do so.[52] He also thought 20,000 too high an estimate of the troops needed to protect the Armenians. They were good soldiers, he said, and of course could expect help from America. He believed 10,000 men would be enough.[53] Apparently no one else thought so, but Lord Curzon stuck tenaciously to his figure.

The remainder of the third and all of the fourth meeting were devoted to Arab questions. The talks were then concluded and the conference separated to meet more formally in the new year, again in London and with the French and Italian prime ministers in attendance.

Several events took place before the new meetings which affected

[50] Ibid., 1st ser., IV, 956-963.
[51] Ibid., 1st ser., IV, 965-966.
[52] Ibid., 1st ser., IV, 967.
[53] Ibid., 1st ser., IV, 968-969.

the positions they could take. Although a clarifying note from Berthe-lot to Curzon[54] had left open the question of expelling the Turks from Constantinople, the British cabinet voted by an "overwhelming majority"[55] against expulsion—and incidentally against the Prime Minister and the Foreign Secretary. As this resolution remained fixed throughout subsequent negotiations, it may be said that the original French position had prevailed through a vote of the British cabinet.

Berthelot's note agreed to the inclusion of the city of Erzerum in Armenia, another point on which the French were willing to yield to British opinion.[56] By this time, however, the British, under pressure from the military, were ready to give it back to the Turks.[57]

On January 19, 1920 the Supreme Council announced the de facto recognition of the Armenian Republic.[58] Five days later an announcement of United States recognition was issued, then retracted. The American government, it appeared, had merely "accepted" the action of its former allies but deferred action of its own.[59]

American supporters of the Armenians who were sure our European allies were selling them out might have been given pause by such contrasting attitudes toward the only existing Armenian state. They weren't. The tireless Gerard announced on February 9 that "our committee will start nationwide campaign against France and England who have already told Armenians they will cut up Armenia."[60] On February 14 he inquired if Mrs. Wilson would receive five Armenian women who would ask her to intercede with the President to prevent the powers from "cutting up Armenia."[61]

---

[54] *Ibid.*, 1st ser., IV, 1024.

[55] Churchill, *op. cit.*, 396.

[56] *BDFP*, 1st ser., IV, 1024.

[57] "Proposals prepared by the Foreign Office, January 16, 1920." *Ibid.*, 1st ser., IV, 1047-1060. Note 54 on page 1059 reveals that the return of Erzerum to the Turks was decided upon as a result of pressure from the General Staff.

[58] *Foreign Relations of the United States 1920* (Washington: Government Printing Office, 1936), III, 775.

[59] *Ibid.*, III, 776. The United States finally extended de facto recognition on April 23, 1920 (*Ibid.*, III, 778).

[60] Wilson Papers, File VI, b. 365, f. 635.

[61] *Ibid.*

"Starting a nationwide campaign against France and England" was not the kind of constructive support which, even at such a late date, might have been helpful to the Armenians. It was, on the contrary, one of the more disheartening of the many outbreaks of political lunacy that disfigured the postwar period.[62] As the Italian premier, Francesco Nitti, expressed it:

> Nothing could be more just than to create a small Armenian state
> which would have allowed the Armenians to group themselves
> around Lake Van and to affirm their national unity in one
> free state. But here also the hatred of the Turks, the agitation of
> the Greeks, the dimly illuminated philanthropy, determined a
> large movement to form a great State of Armenia which should
> have outlets on the sea and great territories.[63]

One need not go so far as to restrict the Armenians to the immediate environs of Lake Van in order to agree that their supporters over-reached themselves. Throughout the spring, with no one in Washington holding out any hope that the United States would act to avert disaster, Gerard continued to refuse support to Allied efforts for a diminished Armenia. On March 6 we find him writing in *The Independent*:

> We must tell our British and French friends in unmistakable
> terms that the retention of the Turks in Constantinople and the
> spoliation of Armenia will seriously affect the friendly sentiment
> which today exists in America for England and France—and
> will provoke most dangerous anti-English and anti-French
> propaganda in America. We must tell them that the conscience
> of America will revolt with an irresistible passion of abhorrence
> and of indignation against those who so complacently offer to
> shake the bloody hands of the Turks and who endanger the

---

[62] It should not be supposed that Gerard was unique. As the energetic chairman of an active organization he spoke and wrote more than most but his views were not exceptional. The *New Republic* articles of the more sophisticated Paxton Hibben, although rich in factual material, take a position indistinguishable from Gerard's.

[63] Nitti, *op. cit.*, 174.

peace of the world under the nefarious influences of greedy financiers and discredited imperialists.[64]

Tell them, in short, that we will call the tune and they will pay the piper.

In February fighting took place at Marash; Admiral deRobeck telegraphed that it was still uncertain whether it portended a "definite forward movement" on the part of the Nationalists. There was evidence, however, that they were in communication with the Bolshevists. An early peace and solidarity among the Allies were vital; if the terms of the peace called for the separation of Constantinople or Smyrna from Turkey or the creation of "even a relatively great Armenia," the Allies "must be definitely prepared to impose them by force."[65]

On the eve of the London conference the Turkish government made further concessions to the Nationalists by jettisoning several ministers and replacing them with men sympathetic to Kemal's party,[66] a development which could only make the struggle for Armenia of even more dubious outcome.

The conference met on February 12, 1920. In his opening speech Lloyd George explained somewhat disingenuously the delay in coming to grips with the Turkish problem as

... due to the fact that President Wilson had led the conference to expect that when he returned to the United States of America he would be in a position very shortly to give a decision as to whether the United States of America would accept a mandate. He had hoped to do so at the latest by August or September. The difficulties, however, had proved to be greater than he had anticipated. The result was that, instead of giving a reply in September, he was not able to give a reply today, nor was he likely to do so three months hence. Hence it was right for the other Powers concerned to try to bring the matter to a conclusion.[67]

[64] *The Independent*, CI, 345.
[65] *BDFP*, 1st ser., IV, 1085-1087.
[66] *Ibid.*, 1st ser., IV, 1088.
[67] *Ibid.*, 1st ser., VII, 1-2.

This summation leaves several nagging questions unanswered. Granted it was right to wait until August or September for President Wilson to announce the decision of the United States, why allow the question to drag until February? Moreover, had not the Allies already seriously compromised the chances of a good treaty with Turkey before President Wilson returned to fight out the issue at home? If so, was not Lloyd George's action in regard to Smyrna one of the chief elements in the deterioration of the Allied position?

So far was Lloyd George himself from being troubled by any such reflections that when the question of evacuating Smyrna came up on the third day of the conference, he managed to kill any action on it. Alexandre Millerand, since January at the head of the French government, gave voice to what had probably been French feelings all along; he wanted the Greeks to get out.[68]

The Armenian question came before the conference on February 14. When the previous decision to leave the Turks in Constantinople had been ratified, Lord Curzon reminded his colleagues that they "were pledged to constitute a separate Armenia."[69] On the 16th they set about doing so.

Berthelot opened the discussion by recalling the reduction in the size of Armenia agreed upon in his talks with British leaders in December. The Armenians, he said, were giving up their claim to Cilicia and were willing to have it go to France. He had told them they couldn't have Trebizond either and should solve the question of access by railways. He mentioned Switzerland as an example of a nation that was viable and even prosperous without a seaport of its own. The French, he said, were opposed to a Greater Armenia in which the Armenians would be a helpless minority. "The suggestion had merely been put forward by the entourage of President Wilson on grounds which could not bear examination."[70]

Reverting to Cilicia, Berthelot said that the Turks would exercise

68 *Ibid.*, 1st ser., VII, 54-56.
69 *Ibid.*, 1st ser., VII, 43.
70 *Ibid.*, 1st ser., VII, 84.

genuine sovereignty, subject only to financial and administrative control. Order would be maintained by a native gendarmerie. The French did not intend to make the province a closed preserve for their own enterprise. On the contrary, they expected to pursue a liberal policy provided three conditions were met: their existing concessions in Cilicia would have to be continued, they must be permitted to collect prewar debts from Turkey, and German property and enterprises would have to be liquidated.[71] In response to a reminder from Curzon that 75,000 Armenians in Cilicia would require protection from a Turkish majority, Berthelot replied that the French had no intention of withdrawing their troops without adequate guarantees.[72]

Lloyd George objected that if the French named officials and instructors, as they proposed to do, other than at the request of the Turks, they were in effect taking a mandate for Cilicia and thus bringing the conference into conflict with the United States. Berthelot, unmoved, replied:

> The United States had done nothing in regard to Turkey. She had not gone to war with Turkey. She would accept no mandate. She would help in no way. Consequently, the conference could not entirely be guided by the wishes of the United States of America.[73]

Lloyd George continued to take exception to the French proposal. In his opinion it "went entirely against the views of President Wilson." The conference "should not place itself in such a position that when the terms of peace came to be placed before Turkey, the latter should have the support of America in opposing them."[74] Why the United States should be expected to swallow British mandates in Mesopotamia and Palestine and a French mandate in Syria only to gag on another French mandate for Cilicia the voluble Prime Minister did not make clear, nor did he explain how the French were to guarantee the

[71] Ibid., 1st ser., VII, 89-90.
[72] Ibid., 1st ser., VII, 94.
[73] Ibid., 1st ser., VII, 96.
[74] Ibid.

safety of an Armenian minority in a state in which they exercised only administrative and financial guidance while enjoying some business concessions.

Disagreement on the French right to appoint personnel implied no similar disagreement on their right to a sphere of influence for economic development. Spheres of influence were taken for granted, the only friction arising over the limits of the three spheres. As formalized on February 26, these were to be Adalia for Italy, Cilicia for France, and Kurdistan for Great Britain.[75] It was also agreed on March 3 that the Tripartite Agreement which was to accompany the peace treaty should provide that each of the powers would be responsible for the protection of minorities in its sphere.[76] Presumably this meant that not only France but Great Britain and Italy as well would exercise some control over the government of their spheres, at least in the domain of the police power.

On February 28 discussion turned again to the massacres at Marash. There was disagreement on the extent of the violence—the French, whose soldiers were there to prevent it, tended to underrate it—but none on the need for obliging the Turks to stop it and to refrain from similar outbreaks. The problem was that there was no threat which could be expected to have any deterrent effect on the Turks. Their government could do nothing for, as Paul Cambon pointed out, it could not control the Nationalist movement.[77]

No more could the Allies. That simple fact, which should have been recognized as the weakness of their position months earlier, was by now a commonplace at the highest levels. Admiral deRobeck telegraphed from Constantinople on February 29: "The Allied High Commissioners are flouted, not by the responsible Government, but by the Nationalist organization which the Government cannot control." Advocating that "preparations should be made at once for effective action," deRobeck summed up the Allied dilemma:

By effective action is meant the occupation of Constantinople,

[75] *Ibid.*, 1st ser., VII, 256-259.
[76] *Ibid.*, 1st ser., VII, 381.
[77] *Ibid.*, 1st ser., VII, 291-297.

together with such other measures as the military authorities may consider possible. The drawback to this course lies in the danger for Allied subjects and Christians in the interior.[78]

The great powers, in short, had dawdled so long that they were at the mercy of an inferior power. The Nationalists had put them in a position they could not break out of without inflicting serious, perhaps fatal, injury on the people they were trying to aid.

As they had failed to keep Turkey weak, they had equally failed to keep themselves united. Admiral deRobeck disclosed that the British and French High Commissioners were acting without taking their Italian colleague into their confidence. "I have fullest confidence in personal character and loyalty of Italian High Commissioner," he telegraphed, "but there are, unfortunately, too many evidences that official Italian policy here is strongly pro-Turkish."[79]

Nonetheless, the Allies fatuously went ahead with their plan to impose harsh terms on Turkey. These, as communicated to the Allied high commissioners on March 5, included the cession of Eastern Thrace as far as the Chatalja line (i.e., virtually all of Eastern Thrace except the immediate environs of Constantinople) to Greece, international control of the Straits with an international armed force to be maintained in the zone, close financial supervision of the Turkish government, the cession of Smyrna to Greece under Turkish "suzerainty" (how this was to work was not explained), an independent Armenia, to include Erzerum, and the probable recognition of an independent Kurdistan.[80]

On March 12 the conference formally requested the League of Nations to become responsible for the safety of Armenia.[81] On the 16th the Allies began a full-scale occupation of Constantinople,[82] a show of force designed to convince the Turks their former enemies were not to

[78] *Ibid.*, 1st ser., VII, 378.
[79] *Ibid.*, 1st ser., VII, 422.
[80] *Ibid.*
[81] *Ibid.*, 1st ser., VII, 478-479. The League of Nations had come into existence in January 1920.
[82] *Ibid.*, 1st ser., VII, 507.

be trifled with—but of doubtful effect on the Nationalists in far-off Marash and Erzerum. Indeed, the effect in Constantinople, if any, must have been to weaken pro-Entente feeling and to strengthen Mustafa Kemal's following in the capital.

March 12 was also the day on which the decisions of the conference were communicated to the American government by the French ambassador, Jules Jusserand, in Washington. The note inquired whether the United States intended

> ... to desist from influence in Eastern affairs or whether on the contrary, as the President of the Council would prefer, it proposes by taking part in this work to claim its share of influence, action, and responsibility in the definitive and general re-establishment of peace.[83]

The American reply, signed by the new Secretary of State, Bainbridge Colby, but obviously at least in part the work of President Wilson, was a commentary on all points of the proposed settlement. With reference to Armenia it reiterated American concern, declaring that "the Government of the United States is convinced that the civilized world demands and expects the most liberal treatment for that unfortunate country."[84]

Read without consideration of the circumstances, it seems a moderate document, at fault only in ignoring the problem of inducing the Turks to accept its sensible proposals. Read in the light of American unwillingness to share the burden of making a difficult peace, it is easy to understand that it was received by the conference with some resentment. As Lloyd George later described it:

> It was an intimation that America meant to leave us in the lurch, dropping a tract in our collection box to meet the crushing expenses of a policy for which the American President insisted on retaining a leading share in the responsibility.[85]

[83] *Foreign Relations of the United States 1920,* III, 750-753.
[84] *Ibid.*
[85] Lloyd George, *op. cit.,* II, 1301.

The belief of the British War Office that the Allies were taking a wrong tack entirely was expressed by Secretary of State for War Winston Churchill in a letter to the Prime Minister on March 29, 1920:

> With military resources which the Cabinet have cut to the most weak and slender proportions, we are leading the Allies in an attempt to enforce a peace on Turkey which would require great and powerful armies and long, costly operations and occupations. . . . Try to secure a really representative Turkish governing authority, and come to terms with it. As at present couched the Turkish Treaty means indefinite anarchy.[86]

On April 11 the Council of the League of Nations replied negatively to the request to guarantee the security of Armenia. It pointed out that the League was not a state and had neither an army nor financial resources of its own. It had less effect on public opinion in the east than in Europe. Nor could the Council forget the "bitter disappointment" of the Armenians at the failure of treaty provisions to protect them in the past. Article 22, moreover, did not authorize the League to exercise mandatory authority; the best way to handle the problem was to call on a single nation to take the mandate. While ready to help find the mandatory, the League would wish to be reassured on three points:

1) Would the Supreme Council advance capital to Armenia or at least guarantee the safety of capital which might be found elsewhere?

2) Since a large portion of the territory proposed for an Armenian state was occupied by Turkish troops, would the Allies be ready to use force to put them out?

3) Could provision be made for Armenian access to the sea? The Council thought this necessary not only for economic reasons but to insure communications between Armenia and the mandatory.[87]

The results of the London conference, therefore, were merely a somewhat more precise definition of Armenian boundaries than the

[86] Churchill, op. cit., 401.

[87] League of Nations, Official Journal (London: Harrison and Sons), April-May, 1920, 85-87.

powers had reached previously and an agreement among the three principal powers on zones of economic advantage in Turkey, which generally followed the lines of the secret wartime treaties. A program to put these aims into effect was no nearer than before. On the contrary, the French defeat at Marash and the increasing weakness of the Turkish government had made the possibility of imposing a settlement more remote than ever.

It is impossible to leave the subject of the conference without recording a curious note, trivial enough in itself but indicative of the strength and pervasiveness of the ideal of self-determination of nations. The plenipotentiaries actually spent some time in discussing an autonomous Lazistan.[88] There was no evidence that the Lazes had asked for a state of their own, believed they could manage one, or particularly wished to try.

On April 18 British, French and Italian negotiators again assembled, this time at San Remo on the Italian Riviera, to complete their work on the Turkish treaty. At the outset they faced the question of what notice to take of the United States. Berthelot continued to favor not taking much:

> In his view it was impossible that the Allies should waste time
> in explaining to the United States step by step why they took this
> action or proceeded on such-and-such lines, and so forth. In
> the special conditions at present obtaining, it was out of the
> question that they should wait for the sanction of the United
> States.[89]

Lloyd George, who had complained at London that the Americans "appeared to assume responsibility for the sole guardianship of the Ten Commandments and the Sermon on the Mount"[90] was of much the same mind as Berthelot:

> He thought it was intolerable that the Allies should continue

---

[88] *BDFP*, 1st ser., VII, 281-282.
[89] *Ibid.*, 1st ser., VIII, 20-21.
[90] *Ibid.*, 1st ser., VII, 428-429.

to conduct correspondence with the United States on the subject. If they did so, the treaty would never be concluded at all.[91]

At the same time he saw advantages in asking the United States to assist Armenia:

If Americans refused to assist, the Allies would be no worse off, and, in one respect, they would be better off. President Wilson would continue to lecture the Allies about the way they were handling the Turkish question, but if the Allies could retort that they had asked America to come in and assist, and that America had refused, the United States could not continue to complain of the inability of the Allies to protect Armenia.[92]

On April 22, after the Turks had been invited to Paris to receive peace terms,[93] Lloyd George again took up the question of Erzerum. The Armenians, he said, could not control it; to award it to them would make the whole treaty unenforceable. He again ran into opposition from the French who, having given in to the British stand, now accepted it in good faith. Berthelot reminded him that Erzerum was a powerful fortress and in addition commanded the railroad. Without it Armenia was a virtual impossibility. Curzon backed Berthelot, emphasizing strategic considerations. Nitti came in on Lloyd George's side. He feared that if the Turks, who were going to lose Thrace and Smyrna, were asked to give up Erzerum too, they would refuse to sign the treaty. Lloyd George pointed out that the Allies could enforce their will in Thrace, Constantinople, and Smyrna, but would have no chance to help the Armenians.[94]

It was an unnecessary reminder. Throughout the discussion it had been accepted that the Allies could do nothing to help the Armenians, other than to furnish officers, arms, and money, hoping they would be enough to enable the Armenians to drive the Turks out of their territory. On April 23, President Aharonian appeared at San Remo and

91 *Ibid.*, 1st ser., VIII, 21.
92 *Ibid.*, 1st ser., VIII, 63.
93 *Ibid.*, 1st ser., VIII, 83.
94 *Ibid.*, 1st ser., VIII, 108-112.

gave a highly optimistic estimate of possibilities. He placed a low value on Mustafa Kemal's troops and was confident that the Armenians could put 40,000 men into the field against them. If the Allies would arm and equip them and lend them the prestige of association, it would be possible to expel the Turks from Erzerum.[95] Marshal Foch took a less sanguine view[96] as did the Allied military advisors in a report submitted on the day of Aharonian's appearance. They called attention to the fact that the Armenians were obliged to get supplies over the rail line from Batum through Tiflis, a resource which had proved unreliable in the extreme. In their opinion the Armenian force was a weak one and could not conquer the Turks, particularly in their stronghold at Erzerum.[97]

Lloyd George seized the opportunity for a solo flight. He began sensibly enough by reminding his colleagues that decisions of the kind they were making with reference to Erzerum could not be made by conferences. With better than 10,000 Turkish troops in the city and determined to hold it, nothing was to be gained by insisting on their leaving. Without the backing of adequate force the Armenians would not get Erzerum, whatever the conference decided, but only another opportunity to be massacred.

At this stage of his argument the Prime Minister became carried away by his own persuasiveness. If the Armenians were to be denied Erzerum on the ground that they couldn't take it, what claim had they to any of Turkish Armenia? They couldn't take any of it. So, with the air of happy discovery with which he was able to surround a preposterous suggestion, Lloyd George advocated restricting Armenia to the territory already controlled by Armenians, that is, the former Transcaucasian province of Erivan.[98] The unanimous aim of

---

[95] *Ibid.*, 1st ser., VIII, 120-121. In January Gerard had quoted Aharonian as needing 10,000 foreign troops to bring the Armenian army up to 30,000 (Gerard, "Save Armenia!" in *The World Outlook*, VI, 8). Now the 10,000 seemed to be already in existence and added to, rather than subtracted from, the 30,000 needed.

[96] *BDFP*, 1st ser., VIII, 122.

[97] *Ibid.*, 1st ser., VIII, 131.

[98] *Ibid.*, 1st ser., VIII, 140.

British statesmen, "the redemption of the Armenian valleys forever from the bloody misrule with which they had been stained by the infamies of the Turk,"[99] at last had come to this—that the Armenians would have a state of their own but every square inch of it would be in the former Russian Armenia. Turkey was to yield nothing at all. In Lloyd George's later account of the peace treaties, in which he proudly set forth the determination of the British to do justice to the Armenians, there is characteristically nothing to suggest that he was ready at a crucial period in the negotiations to give up altogether the project of an Armenian state in eastern Turkey, nor that his egregious proposition was resisted by the supposedly Turcophile French.

The upshot of the new falling out over boundaries was a decision to shunt the problem off on the conference's favorite whipping boy, President Wilson. On April 24, when Lloyd George proposed that the United States be asked to accept the mandate, Millerand suggested that, whether or not the offer of the mandate was accepted, the President should be asked to fix the limits of the state. The French Premier's proposal was confined to the question of the boundary in the vilayet of Erzerum[100] but it was quickly extended to include the entire Turkish-Armenian border. Wilson's discretion was not to be unlimited, for the Turkish portion of the Armenian state could only be taken from the four vilayets of Van, Bitlis, Erzerum, and Trebizond.[101]

It was unfortunate that French designs on three of the six vilayets to which the Armenians had the strongest claim should have made it necessary to substitute Trebizond, whose majority was Turk and whose largest minority was Greek. Nonetheless, in the light of anticipated Armenian population, the size of the proposed state was realistic. Whatever its defects, it could offer the Armenians a chance for self-determination if the United States could be induced to throw its strength and prestige behind it.

[99] See above, page 74.
[100] *BDFP*, 1st ser., VIII, 145.
[101] *Foreign Relations of the United States 1920*, III, 779-781.

The Allied note was forwarded to Secretary of State Colby on April 28. On May 17 he accepted for the President the task of arbitrator for the Armenian boundary[102] and on May 24 Wilson asked permission of the Senate to accept the mandate.

[102] *Ibid.*, III, 783.

10

The Mandate in the Senate

*T*HROUGHOUT THE FALL, winter, and spring of 1919-1920 the American government was besieged by resolutions and appeals on behalf of Armenia that numbered in the thousands, it may be in the hundreds of thousands. These came from individual citizens and from organizations of all kinds, many of them of a religious or charitable nature. The House of Bishops of the Protestant Episcopal Church, for example, petitioned the President and Senate from its assembly in Detroit on October 18, 1919, urging "the acceptance of a mandate for Armenia, if it be offered this country, as an opportunity for unselfish service in restoration of the peace of the world."[1] The Near East Relief Society at its convention in New York on October 15, 1919 petitioned Congress for relief of "100,000 Christian and Jewish women and girls held captive in the harems . . . of the former Ottoman Empire, forced to live in suffering and degradation far worse than death."[2]

[1] *CR*, 66th Congress, 1st Session, LVIII, 7353.
[2] *Ibid.*, 7107.

Senator John Sharp Williams of Mississippi presented the resolution of the Near East Relief Society to the Senate. He also presented resolutions from the American Board of Commissioners for Foreign Missions at their annual meeting in Grand Rapids on October 23, 1919, urging action to protect the people of Armenia, whose very existence was threatened,[3] and of the Armenian National Union of America on October 27, 1919, asking "the adoption of such resolutions as shall afford to the Armenian people immediate protection."[4] As for James W. Gerard and the American Committee for the Independence of Armenia, their appeals were constant and made use of all media; they were now asking, however, for complete independence with American help. They had turned against the mandate in the previous December, believing the territory allowed to Armenia under such an agreement would be too small. Magazines and newspapers were uniformly sympathetic to Armenia,[5] although not all of their comments were favorable to the mandate.

As the meetings of the European Allies in the spring of 1920 brought the issue closer to a showdown, agitation for the Armenians continued at a high level of intensity. On April 2 an appeal for the mandate signed by President Mary E. Woolley and 581 members of the faculty and student body of Mount Holyoke College was sent to the President, the President of the Senate, and the Speaker of the House.[6] James L. Barton told the *New York Times* we would be assuming the role of Pontius Pilate if we refused.[7]

If the approaching decision stimulated support, it also increased re-

---

[3] *Ibid.*, 7867. On October 24 the same resolution was voted by the National Council of Congregational Churches.

[4] *Ibid.*

[5] In all of the American periodical literature I have seen, the only article even moderately favorable to the Turks was written by an Englishman, P. Edmonds, a soldier who had been imprisoned by them. *The World Outlook*, VI, (January, 1920), 9.

[6] *New York Times*, April 3, 1920, 20. The language of this appeal is strongly reminiscent of that of General Harbord's report which the President sent to the Senate the following day.

[7] *Ibid.*, April 5, 1920, 4.

sistance. Herbert Hoover, whose prestige was so high that he was considered by both parties as a candidate for the presidency, reiterated his opposition in April.[8] Although Hoover objected to the expense of a mandate, that was not the principal ground of his hostility. He feared inevitable involvement in the politics of the Old World and the loss of our moral standing that would follow such involvement. Here he was on ground from which he could appeal to large numbers of Americans whose emotional commitment to non-involvement included a strain of fervent belief that ours was a morally superior nation.

Many other leaders, although willing to help Armenia in other ways (usually not specified), were opposed to accepting the mandate. Nor can we overlook the judgment of Undersecretary Polk that the American people as a whole were not interested.[9] The volume of appeals proves that a large number were deeply concerned; it does not prove they were more numerous than those who weren't concerned. In any case, we must conclude that even if the majority favored the mandate, it did not favor it with that fervor which characterized either those who fought hard for it or those who bitterly opposed it. 1920 was an election year. The Republicans could hardly have escaped chastisement at the polls in the fall if they had voted contrary to the strong conviction of the mass of the people.

In the absence of such a strong conviction the decision was up to the Congress.[10] The action of the Senate at least could hardly be in doubt. We have seen that Englishmen in a position to know believed unanimously that the Senate would do nothing. There was further evidence in the adverse vote on the treaty with Germany in November and again in March, for it was the inclusion of the Covenant of

[8] *Ibid.*, April 11, 1920, 18.

[9] Polk to Bristol, June 3, 1920. Polk Papers, dr. 78, f. 71.

[10] The constitutional question whether it was up to the Senate alone under its power to reject or ratify treaties is not considered here. Wilson sent his request to both houses and each assigned it to the appropriate committee. The House ultimately did not act upon it but only because it chose to consider the adverse vote of the Senate as effectively defeating the proposal, not because it thought the matter exceeded its powers.

the League of Nations in that treaty that caused its defeat. Would a body which was unwilling to become a member of the League consider accepting responsibility for another nation under the League's authority? There had also been a consistent failure to act on resolutions in favor of Armenia,[11] none of which had gone so far as to mention a mandate.

There had been bitter complaints that on this as on other matters the President had failed to keep the Senate informed.[12] Above all, the rift between the executive and the Senate had not closed with the passing months. It had probably widened. The Republicans, emboldened by two major victories in foreign policy, were in no mood for anything short of total triumph.

The President sent the Harbord Report to the Senate on April 3, 1920, "several months after it ceased to have any practical value," as the *New York Times* complained editorially. It had been evident for some time, the editors maintained,

> . . . that we are cutting ourselves off from any participation in the Near Eastern settlement; . . . perhaps that is right, perhaps it is wrong; at any rate, the Senate and the public could have formed opinions on the basis of better information if it had been given out long ago, and if the Crane-King report on the Near East, which still slumbers in executive retirement, had been given out also.[13]

The only successful resolution (SR 359), introduced by Republican Senator Warren G. Harding of Ohio, passed the Senate on May 13, 1920. It extended congratulations to the Republic of Armenia on its recognition as a state, expressed good wishes for its future and rec-

---

[11] In addition to the resolutions mentioned in the last chapter, which had been tabled during the previous session, the Senate failed to act on two resolutions introduced by Senator William H. King, Democrat of Utah, which called for help, including military help, for Armenia.

[12] See, for example, Senator Frank B. Brandegee, Republican of Connecticut, on October 17, 1919. Senator King, who opposed Brandegee on the Armenian issue, agreed with him that the Senate did not have enough information. *CR*, 66th Cong., 2nd Sess., LXIX, 7051-7054.

[13] *New York Times*, April 6, 1920, 10.

ommended the despatch of an American warship to Batum with Marines to guard the railroad to Baku for the protection of American property. Harding told the Senate this was only the "ostensible" reason for the action; its "real object" was "to guarantee for Armenia the maintenance of a communication to Erivan through Batum."[14]

On May 24, following receipt of the request from San Remo, President Wilson sent a message to both houses of Congress asking permission to accept the mandate for the United States. Alluding to the Harding resolution which he had recently signed, he wrote:

> I cannot but regard it as providential, and not as a mere coincidence, that almost at the same time I received information that the conference of statesmen now sitting at San Remo . . . had formally resolved to address a definite appeal to this Government to accept a mandate for Armenia.

He had also been asked personally to fix the Turkish-Armenian boundary and had thought it his duty to take on "this difficult and delicate task." He recognized that he was facing the Congress with a critical decision, but again felt it his duty to do so.

> I know from unmistakable evidences given by responsible representatives of many peoples struggling towards independence and peaceful life again that the Government of the United States is looked to with extraordinary trust and confidence, and I believe it would do nothing less than arrest the hopeful processes of civilization if we were to refuse the request to become the helpful friends and advisers of such of these people as we may be authoritatively and formally requested to guide and assist.

The message closed with an appeal to the Christian sentiments of the American people.[15]

The temptation to throw the Senate's own resolution in its face while asking for some tangible evidence of the good will so freely offered the Armenians must have been strong and, in view of the

---

[14] *CR*, 66th Cong., 2nd Sess., LXIX, 6978.
[15] *Ibid.*, 7533-7534.

record of the 66th Congress, it is hard to blame Wilson for yielding to it. Nonetheless, the association of the President with providence could hardly fail to evoke memories of earlier controversies; if it had any effect at all, it must have been to stiffen resistance. It was also a mistake to word the appeal in such a way as to suggest that other struggling nations had the same claim as Armenia on our guidance and protection. There was a better chance of persuading Americans to abandon the tradition of more than a century if Armenia was represented as a special case—as in truth it was—than as the first of a series of undertakings of unspecified duration in unspecified localities.

As if the antagonism of the Senate was not affliction enough for the President, he now found himself in dubious battle with the powerful American Committee for the Independence of Armenia, which had upheld him in the past. In a message to the Senate Committee on Foreign Relations, Gerard pointed out that the President was empowered to draw the Turkish-Armenian border only within the vilayets of Trebizond, Erzerum, Van and Bitlis. He accused the French and British of taking away Armenia's most fertile provinces—Kharput, Sivas, Diarbekir, and Cilicia. If this was what a mandate meant, he preferred outright independence with "full rights of nationhood."[16]

The *Times'* editorial of May 26 conceded that the measure had no chance and commented scathingly on the success with which some of the participants in the controversy had brought discredit on all generous impulses:

> Not everyone would go so far as the Borah-Johnson group, who would have us believe that the Good Samaritan was a fool to run the risk of being blackjacked and robbed by the man he befriended, but our vehement patriots have managed to attach a moral stigma to anything that looks like disinterested aid to others. And they control Congress.

Looking for any good effects that might be anticipated from in-

16 *New York Times*, May 26, 1920, 2.

evitable defeat, the editors could find none for Armenia. "If there is to be any salvation for Armenia," they predicted, "it must come from Russia; that is years in the future." However, "one really good result" might be hoped for in America.

> Our evident unwillingness to live up to our expressions of
> Christian sympathy will, it may be hoped, abate in some degree
> our conviction that we are the most moral, altruistic, and benef-
> icent people on the face of the earth.[17]

On the same day Congressman William E. Mason of Illinois introduced a resolution in the form of fifteen questions for President Wilson (HR 570). Some of them were sensible enough. The Congress had a right to know what boundaries were in dispute between Armenia and its neighbors, how great our military commitment could be expected to be, and how troops were to be raised. Others were tendentious in the extreme. Mason asked for an estimate of the number of men necessary in case of war with Turkey, with Russia, and with Turkey and Russia at the same time. He inquired whether our soldiers were to be used as laborers as they had been in Russia and Siberia, or as policemen, as in Germany. What arrangements had been made for the return of "our soldier dead who may lose their lives in Armenia?" Had the President made an effort to exchange mandates with Great Britain so as to give the oil fields of Persia to us and Armenia to the British? (Obviously any claim the British might have on the Persian oil fields was not derived from a mandate.) Finally, if the President were granted power to accept a mandate, would he be governed "by the so-called covenant for a League of Nations . . . rejected by the Senate of the United States . . . or by the Constitution and laws of the United States?" The questions, by no means untypical of much Congressional opposition to Wilson, were followed by a choice selection of historical quotations, headed, it need hardly be said, by an excerpt from Washington's Farewell Address.[18]

---

[17] *Ibid.*, 10.

[18] *CR*, 66th Cong., 2nd Sess., LXIX, 9094.

Defections appeared even in the ranks of the loyal Democrats. Senator Gilbert M. Hitchcock of Nebraska, the minority floor leader, announced that he would not support the mandate; it was believed that other Democrats would also refuse to do so.[19] In the face of such apostasy the unanimous opinion in favor of a mandate which was conveyed from the Methodist Episcopal General Conference at Des Moines was a rather feeble blow on the President's side.[20]

On May 27 the Foreign Relations Committee voted eleven to four to report the proposal unfavorably.[21] On May 29 its chairman, Senator Henry Cabot Lodge of Massachusetts, the majority floor leader and Wilson's bitter foe, offered a resolution (SCR 27) declining to give the executive power to accept the mandate.[22]

There was little disposition to indulge in a prolonged debate on the resolution. May 29 was a Saturday; the Senate, particularly on the Republican side, was eager to recess by the following Saturday in order to be on hand in Chicago for the opening of the Republican National Convention on Tuesday, June 8. Lodge, therefore, asked for an early vote. He wanted to know if a date for voting could be agreed upon by Monday if the matter were allowed to go over until then. Hitchcock was a bit hesitant, explaining that, although he intended to vote against the mandate, he was reluctant to do so by voting for a resolution which, as it stood, could only have the effect of disheartening the Armenians and encouraging their enemies. He therefore intended to propose an amendment providing for a joint American-Armenian committee to issue and sell bonds for Armenia in the United States. As he believed his amendment needed more work, he did not want the vote rushed.[23]

Lodge replied by presenting various statements from Armenian authorities which he had received through Gerard and in which the

19 *New York Times*, May 27, 1920, 1.

20 *Ibid.*, 6. The Methodists' resolution was cited by Senator Robinson in the ensuing debate. *CR*, 66th Cong., 2nd Sess., LXIX, 8056.

21 *New York Times*, May 30, 1920, 1.

22 *CR*, 66th Cong., 2nd Sess., LXIX, 7714.

23 *Ibid.*, 7875.

needs of the country were detailed. These included food and finance and political help in their relations with the great powers or the Supreme Council; no mention was made of a mandate. The Republican floor leader was cordial toward Hitchcock and his proposal and apparently anxious to assure him that the door would not be closed to all help for Armenia if the United States refused to assume a mandate.[24] He may have been trying to guard against a last-minute rallying of the Democrats, for while he did not need their vote to win, a substantial defection from the President's party would be helpful in burying the issue.

When John Sharp Williams asked to make a statement, Lodge, still cordial, readily assented. The Mississippian announced that he was ready to vote right away. He acknowledged that he was in a very small minority and was going to be beaten, but he saw no reason for backing away from the issue. In a strong plea for acceptance of responsibility, he went beyond the plight of Armenia to arraign the prevailing attitude of postwar America:

> I for one do not see how my country can take itself out of
> the world. It is a part of it and the earth now is a very narrow
> place, with its aeroplanes and its wireless and all the other
> things which bring its peoples close together. Even if it were
> advisable to *be* off the earth, we can not *get* off it, nor can we
> escape and shirk the burdens and responsibilities of a situation
> while we accept all of its advantages.[25]

A fellow-Democrat who was not ready to vote was Andreius A. Jones of New Mexico. He charged that the Foreign Relations Committee had not done enough work on the question or at least had not brought in a report embodying the results of its work. He argued that under Article 22 of the Covenant it was possible to define a mandate as limited to "administrative advice and assistance," a point the committee had not considered.[26] Although this opinion recurred

24 *Ibid.*, 7876.
25 *Ibid.*, 7877.
26 *Ibid.*, 7888.

during the debate, it is hard to see that the committee was at fault in not considering it. However acceptable it might have been as an interpretation of Article 22, it had no relation to the debate over Armenia.

By this time the floodgates were open and Lodge's efforts to set the question aside until Monday were unavailing. Senator Hoke Smith of Georgia delivered an attack on the President's proposal from the Democratic side that was not excelled in exhaustiveness nor perhaps in acidulous phraseology by any Republican in the subsequent debate—although Brandegee of Connecticut and Borah of Idaho were hard men to beat in the application of acid. Smith outlined the five arguments against the mandate which the debates of May 31 and June 1 merely reiterated:

1) The proposition was ambiguous because no one knew exactly what Armenia was.

2) It was ambiguous because no one knew exactly what a mandate was.

3) There was no authority under the Constitution to tax Americans for altruistic service to other peoples nor to send an American army to protect one people against another.

4) Americans were being swindled by the slick British and French who had "taken the rich oil wells and copper mines." (Senator Lodge had said earlier the same day: "There are three banks and a poorhouse over there, and we have been given the poorhouse.")[27]

5) The assumption of responsibility for Armenia would commit us to the acceptance of other similar obligations. In reply to his fellow-Democrat Charles S. Thomas of Colorado who had asked if, having agreed to the Armenian mandate, we could decline others, Smith said probably not. When Thomas asked if, on the principle that charity begins at home, we should not assume a mandate for Mexico—which would have been impossible under Article 22—Smith re-

---

[27] *Ibid.*, 7889. Lodge made no claim to have originated this *mot*, nor did Senator Irvine Lenroot (R.-Wis.) who had used it in a speech at New York on May 20. *New York Times*, May 21, 1920, 4.

torted: "The objection to a mandate over Mexico is that it is so near home it might contribute to the welfare of our own people."[28]

When debate was resumed on Monday, Hitchcock brought forward his amendment providing for the sale of Armenian bonds in the United States.[29] Following this, James A. Reed of Missouri took the floor to deliver what was probably the most virulent speech of the entire debate. One of the Democratic irreconcilables who had joined with the Republicans to defeat the League of Nations, Reed began by calling attention to the widespread protest among Moslems against domination by the west. He had been reading Lothrop Stoddard's *The Rising Tide of Color* and was full of the subject. (He had perhaps not noticed that a large percentage of Moslems, including all of them in the vicinity of Armenia, were white.) He argued that since Armenia cut the Moslem world in two—surely an exaggeration if it was to be restricted to four vilayets and Erivan—the United States would have to fight against Moslems.

Turning to the Harbord Report he noted that the Armenians themselves had been guilty of massacres:

So that it is a case of eastern barbarism on both sides, each
of them responding to the hate of centuries, each of them pur-
suing the same methods and tactics. Over this cesspool of
criminality, of cruelty, of villainy, of race hatred the United
States is asked to assume control, and to do it because the countries that have, speaking broadly, stolen the lands of these
people all over the world decline to take control because it is
expensive.

Disclaiming any racial feelings of his own, Reed declared that if the Armenians were what they ought to be—again "speaking broadly"—"the things that have occurred never would have happened."[30]

On June 1, the date fixed for a vote, Senator Thomas asserted that the Turks within the boundaries of Armenia would want religious

---

[28] *CR*, 66th Cong., 2nd Sess., LXIX, 7889-7890.
[29] *Ibid.*, 7964.
[30] *Ibid.*, 7967-7970.

liberty which the Armenians wouldn't want to grant them. If this was so, it was a good argument for establishing a mandate rather than a completely independent Armenia (which was in any case a will-o-the-wisp), but Thomas declared he was in sympathy with the Armenians and would vote for "any measure short of control."[31] In other words, having pointed to a frustration of the Turkish desire for religious freedom as a source of trouble, he announced his willingness to vote for anything that would not oblige the Armenians to give it to them.

Senator Joseph T. Robinson of Arkansas replied to Reed with a moving appeal to humanity and reason. He referred to the sympathy and support for the Armenians which had manifested itself in the Senate only two weeks before with the passage of the Harding Resolution, defective though it was. He preferred a mandate, whatever its difficulties, to the kind of military intervention called for by that resolution. He deplored the kind of equivocation that was willing to aid Armenians only under the guise of securing American property. He favored the amendment offered by Senator King which called for the United States to enter agreements with our allies for help to the Armenians.

He called Reed to account for condemning the Armenians because they had submitted to persecution and equally because they had fought back. To the charge that they were somehow at fault for the things that had happened to them, he replied succinctly: "Mr. President, the Armenians are arraigned in the Senate because they have been massacred." Getting to the heart of the matter, Robinson summed up his position:

I do not justify the demand here presented for assistance to the Armenians . . . solely on the ground that they are a Christian and a long-suffering people. I justify it as well on the ground of political morale and common decency. We encouraged them to enlist under the banner of the Allies . . . Not by the rules of mercy and humanity alone but by the law of justice, the Arme-

. [31] *Ibid.*, 8052-8053.

nians are entitled to protection at the hands of other Christian
peoples. Armenian men are entitled to live and toil. Armenian
women are entitled to immunity from outrage. . . . The one
reward which the surviving Armenians claim is the right to
live, to enjoy religious freedom and civil independence.[32]

Senator Brandegee took the floor to reiterate the charge that the
language of the President's message would oblige us to accept a mandate not only over Armenia "but for any other people."[33] His speech
was distinguished by the sudden outbreak of a demonstration for
Ireland which was quelled only by the expulsion of a number of persons from the galleries.

Senator Medill McCormick, Republican of Illinois, wanted to know
why Mesopotamia was not being given to the United States, if we
were a disinterested people suitable for guiding the freed populations
of Asia. Why not Jerusalem if we were the protectors of Christians?
He predicted bloodshed if the President had his way:

If we put our hand to the plow now, we can never turn back. We
shall plow the furrow which will be sown with salt and fertilized
in the blood of our young men. The tender of this mandate
brings home the reality behind the irridescent vision of the
League of Nations.[34]

McCormick was representative of the opposition to the President
in his fear of a major military involvement, although he expressed
it in somewhat more purple prose than the others. It was a genuine
fear, but it is not certain that it was justified. While the Turks probably would have fought the whole world for Smyrna, it is at least
doubtful that they would have fought the United States for the rather
restricted Armenia of the King-Crane Report. Much of the disturb-
ance in and around Armenia was sustained by the shrewd percep-
tion of Armenia's neighbors that none of the great powers was going
to act with any determination to stop it. The arguments of the ma-

[32] *Ibid.*, 8053-8055.
[33] *Ibid.*, 8056.
[34] *Ibid.*, 8060.

jority were open to attack on this point, yet only Senator Williams predicted that "the mere presence of the American uniform would very nearly, if not quite, settle the issue."[35]

Similarly the Democrats failed almost entirely to attack their opponents' persistent misuse of the estimates of the cost of the mandate in the Harbord Report. Senator Thomas J. Walsh, Democrat of Montana, charged in the closing hours of the debate that estimates intended to cover all of Asiatic and European Turkey were being applied by the opposition to Armenia alone. Although some copies of the report were available and it had been ordered printed in the *Congressional Record* of May 29, Walsh may not have seen it when he prepared his remarks. He had apparently only become aware of the misuse of the figures through an article by Stephen Bonsal in the *Baltimore Sun* of May 30. Bonsal, a member of the American Commission to Negotiate Peace, had written, on the authority of one of General Harbord's associates in the mission, that estimates for Armenia alone had been made but were not included in the report. According to these, the mandate would require 10,000 men and $14,000,000 rather than 59,000 men and $84,000,000 as charged by the Republicans. Moreover, even the $14,000,000 estimate assumed the country would produce no revenue of its own.[36]

The weakness of the Democratic position was dramatically exposed by Attlee Pomerene, Democrat of Ohio, who reminded the Republicans that the blood of the Armenians would be on the head of the American government if we refused to help them and then announced that he would vote against the mandate. The proposal was too vague, he said, and should go back to committee.[37]

As the time for a vote was approaching, Hitchcock moved to send the resolution and all amendments back to committee. He charged the matter had been reported out after the briefest of deliberations. The attitude of the committee had been one of "peremptory refusal." He echoed complaints by Walsh and others that no information was

35 *Ibid.*, 7877.
36 *Ibid.*, 8064.
37 *Ibid.*, 8062.

available to the Senate which would make a vote possible.[38] This was
too much for Senator Williams, who had been silent since his statement of the previous Saturday. He rose angrily to remind his colleagues that sending the question back to committee meant delaying
action a full six months since the Congress would not meet after
adjournment until the first Monday in December:

> Mr. President, it is out of all reason, it is out of all courtesy,
> it is out of all comity of nations, that the United States should
> receive, through its Executive, from the great civilized powers
> of the world an international invitation and deliberately send
> it to a committee to sleep "until after the conventions."[39]

It is doubtful that many of the Republicans shared the Senator's
delicacy of feeling toward the great civilized powers of the world,
but they were equally determined not to send the resolution back to
committee. Knowing they had the votes and believing they had the
country with them, they wanted to dispose of the question before the conventions. The motion was defeated by forty-three nays
to thirty-four yeas.[40]

Brandegee, who had been one of the most vitriolic enemies of the
mandate, then sought to embarrass the Democrats by introducing a
resolution to accept it. Since a vote against Lodge's resolution could
later be defended on the ground that the objector didn't like its word-
ing or wanted more study of the subject, Brandegee, by calling for a
vote on acceptance rather than rejection, was challenging the Democrats who really wanted the mandate to stand up and say so. Twelve
of them did and were snowed under by sixty-two nays.[41]

Hitchcock's amendment providing for the sale of Armenian bonds
was next to come to a vote and was rejected by forty-one to thirty-

---

[38] *Ibid.*, 8069.

[39] *Ibid.*

[40] *Ibid.*, 8070.

[41] "It is offered, as he frankly states, for the purpose of putting someone in the
hole." Walsh (Montana) in debate of June 1, 1920. *Ibid.*, 8064. For the vote
on Brandegee's resolution see *Ibid.*, 8071.

four.[42] Another offered by Senator Key Pittman, Democrat of Nevada, to provide advice and assistance without military commitment, was rejected by a voice vote. Senator King's resolution (SCR 29), offered as an amendment, to provide protection for Armenia in cooperation with the other powers failed of acceptance by forty-six to twenty-eight.[43]

With all the amendments disposed of, the original resolution was moved and carried by fifty-two to twenty-three.[44] The mandate was dead in time for the conventions.

Senator Lodge had written to Henry White on August 19 of the preceding year: "Do not think I do not feel badly about Armenia. I do, but I think there is a limit to what they have a right to put off on us."[45] He must have felt with satisfaction that the limit had been reached and not passed.

Polk summed up the situation for Bristol in a letter of June 3:

Congress would not do a blessed thing. . . . Of course, the President's suggestion in regard to a mandate for Armenia was hopeless to my mind, from the start, as Congress was entirely against it and the American people more than indifferent. At least he was honest. The proposal of the Senate to send a warship to Batum with sufficient landing force to keep the railroad open was not even a respectable relief and must have caused no end of amusement at Constantinople, that is, if they pay any attention at all to what we do.

He ended his letter with a hope that a strong Russia would grow up and meet Near Eastern problems "directly and honestly, which is more than you can say for what has been done up to date."[46] In two weeks the mover of the resolution which was "not even a respectable relief" had been designated by the Republicans as Wilson's succes-

---

42 *Ibid.*, 8072.
43 *Ibid.*, 8073.
44 *Ibid.*
45 Nevins, *op. cit.*, 466.
46 Polk Papers, dr. 78, f. 71.

sor. The Russians, without waiting to grow up, regained control of Transcaucasian Armenia in less than a year.

At Chicago the Republicans reaffirmed their opposition to the mandate. After condemning Wilson for asking the Congress for it, the platform declared that its acceptance "would throw the United States into the very maelstrom of European quarrels." It then misapplied General Harbord's cost estimates as the party's speakers had done in the Senate and on the basis of this misuse charged that "no more striking illustration can be found of President Wilson's disregard of the lives of American boys or American interests." The platform stated in conclusion:

> We deeply sympathize with the people of Armenia and stand
> ready to help them in all proper ways, but the Republican Party
> will oppose now and hereafter the acceptance of a mandate
> for any country in Europe or Asia.[47]

The Democrats were as far from advocating the acceptance of a mandate, but instead of trumpeting their opposition defiantly as the Republicans had done, they called as little attention to it as possible. This is the best the President's party could do for the nation Americans had believed only a few years before to be more in need of self-determination than any other:

> We express our deep and earnest sympathy for the unfortunate
> people of Armenia, and we believe that our Government, con-
> sistent with its Constitution and principles, should render
> every possible and proper aid to them in their efforts to establish
> and maintain a Government of their own.[48]

The plank would have been quite different if the Platform Committee and the Convention had heeded a last-minute appeal from the President. A few hours before leaving for the convention, Secretary of the Treasury Carter Glass called at the White House. As he was on the point of leaving, Wilson handed him a slip of paper, saying: "I wish you would get this into the platform."

[48] *Ibid.*, July 3, 1920, 4.
[47] *New York Times*, June 11, 1920, 3.

Glass opened the paper on the train to discover that the suggested plank dealt with Armenia. Typed by the President himself and initialed W.W., it read:

> We hold it to be the Christian duty and privilege of our Government to assume responsible guardianship of Armenia which now needs only the advice and assurance of a powerful friend to establish her complete independence and to give her distracted people the opportunities for peaceful happiness which they have vainly longed for through so many dark years of hopeless suffering and hideous distress.[49]

Glass, who fought hard and successfully for the plank approving the Covenant of the League of Nations, admitted that Democratic opposition to the President's Armenian policy was "overwhelming."[50]

---

[49] Note of June 19, 1920 by Carter Glass, cited in Rixey Smith and Norman Beasley, *Carter Glass: A Biography* (New York and Toronto: Longmans, Green & Co., 1939), 208-209.

[50] Stephen Bonsal, *Suitors and Suppliants: The Little Nations at Versailles* (New York: Prentice-Hall, Inc., 1946), 197.

$\mathcal{D}$ecline and $\mathcal{F}$all

O N M A Y 3 0 James W. Gerard addressed a mass meeting to
celebrate the second anniversary of Armenian independence at Carnegie Hall. Assuming the defeat of the mandate was inevitable, he
called for the President to use executive authority to aid and protect
Armenia, citing as precedents the American relation to Liberia and
the action of President Taft in Chile in 1912.[1]

Equally undaunted, the government of the Republic of Armenia
wrote to its legation in Washington on June 10 expressing confidence
that President Wilson would support the just cause of Armenia and
would define such boundaries as would assure political and economic
life to the state. It directed the legation to call attention to certain
needs of the republic, such as munitions and supplies for an army of
50,000 men (up by two-thirds since January), a small international
force to fight beside the Armenians, and the setting aside of perhaps

[1] *New York Times,* May 31, 1920, 18.

$200,000 from the indemnities paid by the Central Powers, to be used for repatriation of the Armenians.[2]

These are symptoms, among many, of a substantial pressure in favor of Armenia which was to go on for several years.[3] Unfortunately, these good people were merely whistling as they passed the graveyard. So far as the United States officially was concerned, although it would have taken a brave man in either party to say so, Armenia was dead. The Congress would not only accept no mandate, but it would not, as Polk had expressed it, "do a blessed thing." Without the consent of Congress, Wilson believed he could not send the necessary troops to Armenia nor appropriate money for the use of the Armenians. He was, in fact, left with the melancholy privilege of defining boundaries for a state which had very little chance of existence.

The Armenians had only two hopes left—the League of Nations and France. The League might admit Armenia to membership; if so, the protection that could not be provided under Article 22, since no state would take a mandate, could be furnished to Armenia as a member state under Article 10. If this failed, France was still holding Cilicia and was expected to continue to hold it. Some Armenians had been repatriated at the expense of the French taxpayers, who would probably be willing to bring in more refugees if other members of the League would help to defray expenses.

One thing that offered no help at all, although played out with elaborate seriousness, was the Treaty of Sèvres, by which the Allies finally made peace with Turkey.[4] Signed on August 10, 1920, it obliged the Turks to agree to the creation of an Armenian state along the lines laid down at San Remo. This was but one of the many terms dictated to the losers, who showed no signs of complying with them. At the

[2] NA, State Department 860J.01/407.

[3] The State Department records in the National Archives contain 603 communications about Armenia from individuals, churches, and organizations between the dates of November 19, 1920 and February 12, 1922. Impressive as this figure is, it is far from presenting the full picture since it is not likely that it includes all correspondence received by members of Congress. The letters to the editor of the New York Times are another clue to the persistence of interest in Armenia.

[4] British and Foreign State Papers, 1920, 652-776.

same time France, Great Britain, and Italy signed a tripartite agreement which divided Turkey into spheres of economic interest.[5] The Turks were not even consulted about it.

The treaty, running to more than a hundred pages of printed text and dealing with everything imaginable down to the ferryboats on the Bosphorus, was an egregious piece of mummery. The Italian government was so little in sympathy with the instrument to which it was putting its hand that Count Sforza, the foreign minister, made a point of speaking generously of the Turks in the Chamber on the day before the signing.[6] The French, concerned with their investments and with their position in Syria, were not at all averse to coming to terms with the Turks.[7] The British were at last preparing to evacuate Batum.

The Nationalist movement had, in the meanwhile, become in effect the government of Turkey. In spite of the opinion at London and San Remo that Ankara and Constantinople were in collusion, the Sultan's government had actually made an attempt to oppose Kemal's forces in the spring of 1920. It was the last. In April the Sultan dissolved the parliament. In the same month the Grand National Assembly met in Ankara for the first time. No doubt there was still some support for the official government but it lost whatever effectiveness it may have had by accepting the humiliating treaty. By fall the Nationalists were in virtual command of the country internally and ready to move against the Armenians who had occupied the coal mines at Olti while the Turks were busy fighting the French further south. Moreover, the Turks no longer stood alone against the might of the victorious Allies. The alliance with the Bolshevist government of Russia, although not formalized until the following March, was to all intents and purposes already in effect.

[5] Ibid., 797-803.

[6] Mandelstam, La Société des Nations et les puissances devant le problème arménien (Paris: A. Pedone, 1925), 158.

[7] Mandelstam, (Ibid., 177) wrote that the treaty was "plutôt subi qu'accepté" by both France and Italy. Briand insisted in the Chamber of Deputies on July 25, 1920 that France had no right to evacuate Cilicia (L'Asie française, CLXXXIV, 241) but it is doubtful that any of the Allies took him seriously.

The new friendship for Russia was in no sense ideological. Geoffrey Lewis has made that clear in relating the "curious episode of the two Communist Parties in Turkey."

> The first of these was founded in May 1920, by a number of members of the Grand National Assembly, acting on orders from Mustafa Kemal. It had no connection with the Third International and engaged in no political activity; its sole purpose was to show the Russians how friendly the new Turkey was to the ideas of the new Russia. The second Communist Party of Turkey was founded two months later. It was affiliated to the Third International and aimed at establishing an orthodox dictatorship of the proletariat. Its activities were abruptly terminated by the Independence Tribunals in 1921. In July 1922, when the Nationalists were certain of victory over the Greeks, all Communist activity was proscribed. For Mustafa Kemal never swerved from his aim: Turkey was to become a Western State, a European state; France and Britain were his models, not Russia.[8]

The Russians were more troubled by the ideological discrepancies between the two movements, particularly when backing Kemal meant helping to suppress Turkish communism, but, like the Turks, they recognized that they could not stand alone against the west.[9]

On September 13 Turkish armies invaded Armenia, demanding the return of Kars and Ardahan, ceded to Turkey in the Treaty of Brest-Litovsk but occupied by the Armenians. The latter countered by two appeals to the League of Nations—to the Assembly for admission to membership and to the Council, sitting in Brussels, for defense of Armenia and enforcement of the Treaty of Sèvres.

Neither of these pleas came to anything. The Assembly, acting on the recommendation of its Fifth Committee, rejected Armenia for membership because, as a former territory of the Russian Empire, it

---

[8] Geoffrey Lewis, *op. cit.*, 113.

[9] For a discussion of the alliance from the Russian point of view see Walter Z. Laqueur, *The Soviet Union and the Middle East* (New York: Frederick A. Praeger, 1959), 25-29.

was currently under the threat of reintegration by the Bolsheviks. Georgia, Lithuania, Latvia, and Esthonia were rejected for the same reason. The members of the committee could not see how the guarantees of Article 10 could be offered to those states, and despite an abortive effort by Lord Robert Cecil, representing South Africa, to bring them in without such guarantees, reported unfavorably on the applications.[10] The foreign ministers of the three European Allies intervened to throw their weight against the admission of Armenia in a note from London.[11] If anyone had had any doubt which way the great powers were preparing to jump, this action should have dispelled it.

The Council of the League heard the complaints of the Armenians the last week of October. It replied that the Treaty of Sèvres was not yet in force and in any case the powers which had signed it had the obligation to enforce it. The Council reminded the powers of the correspondence of March and April on the subject of Armenia and repeated its willingness to consult.[12]

When this reply was reported to the Assembly on November 20, various proposals were put forward. Their futility was summed up by the French delegate René Viviani who said: "We are a powerless Assembly, because we have been entrusted with a responsibility without having been given any real authority."[13] All that could be done, he said, was to find a power that would take the necessary measures to halt hostilities. He also seized the occasion to remind his colleagues that if the French proposal for an armed force under the command of the League of Nations had been adopted, they would not find themselves in such a frustrating position.

Following Viviani's suggestion an appeal went out to the nations to mediate. Response was meager. Spain expressed its readiness to "cooperate in any action of a moral and diplomatic nature." Brazil was

---

[10] League of Nations, *Records of the First Assembly: Meetings of the Committees*, 2 vols., II, 195-199.

[11] *BDFP*, 1st ser., VIII, 849.

[12] League of Nations, *Official Journal*, 1920, no. 8, 90.

[13] League of Nations, *Records of the First Assembly: Plenary Meetings*, 190.

willing to assist in "putting an end to Armenia's desperate position."
President Wilson, explaining that without the consent of Congress he
could not officially intervene in any way, offered his personal media-
tion.[14]

A far more interesting proposal, perhaps too farsighted to be acted
on favorably in the League's first session, was made by M. Jonnesco of
Rumania. He advocated that an international force of 40,000 men, to
be drawn proportionally from the member states, be sent to protect
the Armenians until peace could be restored. Rumania, he said, was
ready to provide its share of such an expeditionary force.[15]

The Assembly's sole action was a resolution of December 18, 1920
affirming its continued collaboration with the Council, which had
been empowered to "refer" to the members in the interests of Armenia,
and noting that

> . . . in response to the initiative taken by the League, universal
> sympathy has already been shown for Armenia, and that Ar-
> menia has received offers of mediation on her behalf from Presi-
> dent Wilson, Spain and Brazil.[16]

By the time this sonorous bromide had received the assent of the
delegates, the war was over. Armenia, badly beaten, was forced to sign
an armistice which left Kars and Ardahan under the control of the
Turkish Nationalists and the rest of the Republic in the hands of the
Russians.[17] As Bristol telegraphed to the Secretary of State on November 30: "Armenia is finished. . . . The Bolsheviks and Nationalist Turks
are in accord."[18] By early December Armenia had accepted not only
defeat but extinction: "It is officially announced at Erivan, December
2nd, that Armenia is declared Soviet republic."[19]

---

[14] League of Nations, *Official Journal*, 1920, no. 8, 92-93.

[15] League of Nations, *Records of the First Assembly: Plenary Meetings*, 672.

[16] *Ibid.*, 729.

[17] The brief military action in the fall of 1920 restored the pre-1878 boundary
between Russia and Turkey, which has remained in force until the present despite an attempt by Russia in 1946 to claim the districts of Kars and Ardahan
for Soviet Armenia.

[18] *Foreign Relations of the United States 1920*, III, 805.

[19] Moser, Consul at Tiflis, to Secretary of State, December 4, 1920. *Ibid.*, III, 806.

Wilson's boundary decision had been transmitted by Colby to the Allies on November 24; hence, although there was no longer an Armenian state, it was possible at last to know what its boundaries were. American experts had traced a workable line between Armenia and Turkey, taking into account both ethnic factors and those relating to the viability of the new nation.[20] The most controversial point was the inclusion of the port of Trebizond in Armenia. It was conceded in Wilson's message that the vilayet was predominantly Turkish and that the Christian minority was far more Greek than Armenian. However, the new state needed a port on the Black Sea and Trebizond was the only one available. The President expressed the hope that the Armenians would so conduct themselves that the inevitable minorities would work as hard for the success of the state as the Armenians themselves.

Having determined the boundaries of a nonexistent state, the President appointed former Ambassador Morgenthau as his personal representative to mediate a quarrel that had ended.[21]

The movement among the Allies to modify the Treaty of Sèvres, which had begun when they signed it, was gaining momentum. Venizelos had been defeated in the Greek elections and his government had resigned on November 14. King Constantine had again assumed control despite a warning from the Allied ministers meeting in London that his return would have an unfavorable effect on Greek relations with the Allies. The British therefore veered to the position the French and Italians had maintained virtually since the treaty was signed—that it should be revised. The Armenians would be sacrificed first.

It would be pointless as well as dispiriting to follow in detail the steps by which Armenia was scaled down from the free and inde-

[20] Wilson's decision and accompanying explanation in *Ibid.*, III, 789-804. The boundary as defined by Wilson appears to correspond closely to that recommended by the King-Crane Commission. The Wilson map will be found inside the back cover of the State Department publication cited above; a copy of the King-Crane is among Professor Yale's papers at Ann Arbor.

[21] *Ibid.*, III, 807.

pendent state of Article 88 of the Treaty of Sèvres to a small "national home" with a semi-autonomous status under a Turkish government, thence to a smaller "national home" around Lake Van with no government of its own but in which the Turks would allow them to speak and teach their own language, practice their own religion, and preserve their own culture, and finally in the Treaty of Lausanne to nothing at all. Since there was no longer any intention to force the Turks to accept an Armenian state, it matters little what it was called. Only Greece was still trying to force anything on the Turks and since May 15 of the previous year the efforts of the Greeks had made things worse for the Armenians.[22] Nor had they in any case a chance of prevailing over the Turks, for after the fall of Venizelos, British naval and military aid stopped while the French and Italians openly sided with the Turks.

Cilicia was the last hope for the Armenians and it will be seen from the foregoing that it was a feeble reed. As in Syria, the French had wanted the British out, but when Cilicia was turned over to their sole control, they failed to put in a force adequate to hold it against the Nationalists.[23] Their defeats at Marash and elsewhere had increased their eagerness to come to terms with their former enemies. While the Allies met again at London in the spring of 1921, Foreign Minister Briand concluded a pact with his Turkish counterpart, Bekir Sami Bey. Briand agreed that the French would withdraw their troops from Asia Minor and readjust the border with Syria in favor of the Turks in return for economic advantages in the exploitation of railroads and mines in Cilicia and the vilayets of Kharput, Sivas and Diarbekir. The French also attempted to provide for the safety of minorities by leaving some of their officers in charge of the police. Even this was too great an

---

[22] As an example of the disposition to sacrifice the Armenians to everyone else's blunders, it is interesting to note that the London Conference of 1921 took nothing of any significance from the Greeks but gave up entirely on an independent Armenian state. The stages of the decline of Allied claims for Armenia are admirably traced in Mandelstam *La Société des Nations et les puissances devant le problème arménien.*

[23] General Brémond's account (*La Cilicie en 1919-1920*) makes clear that French weakness, rather than Turkish strength, determined the failure to hold Cilicia.

infringement of Turkish sovereignty. The pact was rejected by the Grand National Assembly at Ankara. Bekir Sami Bey was obliged to resign and a new cabinet was formed. A Turkish-Italian agreement, also concluded at London, brought about the withdrawal of Italian forces from Adalia.

Succeeding months saw new fighting between Turkish and French troops north of Alexandretta from which the French were forced to retire. In the fall their representative Franklin-Bouillon was finally able to negotiate with Yusuf Kemal Bey, the new foreign minister, an agreement the Turks could accept. The Ankara Pact gave up on the protection of minorities altogether beyond an assurance by the Turks that they intended to live up to the terms of their own National Pact.[24]

It can hardly be doubted that France could have imposed its will on Turkey had the required number of troops been sent into Cilicia and backed by a determination to impose it. It was the will that was lacking. Nor was there any want of reasons why it should be. Four of them at least are fairly obvious:

1) As already suggested, the French interest was chiefly commercial. If the Turks, who were not in a position to develop their own resources, were willing to give priority to French companies, why offend them by a costly attempt to impose a political control that was not necessary for the exploitation of the region?

2) The French people had no such emotional attachment to Cilicia as to Syria. It was therefore possible for the government to sacrifice Cilicia to secure Syria. A constant struggle with Turkey would have jeopardized Syria; a friendly Turkey could guarantee the French position there.[25]

3) The French, like the Italians, were angered at the primacy of Great Britain in the award of mandates. To continue the struggle with

[24] *British and Foreign States Papers, 1921,* 771-773.

[25] The importance to France of Turkish friendship was demonstrated eighteen years later when the French ceded the sanjak of Alexandretta from Syria to Turkey on the eve of the Second World War. Needless to say, there was nothing in the League Covenant that empowered a mandatory to cede a portion of the mandated territory to a foreign state.

Turkey would be, they believed, merely sacrificing their own interests to those of the British.

4) France had made sacrifices in the World War second to none. The French people would not stand for further loss of life in a conflict in which no basic French interest was at stake.[26]

Whatever the reasons for it, the Ankara Pact had not only brought to an end all hope of resettling Armenians in Cilicia but produced a new exodus from that province. The status of minorities in Turkey had been restored to exactly what it had been before the war—a matter entirely at the discretion of the Turks. This does not mean that their sitation has been as bad under the Turkish Republic as it was in the late days of the empire. It remained deplorable so long as the Turks were fighting to rid their country of Greek invaders but after the Treaty of Lausanne it became much better and, in spite of some lapses, it has remained better than in some European states. The Nationalists were in earnest in their desire to westernize the country. They therefore approached the ideal of treating all citizens equally. The pusillanimity and false dealing of the Allies cannot, however, be excused on the ground that they foresaw a Turkish change of heart which would render their intervention unnecessary. With some honorable exceptions —Arnold J. Toynbee was one—the western attitude toward the "Kemalists" was that they were a gang of thugs. This view received frequent expression during the 1920's in the United States, particularly in connection with the debate over ratification of the American treaty with Turkey.

With the French collapse the Allied position crumbled rapidly until the final surrender at Lausanne.[27] Meeting in that city from November

---

[26] The will of the nation was invoked by the French ambassador in London, M. de Montille, in his reply of November 17, 1921, to Lord Curzon's complaints about the Ankara Pact. *British and Foreign State Papers, 1921*, 298-308. On December 7, 1921, Prime Minister Briand told Armenian representatives Aharonian and Noradunghian the French people would not support a war against the Turks in Cilicia. "From Sardarapat to Sèvres and Lausanne. Part VIII" in *The Armenian Review*, XVII, no. 4 (Winter 1964), 53.

[27] The British made a last-minute stand at Chanak on the Asiatic shore of the Dardanelles. Although deserted by their allies, they were prepared for battle to

20, 1922 to February 4, 1923 and again from April 23 to July 24, 1923, Turkish and Allied representatives wrote a treaty which reversed that of Sèvres in virtually every significant respect.[28]

The only territorial point which the Turks were obliged to concede was the province of Mosul, originally earmarked for France in the Sykes-Picot Agreement but conceded to Great Britain by Clemenceau in December 1918. As it contained some of the world's richest oil deposits, the Turkish argument that its Kurdish population belonged to Turkey had not the same cogency as their claim to the Armenian poorhouse. The British stood firm, Lord Curzon turned on a dazzling, if somewhat irrelevant, display of ethnological erudition —for if the Kurds weren't Turks, they certainly weren't Arabs either —and saved Mosul for Britain's Iraqi mandate. (The British position in Cyprus and Egypt was also conceded, but it was not in serious dispute.) The Greeks got none of the Turkish territory they had sought but were compensated by the annexation of Western Thrace which the American delegation had always wanted to award to Bulgaria. Armenia was compensated nowhere. As their leaders protested in a note to the powers on August 13, 1923, peace had been concluded "as if the Armenians did not exist at all."[29]

prevent the Turks, moving north after their victory at Smyrna, from entering the demilitarized zone of the Straits and attempting to take Constantinople. The cabinet was divided and the public showed little heart for a policy which could have meant war, not only with Turkey but with France as well. Fortunately, the Turks, after entering the demilitarized zone, withdrew the next day and France was persuaded to join Great Britain in negotiating an armistice at Mudania. The most immediate result of the crisis was the fall of Lloyd George's Coalition Government.

Some British writers have treated the stand at Chanak as something of a victory for Great Britain (e.g. Winston Churchill, its leading advocate in the cabinet). Their attitude is puzzling. In the face of Turkish resolve, French and Italian hostility, and strong opposition at home, the determination of the government may well seem courageous and even grand, but its grandeur arises purely from its gratuitous character. Churchill and his supporters were saying in effect to the Turks: "We will fight and shed blood to keep you from taking by force what we are now eager to give you by treaty."

[28] *British and Foreign State Papers, 1923*, I, 543-591.

[29] *New York Times*, September 12, 1923, 30. The final chapters of Harold Nicol-

Although our government was not a party to the Treaty of Lausanne and had been represented at the conference only by observers, it negotiated a separate treaty with the Turks in the same city.[30] Dealing with such matters as commercial concessions, capitulations, and the rights of foreign religious and educational institutions, it was signed on August 6. Turkey's Grand National Assembly ratified it promptly on August 23, but it ran into serious trouble in the United States. Those Americans who were still outraged by the failure to help Armenia seized on the pact as a new manifestation of the old issue and persuaded themselves that by opposing it they were somehow helping the Armenians. They attacked the treaty on various grounds, among them the surrender of the capitulations under which American missionaries had operated in Turkey for almost a century, but the chief complaint was that the Armenians would be "sold out" if the treaty were ratified.[31]

Nathaniel Peffer, a journalist later known for his work in China, answered this charge in two articles.[32] The Armenians, he wrote, had already been as thoroughly sold out as they could be. Further agitation of the issue would only impede current attempts of Turkish and Armenian leaders for reconciliation. The best thing that could happen

son's work on Curzon, in which Lausanne is represented as a diplomatic triumph for Curzon and the British, constitute one of the most curious productions I have encountered. They are explicable only on the assumption that Nicolson had come to consider France and Italy, rather than Turkey, as the enemy.

[30] *Foreign Relations of the United States, 1923*, II, 1153-1166. The American observers were Richard Washburn Child, Ambassador to Italy, Joseph C. Grew, Minister to Switzerland, and Admiral Bristol. Grew was responsible for negotiating the Turkish-American treaty.

[31] An unsuccessful attempt had been made by the American negotiators to insert a clause protecting the rights of minorities in Turkey. Joseph C. Grew, *Turbulent Era. A Diplomatic Record of Forty Years, 1904-1945*, 2 vols. (Boston: Houghton Mifflin Co., 1952), I, 588-589. Previously the American observers at the Lausanne Conference had assisted Americans interested in Armenia in placing a statement before the Conference. *Ibid.*, I, 524-525.

[32] "Armenians and the Lausanne Treaty," in the *New Republic*, XXXVII (February 20, 1924), 333-334; "Hands off Turkey!" in *Asia*, XXXIV (April 1924), 267-271.

to the Armenians, Peffer argued, would be for the west to leave them alone.

Such reasoning had no effect at all on Gerard and those who shared his view. Nor was it to be expected that it would entirely win over the Democrats who had seen their best efforts in the international realm destroyed by a rancorous Republican opposition in Congress. The battle continued in press and pulpit for three and a half years with Gerard, Senators William H. King and Claude Swanson, Charles W. Eliot of Harvard, former Secretaries of War Lindley M. Garrison and Newton D. Baker, Bishop William H. Manning of the Episcopal Diocese of New York, and Professor Herbert Adams Gibbons of Princeton, among numerous others, opposing ratification.

A number of Americans with experience in the middle east, including some like James L. Barton who had worked long and hard for the Armenians, supported the other side. They believed rejection would result in the closing of all American institutions in Turkey.[33] They were answered hotly but not adequately; those who took Gerard's view appeared little concerned with the practical effects of a refusal to ratify.

Not all Armenians opposed ratification; some apparently thought with Peffer that they could do better if powers which had no intention of helping them stopped infuriating the Turks by fussing over them. John Arschagouni, M.D., wrote in this sense to the *New York Times* on October 14, 1923:

> Western civilization in its nudity showed that it lacked a back-
> bone; that justice, humanity, even so-called Christianity, were
> merely subterfuges; that greed and jealousy against each
> other crushed all rights. . . .
> Turkey is on her feet again, her army entered Constantinople
> yesterday. Let her have time to realize that Armenians were
> merely victims of European jingoism, and then she will look to
> that nation with the same far-sightedness as their ancestors . . .[34]

When the Senate finally rejected the treaty on January 18, 1927,

[33] *New York Times*, November 26, 1923, 4.
[34] *Ibid.*, October 14, 1923, Section IX, 8.

it did so after two weeks of executive session. As fifty Senators voted for ratification to thirty-four against, the measure failed by six votes of the necessary two-thirds. The importance of Armenia as motive for the opposition was apparent in Senator King's statement to the press:

> Obviously it would be unfair and unreasonable for the United States to recognize and respect the claims and professions of Kemal so long as he persists in holding control and sovereignty over Wilson Armenia—now a "No Man's Land," while nearly a million Armenian refugees and exiles are people without a country.[35]

King's sincerity is not in question, but the outcome was rather a Democratic revenge against the Republicans than a victory for the Armenians over the Turks.

On the other hand, the fear that American institutions in Turkey would be closed proved unfounded. Robert College and the American College for Girls continue to flourish on the Bosphorus under an American administration and an American board. The Republic of Turkey, which crushed Armenia through its alliance with the Bolsheviks, has become a favorite of the American government and people for its stand against communism.

The Armenians who came to the peace conference with bright prospects for a state of their own, emerged from the disorders of the early 1920's with nothing but the minute state of Erivan which had become the Armenian Socialist Soviet Republic. To what extent the Armenians of that state enjoy a national life and culture of their own lies outside the scope of this inquiry, yet it is safe to say that, whatever benefits they have derived from their association with the Soviet Union—and survival must be accounted a benefit—they failed utterly to achieve their aim of a sovereign, independent state of their own.

While it is impossible to state categorically that the Armenians were in no way to blame for what happened to them—one senses,

35 *Ibid.*, January 19, 1927, 1.

for example, that they made a less favorable impression on the peace conference than their neighbors, the Georgians, who had a much weaker case—the important reasons for their failure must all be laid at the door of their western friends. In the first place, the western powers delayed the treaty with Turkey until the Turks had grown strong enough to have their way. According to all contemporary opinion, they would have accepted virtually any treaty in the months following the Armistice. The delay became perilous in the extreme when, under the influence of Lloyd George and Venizelos, the great powers landed a Greek force at Smyrna and persisted in keeping it in Turkey until the Turks drove it out three years later. The mood produced in Turkey by an attempt to subordinate the nation to a neighbor which had not beaten the Turks in the field and for which they cherished a long—and richly reciprocated—animosity made the demand for the reintegration of Turkey irresistible.

Since, however, some pro-Allied or at least pro-Constantinople sentiment remained in Turkey until well into 1920, the Allied position might not have been irretrievable even then. Instead of retrieving it the Allies allowed it to deteriorate at an accelerating pace by rivalries among themselves and by continued procrastination under the fanciful excuse that they were waiting to see what the United States would do.

The American people, who had more persistently expressed devotion to Armenia than any of their allies, shabbily refused to do anything at all. For this there can be no forgiveness, but it in no way excuses the dawdling of the Allies, since the action of the Senate had been freely forecast by European observers for almost a year.

The ultimate blunder of the Allies was their attitude toward the Russian Revolution. It need not be argued here to what extent the hostility of the west toward communism was justified nor to what extent a more sympathetic reception of the new government might have mitigated those features of it which the west found objectionable. Whatever its justification, it sealed the fate of Armenia. The point is too simple to require discussion: the one development an Armenian state could never surmount was a genuine rapprochement between Russia and Turkey. That development the western attitude toward the Turks and the Bolsheviks made inevitable.

A final reflection may bring this indictment to an end. The Allies' refusal to help Armenia was bad enough, but they crowned their offense by their unwillingness to let it alone. By constantly placing it on the agenda, by constantly discussing it, by constantly intimating that they still intended to do something for it, they blocked any chance the Armenians might have had to create a place for themselves by direct negotiation with the Turks. This was perhaps a forlorn hope, but we cannot know that it was, since it was never put to the test. It is clear that much of the Turkish animus toward the Armenians arose from resentment at foreign intervention in their behalf; it would be of the greatest interest to know what would have happened if Turks and Armenians could have talked together with an absolute assurance that no such intervention would complicate the issues between them.

If there is any consolation in this sad story, it is that the Armenians have survived—not as a state, but as a people. This was not enough in 1919, the heyday of national self-determination, which identified the nation with the sovereign political state, but it may be enough in years to come when the falsity of this equation becomes apparent and when the sovereign political state, once a refuge, threatens to become a sepulchre. A free and independent, fully sovereign Armenia between Turkey and the Soviet Union appears today beyond the bounds of possibility, but an Armenia which would take its place, along with Turkey and the Soviet Union, as a member state in a world federation could offer life and justice to an ancient, long-suffering, and tenacious people.

Bibliography

UNPUBLISHED MATERIAL

Abbott, Freeland. American Policy in the Middle East: a study of the attitudes of the United States toward the Middle East, specially during the period 1919-1936. Doctoral thesis, The Fletcher School of Law and Diplomacy, Tufts University, 1951.

Bryson, Thomas A. III. Woodrow Wilson, the Senate, Public Opinion, and the Armenian Mandate Question 1919-1920. Doctoral thesis, University of Georgia, 1965.

Cook, Ralph E. The United States and the Armenian Question. Doctoral thesis, The Fletcher School of Law and Diplomacy, Tufts University, 1957.

"Files of the Inquiry", papers prepared by the Intelligence Section of the American Commission to Negotiate Peace. Sterling Memorial Library, Yale University, New Haven, Conn.

House, Edward M. Papers and Diary. Sterling Memorial Library, Yale University, New Haven, Conn.

National Archives of the United States. Record Group 59, Files of the State Department.

National Archives of the United States, Record Group 256, Files of the Paris Peace Conference.

Polk, Frank L., Papers. Sterling Memorial Library, Yale University, New Haven, Conn.

Richardson, John Philip. The American Military Mission to Armenia. Master's thesis, George Washington University, 1964.

Sachar, Howard Morley. The United States and Turkey 1914-1917: The Origins of Near Eastern Policy. Doctoral thesis, Harvard University, 1953.

Wilson, Woodrow. Papers. Manuscript Division, Library of Congress, Washington, D. C.

Yale, William. An Analysis of the Syrian-Palestine Situation in 1919: The American Point of View. Master's thesis, University of New Hampshire, 1928.

Yale, William. Papers. University of Michigan Library, Ann Arbor, Michigan.

Yale, William. Recommendations as to the Future Disposition of Palestine, Syria, and Mount Lebanon. Minority report of the King-Crane Commission. Boston University, Boston, Mass.

OFFICIAL PUBLICATIONS

AMERICAN

Harbord, Major-General James G., U. S. Army. *Conditions in the Near East.* Report of the American Military Mission to Armenia. Senate Documents, 66th Congress, 2nd Session, XV, No. 264. Washington, D. C.: Government Printing Office, 1920.

U. S. State Department. *Papers Relating to the Foreign Relations of the United States, 1918-1923.* Washington, D. C.: Government Printing Office, 1930, 1931, 1932, 1933, 1934, 1935, 1936, 1938.

U. S. State Department. *Papers Relating to the Foreign Relations of the United States. Paris Peace Conference 1919.* 13 vols. Washington, D. C.: Government Printing Office, 1942, 1943, 1945, 1946, 1947.

Congressional Record, 1919-1927. Washington, D. C., U. S. Government Printing Office.

BRITISH

Bryce, Viscount. *The Treatment of Armenians in the Ottoman Empire*

1915-1916. Documents presented to Viscount Grey of Fallodon, Secretary of State for Foreign Affairs, with a preface by Viscount Bryce. Blue Book Miscellaneous No. 31 (1916). London: Joseph Causton and Sons, Limited, 1916.

The Parliamentary Debates, 1914-1920. London: His Majesty's Stationery Office.

House of Commons Command Papers. London: Harrison and Sons.

Correspondence Relating to the Asiatic Provinces of Turkey, 1895 (C-7894).

Correspondence Respecting the Conditions of the Populations in Asiatic Turkey and the Proceedings in the Case of Moussa Bey, 1890-1891 (C-6214).

Correspondence Respecting the Disturbances at Constantinople, 1896-1897 (C-8303).

Further Correspondence Respecting the Asiatic Provinces of Turkey and Events in Constantinople, 1897 (C-8395).

Further Correspondence Respecting the Condition of the Populations in Asiatic Turkey, 1892 (C-6632).

Reports Received from Her Majesty's Ambassador and Consuls Relating to the Conditions of Christians in Turkey, 1867 (3854 and 3944).

Woodward, W. L. and Rohan Butler (eds.). *Documents on British Foreign Policy 1919-1939.* 29 vols. London: His Majesty's Stationery Office, 1947, 1948, 1949, 1952, 1954, 1956, 1958, 1960, 1961, 1962.

FRENCH

Assemblée Nationale. Chambre des Députés. Débats 1918 in *Journal Officiel.* Paris: Imprimerie Nationale.

Conférence de la Paix 1919-1920. *Recueil des Actes de la Conférence.* Paris: Imprimerie Nationale, 1923.

Ministère des Affaires Etrangères. *Documents Diplomatiques: Affaires Arméniennes. Projets de Réforme dans l'Empire Ottoman, 1893-1897.* No. 6. Paris: Imprimerie Nationale, 1897.

LEAGUE OF NATIONS

Official Journal, 1920. London: Harrison and Sons.

Records of the First Assembly: Meetings of the Committees, 1920. 2 vols. London: Harrison and Sons.

Records of the First Assembly: Plenary Meetings, 1920. London: Harrison and Sons.

DOCUMENTS

Baker, Ray Stannard and William E. Dodd (eds.). *Public Papers of Woodrow Wilson.* 6 vols. New York: Harper and Brothers, 1927.

Lepsius, Johannes. *Deutschland und Armenien: Sammlung Diplomatischer Aktenstücke.* Potsdam: Der Tempelverlag, 1919.

Mantoux, Paul. *Les Délibérations du Conseil des Quatre (24 mars–28 juin 1919). Notes de l'officier interprète.* 2 vols. Paris: Editions du Centre de la Recherche Scientifique, 1955.

A Speech Delivered by Ghazi Mustapha Kemal, President of the Turkish Republic, October 1927. Leipzig: K. F. Koehler, 1929.

GENERAL WORKS

Albrecht-Carrié, René. *Italy at the Peace Conference.* Published for the Carnegie Endowment for International Peace. New York: Columbia University Press, 1938.

Arpee, Leon. *The Armenian Awakening.* Chicago: University of Chicago Press, 1909.

Atamian, Sarkis. *The Armenian Community.* New York: Philosophical Library, 1955.

Bailey, Thomas A. *A Diplomatic History of the American People.* 6th ed. New York: Appleton-Century-Crofts, Inc., 1958.

Bailey, Thomas A. *Woodrow Wilson and the Great Betrayal.* New York: Macmillan Co., 1945.

Bailey, Thomas A. *Woodrow Wilson and the Lost Peace.* New York: Macmillan Co., 1944.

Baker, Ray Stannard. *Woodrow Wilson and World Settlement.* 3 vols. Garden City: Doubleday, Page and Co., 1922.

Baldwin, Oliver. *Six Prisons and Two Revolutions.* Garden City: Doubleday, Page and Co., 1925.

Beaverbrook, Lord. *The Decline and Fall of Lloyd George.* New York: Duell, Sloan and Pearce, 1963.

Berkes, Niyazi. *The Development of Secularism in Turkey.* Montreal: McGill University Press, 1964.

Birdsall, Paul. *Versailles Twenty Years After*. New York: Reynal and Hitchcock, 1941.

Bonsal, Stephen. *Suitors and Suppliants: The Little Nations at Versailles*. New York: Prentice-Hall, 1946.

Brémond, E. *La Cilicie en 1919-1920*. Paris: Imprimerie Nationale, 1921.

Brémond, E. *Le Hedjaz dans la Guerre Mondiale*. Paris: Payot et cie, 1931.

Bryce, James. *Transcaucasia and Ararat*. 4th ed. New York and London: Macmillan Co., 1896.

Churchill, Winston S. *The Aftermath*. New York: Charles Scribner's Sons, 1929.

Craig, Gordon A. and Felix Gilbert, eds. *The Diplomats 1919-1939*. Princeton: Princeton University Press, 1953.

Cramer, C. H. *Newton D. Baker*. Cleveland and New York: World Publishing Co., 1961.

Davison, Roderic H. *Reform in the Ottoman Empire 1856-1876*. Princeton: Princeton University Press, 1963.

DeNovo, John A. *American Interests and Policies in the Middle East 1900-1939*. Minneapolis: University of Minnesota Press, 1963.

Dugdale, Blanche E. C. *Arthur James Balfour*. 2 vols. London: Hutchinson and Co., 1936.

Edib, Halide. The Turkish Ordeal. New York: The Century Co., 1928.

Eliot, Sir Charles. *Turkey in Europe*. London: Edward Arnold, 1908.

Evans, Laurence. *United States Policy and the Partition of Turkey 1914-1924*. Baltimore: The Johns Hopkins Press, 1965.

Farrère, Claude. *L'Homme qui assassina*. Paris: Flammarion, 1922.

Garnett, David, ed. *The Letters of T. E. Lawrence*. New York: Doubleday, Doran and Co., 1939.

Gates, Caleb F. *Not to me Only*. Princeton: Princeton University Press, 1940.

George, Alexander L. and Juliette L. *Woodrow Wilson and Colonel House: A Personality Study*. New York: John Day Co., 1956.

Gontaut-Biron, Comte R. de. *Comment la France s'est installée en Syrie*. Paris: Plon-Nourrit, 1924.

Grew, Joseph C. *Turbulent Era: A Diplomatic Record of Forty Years 1904-1945*. 2 vols. Boston: Houghton-Mifflin Co., 1952.

Hogarth, David G. *A Wandering Scholar in the Levant.* London: John Murray, 1896.

Hoover, Herbert. *Memoirs.* 3 vols. New York: Macmillan Co., 1951.

Hoover, Herbert. *The Ordeal of Woodrow Wilson.* New York: Mc-Graw-Hill Book Co., Inc., 1958.

Howard, Harry N. *The King-Crane Commission: An American Inquiry in the Middle East.* Beirut: Khayat's, 1963.

Howard, Harry N. *The Partition of Turkey 1913-1923.* Norman: University of Oklahoma Press, 1931.

Howe, Frederic C. *The Confessions of a Reformer.* New York: Charles Scribner's Sons, 1925.

Kazemzadeh, Firuz. *The Struggle for Transcaucasia 1917-1921.* New York: Philosophical Library, 1951.

Kedourie, Elie. *England and the Middle East. The Destruction of the Ottoman Empire 1914-1921.* London: Bowes and Bowes, 1956.

Kinross, Lord. *Ataturk.* New York: William Morrow and Co., 1965.

Kurkjian, Vahan M. *A History of Armenia.* New York: Armenian General Benevolent Union of America, 1959.

Langer, William L. *The Diplomacy of Imperialism 1890-1902.* 2nd ed. New York: Alfred A. Knopf, 1951.

Lansing, Robert. *The Peace Negotiations: A Personal Narrative.* Boston: Houghton Mifflin Co., 1921.

Laqueur, Walter Z. *The Soviet Union and the Middle East.* New York: Frederick A. Praeger, 1959.

Léart, Marcel. *La Question arménienne à la lumière des documents.* Paris: Challamel, 1913.

Lee, Dwight E. *Great Britain and the Cyprus Convention Policy of 1878.* Cambridge: Harvard University Press, 1934.

Lepsius, Johannes. *Armenia and Europe: An Indictment.* Eng. trans. London: Hodder and Stoughton, 1897.

Leslie, Shane. *Mark Sykes: His Life and Letters.* London: Cassell and Co., Ltd., 1923.

Lewis, Bernard. *The Emergence of Modern Turkey.* Issued under the auspices of the Royal Institute of International Affairs. London: Oxford University Press, 1961.

Lewis, Geoffrey. *Turkey.* New York: Frederick A. Praeger, 1955.

Lloyd George, David. *The Truth about the Peace Treaties.* 2 vols. London: Victor Gollancz, Ltd., 1938.

Love, Donald M. *Henry Churchill King of Oberlin.* New Haven: Yale University Press, 1956.

Luke, Sir Harry. *The Old Turkey and the New.* Revised ed. London: Geoffrey Bles, 1956.

Lynch, H. F. B. *Armenia: Travels and Studies.* 2 vols. London: Longmans, Green and Co., 1901.

Mandelstam, André N. *La Société des Nations et les puissances devant le problème arménien.* Paris: A. Pedone, 1925.

Mandelstam, André N. *Le Sort de l'Empire Ottoman.* Lausanne and Paris: Payot et cie, 1917.

Manuel, Frank E. *The Realities of American-Palestine Relations.* Washington: Public Affairs Press, 1949.

Mardin, Serif. *The Genesis of Young Ottoman Thought.* Princeton: Princeton University Press, 1962.

McKee, Irving. *"Ben-Hur" Wallace.* Berkeley and Los Angeles: University of California Press, 1947.

Monroe, Elizabeth. *Britain's Moment in the Middle East 1914-1956.* London: Chatto and Windus, 1963.

Moore, Thomas Emmet. *My Lord Farquhar: A Romance.* New York: The Abbey Press, 1902.

Morgenthau, Henry. *All in a Lifetime.* Garden City: Doubleday, Page and Co., 1922.

Morgenthau, Henry. *Ambassador Morgenthau's Story.* Garden City: Doubleday, Page and Co., 1918.

Nalbandian, Louise. *The Armenian Revolutionary Movement: The Development of Armenian Political Parties through the Nineteenth Century.* Berkeley and Los Angeles: University of California Press, 1963.

Nevins, Allan. *Henry White: Thirty Years of American Diplomacy.* New York: Harper and Brothers, 1930.

Nicolson, Harold. *Curzon: The Last Phase 1919-1925: A Study in Post-War Diplomacy.* Boston and New York: Houghton Mifflin Co., 1934.

Nicolson, Harold. *Peacemaking 1919.* Boston and New York: Houghton Mifflin Co., 1933.

Nitti, Francesco. *Peaceless Europe.* Eng. trans. London: Cassell and Co., Ltd., 1922.

Paillarès, Michel. *Le Kémalisme devant les alliés.* Constantinople and Paris: Editions du Bosphore, 1922.

Pears, Sir Edwin. *Forty Years in Constantinople*. New York: D. Appleton and Co., 1916.

Ramsaur, E. E., Jr. *The Young Turks: Prelude to the Revolution of 1908*. Princeton: Princeton University Press, 1957.

Sanjian, Avedis K. *The Armenian Communities in Syria under Ottoman Dominion*. Cambridge: Harvard University Press, 1965.

Seymour, Charles, ed. *The Intimate Papers of Colonel House*. 4 vols. Boston and New York: Houghton Mifflin Co., 1928.

Shotwell, James T. *Autobiography*. Indianapolis: Bobbs-Merrill Co., Inc., 1961.

Smith, Elaine D. *Turkey: Origins of the Kemalist Movement 1919-1923*. Washington: privately printed, 1959.

Smith, Rixey and Norman Beasley. *Carter Glass: A Biography*. New York and Toronto: Longmans, Green and Co., 1939.

Sykes, Sir Mark. *The Caliph's Last Heritage*. London: Macmillan Co., Ltd., 1915.

Sykes, Sir Mark. *Dar-ul-Islam: a record of a journey through ten of the Asiatic provinces of Turkey*. London: Bickers and Son, 1904.

Sykes, Sir Mark. *The Future of the Near East*. London: Pelican Press, 1918.

Temperley, H. W. V., ed. *A History of the Peace Conference of Paris*. 6 vols. Published under the auspices of the British Institute of International Affairs. London: Henry Frowde and Hodder and Stoughton, 1920.

Toynbee, Arnold J. *Armenian Atrocities: The Murder of a Nation*. London: Hodder and Stoughton, 1915.

Toynbee, Arnold J. *A Study of History*. 12 vols. London: Oxford University Press, 1955.

Toynbee, Arnold J. *The Western Question in Greece and Turkey: A Study in the Contact of Civilizations*. 2nd ed. Boston and New York: Houghton Mifflin Co., 1923.

Vratzian, Simeon. *Armenia and the Armenian Question*. Boston: Hairenik Publishing Co., 1943.

Werfel, Franz. *The Forty Days of Musa Dagh*. Eng. trans. New York: The Viking Press, 1934.

Yale, William. *The Near East: A Modern History*. Ann Arbor: University of Michigan Press, 1958.

Yalman, Ahmed Emin. *Turkey in My Time.* Norman: University of Oklahoma Press, 1956.

Zeine, Zeine N. *The Struggle for Arab Independence.* Beirut: Khayat's, 1960.

PERIODICALS

The periodicals listed below are those that have been examined for purposes of this study. The period covered is roughly 1890-1927 but a few useful articles have been found at earlier dates. The list is not offered as exhaustive; it more nearly approximates completeness in American than in British and French publications.

AMERICAN

The Arena
The Armenian Herald
Asia
The Atlantic Monthly
The Century
The Chautauquan
Current History
The Editor and Publisher
The Forum
The Independent
The Literary Digest
The Missionary Review of the World
The Nation
The New Republic
The New York Times
The North American Review
The Outlook
Scribner's Monthly
The Survey
The World Outlook
The World Today
The World's Work

BRITISH

Blackwood's Edinburgh Magazine
The Contemporary Review
The Dial
The Edinburgh Review
The Fortnightly Review
The Near East
The Nineteenth Century and After
The Quarterly Review
The Saturday Review of Politics, Science, Literature and Art
The Times (London)

FRENCH

L'Asie française
La Revue de Paris
Revue des Deux Mondes
Revue des Etudes arméniennes
Revue Littéraire et Politique (*Revue Bleue*)
Le Temps

Index

Abdul Hamid, Sultan, 16, 27, 29-31, 37-8

Aharonian, Avetis, 82-5, 218-9

American Committee for the Independence of Armenia, 79, 86, 90, 223, 227

Anatolia, 8, 12, 15, 30, 90, 92, 95, 113, 154, 159, 180

Ankara Pact, 248-9

Ardahan, 29, 59, 128, 243, 245

Armenia and Armenians, 2-14; and Harbord Mission, 171-191; and League of Nations, 214, 216; and London Conference, 206-9, 211, 215; and mandate, 77, 91, 98, 158, 162; at Peace Conference, 81-5; in political platforms of 1920, 238-9; population of, 22-3; Republic of, 59, 96, 129, 151, 168; and San Remo Conference, 218-21; and Sykes-Picot Agreement, 62; and U. S. Senate, 199, 225-37

Armenian National Conference, 46

Armenian National Delegation, 74-5, 84

Armenian National Union of America, 67, 89, 223

Asia Minor, 63, 93, 100, 109, 111, 128, 140, 149, 153, 159-60, 162, 180-1, 190

Azerbaijan, 3, 168, 199-200, 206

Balfour, Arthur James, 68, 91, 110-11, 129-31, 196, 206

Barton, James L., 137-140, 166-7, 170, 223, 252

Batum, 29, 83, 170, 192, 207

Berlin, Treaty of, 16, 28, 31, 39, 75

Berthelot, Philippe, 205-6, 208, 211-2, 217-8

Bitlis, 5, 62, 84, 206, 220, 227

Brest-Litovsk, Treaty of, 59, 77, 83, 129, 243

Bristol, Adm. Mark, 101, 115, 154, 170, 177, 200-2, 245

Bryce, Viscount (James), 53, 55, 79, 95, 114, 175

Calthorpe, Adm., 102, 112, 125, 134, 196